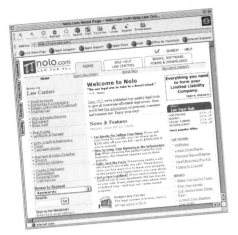

LEGAL INFORMATION ONLINE ANYTIME

24 hours a day

www.nolo.com

AT THE NOLO.COM SELF-HELP LAW CENTER, YOU'LL FIND

- Nolo's comprehensive Legal Encyclopedia filled with plain-English information on a variety of legal topics
- Nolo's Law Dictionary—legal terms <u>without</u> the legalese
- Auntie Nolo—if you've got questions, Auntie's got answers
- The Law Store—over 250 self-help legal products including: Downloadable Software, Books, Form Kits and eGuides
- Legal and product updates
- Frequently Asked Questions
- NoloBriefs, our free monthly email newsletter
- Legal Research Center, for access to state and federal statutes
- Our ever-popular lawyer jokes

Quality LAW BOOKS & SOFTWARE FOR EVERYONE

Nolo's user-friendly products are consistently first-rate. Here's why:

- A dozen in-house legal editors, working with highly skilled authors, ensure that our products are accurate, up-to-date and easy to use
- We continually update every book and software program to keep up with changes in the law
- Our commitment to a more democratic legal system informs all of our work
- We appreciate & listen to your feedback. Please fill out and return the card at the back of this book.

OUR "NO-HASSLE" GUARANTEE

Return anything you buy directly from Nolo for any reason and we'll cheerfully refund your purchase price. No ifs, ands or buts.

An Important Message to Our Readers

This product provides information and general advice about the law. But laws and procedures change frequently, and they can be interpreted differently by different people. For specific advice geared to your specific situation, consult an expert. No book, software or other published material is a substitute for personalized advice from a knowledgeable lawyer licensed to practice law in your state.

How to Create a Noncompete Agreement

by Attorney Shannon Miehe

NOLO

Keeping Up-to-Date

To keep its books up-to-date, Nolo issues new printings and new editions periodically. New printings reflect minor legal changes and technical corrections. New editions contain major legal changes, major text additions or major reorganizations. To find out if a later printing or edition of any Nolo book is available, call Nolo at 510-549-1976 or check our website at http://www.nolo.com.

To stay current, follow the "Update" service at our website at http://www.nolo.com/update. In another effort to help you use Nolo's latest materials, we offer a 35% discount off the purchase of the new edition of your Nolo book when you turn in the cover of an earlier edition. (See the "Special Upgrade Offer" in the back of the book.)

First Edition	JANUARY 2002
Editor	BETH LAWRENCE
Book Design	SUSAN PUTNEY
Book Production	SARAH HINMAN
Cover Designer	TONI IHARA
Index	JEAN MANN
Proofreading	ROBERT WELLS
Printing	CONSOLIDATED PRINTERS, INC.

Miehe, Shannon, 1971-
    How to create a noncompete agreement / by Shannon Miehe.
        p. cm.
    Includes index.
    ISBN 0-87337-714-1
    1. Covenants not to compete--United States. 2. Small business--Law and legisla-
tion--United states. 3. Businesspeople--United States--Handbooks, manuals, etc.
    I. Title.
KF3463.Z9 M54 2001

346.73'0652--dc21   2001030840

For information on bulk purchases or corporate premium sales, please contact the Special Sales Department. For academic sales or textbook adoptions, ask for Academic Sales. Call 800-955-4775 or write to Nolo, 950 Parker Street, Berkeley, CA 94710.

Acknowledgments

Many thanks to the people at Nolo who made this book happen: to my editor, Beth Laurence, for her infinite patience, careful editing and uncanny knack for translating a complicated legal subject into English; to Jake Warner, for dreaming this whole thing up in the first place; and to the other editors and authors at Nolo who encouraged me to keep writing and made me believe I'd actually finish.

About the Author

Shannon Miehe received her undergraduate degree from Stanford University and her law degree from the University of Southern California Law School. Before joining Nolo, Ms. Miehe was a corporate attorney with a large Los Angeles law firm, and spent several years representing small and mid-size entrepreneurial companies in connection with mergers, acquisitions and business formation issues. She edits many of Nolo's small business products, including *Legal Forms for Starting & Running a Small Business*, *The Partnership Book* and *Tax Savvy for Small Business*.

Table of Contents

Introduction

Chapter 1: What's In a Noncompete Agreement?

Chapter 2: When to Use a Noncompete Agreement

Chapter 3: Using Noncompete Agreements for Employees

Chapter 4: Creating a Noncompete Agreement for an Employee

Chapter 5: Using Noncompete Agreements for Independent Contractors

Chapter 6: Creating an Independent Contractor Agreement

Chapter 7: When Workers Depart: Revisiting Your Agreement

Chapter 8: Help Beyond This Book

Appendix 1

How to Use the CD-ROM

Appendix 2

Noncompete Statutes

Appendix 3

Forms for Businesses With Employees

Forms to Use With Independent Contractors

Introduction

Whether you own a bakery, run a yoga studio or operate a small public relations firm, you probably give many of your employees and independent contractors access to confidential details about your business (for example, marketing strategies, production know-how or client lists). And you no doubt invest a lot of time and money training these people in your way of doing business. When a former worker starts a competing business or goes to work for a competitor, a lot of this information—and all of the training—travels with your ex-worker.

How likely is it that a former worker will compete? Consider this—according to the National Federation of Independent Businesses, approximately 50% of all new businesses are started by former employees of small companies. In other words, it's likely that the company you've worked hard to build will be the foundation of a former worker's successful competing business. And since people are changing jobs in record numbers, it's even more likely that your workers will go to work for a competitor and take some of your

trade secrets, like a recipe, manufacturing process or customer list, with them.

Company loyalty—a quaint concept that existed throughout most of the 20th century—has gone the way of hoop skirts and electric typewriters. This change in attitude is reflected in the numbers. According to some studies, the average worker in the United States today will hold more than eight different jobs between the ages of 18 and 32, and employees today are 40% more likely to voluntarily change jobs than they were five years ago. That means your employees and independent contractors are much more likely than ever before to go to work for one of your competitors—and possibly take other employees with them.

Your employees may be invited to leave your business, too. Because the pool of qualified workers is limited (especially in the technology sector), many employers turn to other companies, often competitors, to find highly trained, knowledgeable workers who may want to move on to greener pastures. For instance, a competing company could offer one of your employees a fat pay raise, benefits and other perks in hopes of cashing in on the training you provided.

Although employee turnover can cost you money, it can hurt your business even more when former workers take your trade secrets, and sometimes your customers and other employees, to a competitor. Many employers think they're helpless to stop a former worker from engaging in this kind of behavior, but they're not.

How Noncompete Agreements Can Protect Your Business

Using a carefully written and signed agreement between you and your worker, you can keep a former worker from disclosing your confidential information, stealing your customers or employees and, in most states, from competing against you. This powerful trio of agreements will also make it difficult for competitive businesses to try to profit from your hard-won secrets by poaching or raiding your workforce for your most knowledgeable, experienced employees. After all, if you've effectively silenced (or tethered) an employee with enforceable agreements, there's no incentive to try to hire them away.

Let's Get the Terminology Straight

Lawyers have managed to create some confusion when it comes to the terms used in noncompete agreements. Here's what you have to understand: A noncompete agreement usually consists of three parts, or clauses:

- An agreement not to disclose trade secrets, called a nondisclosure clause
- An agreement not to solicit other employees or customers, called a nonsolicitation clause, and
- An agreement not to compete with a former employer, called a noncompete clause.

Perhaps you can already see the cause for confusion: that part of a noncompete agreement that covers working for competitors—the noncompete clause—*also* uses the term "noncompete."

As we'll explain in "Is a Written Agreement Really Necessary?" below, an employer may use all three clauses, or just one or two, in a noncompete agreement. To try to keep confusion at a minimum in this book, when the noncompete clause is absent from a particular agreement, we'll refer to the agreement as a nondisclosure agreement, a nonsolicitation agreement, or a nondisclosure and nonsolicitation agreement. When all three clauses are present, we'll use the term noncompete agreement.

It would be nice if employers everywhere could choose to include all three clauses in a noncompete agreement. Unfortunately, several states limit your choices. Let's start with what all employers *can* do: All states allow noncompete agreements to control:

- what information of yours a former worker can use or disclose in a competing business (in the agreement's "nondisclosure" clause), and
- whether a former worker can encourage your clients, customers and employees to leave your company (in the agreement's "nonsolicitation" clause).

Not all states, however, allow employers to prevent former workers from competing with them—by working for a competitor or starting a competing business of their own. In the states of California, Montana, North Dakota and Oklahoma, an agreement that limits whom he can work for after he stops working for your business generally won't be enforced. In several other states (Alabama, Colorado, Florida, Oregon and Texas), you can keep a worker from competing against you only in certain circumstances.

In all other states, however, a noncompete agreement can contain a "noncompetition clause," which places legal limits on:

- for whom a former worker can work and what type of business the worker can start or run
- the amount of time a former worker must wait before taking a competing position or starting a competing business, and
- where in the United States a former worker can compete against you.

These rules are summarized in "States That Allow Noncompete, Nondisclosure and Nonsolicitation Agreements," below.

If your state does not allow you to ask a worker to sign an agreement in which the worker promises not to compete, you can still protect yourself against the loss of trade secrets, customers and employees with an agreement containing nondisclosure and nonsolicitation clauses. If your state doesn't permit workers to enter into noncompetition agreements, see Chapter 2, Section B, for more information on these states' laws and how you can use nondisclosure and nonsolicitation agreements to comply with them. But if you do jump ahead, be sure to return to Chapter 1 to learn about creating enforceable nondisclosure and nonsolicitation agreements.

States That Allow Noncompete, Nondisclosure and Nonsolicitation Agreements

Whether you can restrict your employees' abilities to compete, disclose and solicit depends on where your business is located, as shown below.

	California, Montana, North Dakota and Oklahoma	Alabama, Colorado, Florida, Oregon and Texas	All other states
Nondisclosure agreement	yes	yes	yes
Nonsolicitation agreement	yes	yes	yes
Noncompetition agreement	no	limited circumstances	yes

EXAMPLE: Sarah operates her own public relations firm in Chicago. After working by herself for several years, Sarah hires Ann. Although Ann has little P.R. experience she quickly learns the business from Sarah and soon has unrestricted access to Sarah's client database (which contains all kinds of juicy tidbits—and hard-earned information—about the clients). Ann also has frequent contact with Sarah's clients. As Sarah's business grows, she hires more employees but only Ann, her trusted assistant, has full access to the confidential client database. One day, Ann announces she's quitting to form her own public relations firm in the same town.

Sarah also finds out that Ann has made copies of Sarah's confidential client database, solicited some of Sarah's clients and encouraged some of Sarah's employees to join her. Sarah is irritated and worried about what Ann's competition will do to her business.

Luckily, Sarah had the foresight to require Ann to sign a noncompete agreement before Ann started her job. Sarah reminds Ann that she has signed a noncompete agreement that (1) bars Ann from competing against Sarah for a period of six months after she leaves Sarah's company in the same geographic area in which Sarah does business, (2) prohibits her from soliciting Sarah's clients and employees and (3) prevents her from stealing Sarah's confidential information. Ann laughs at Sarah and says, "Just try to enforce it."

Never one to back down from a challenge, Sarah decides to take Ann's advice. Armed with evidence that Ann has pilfered Sarah's client list and confidential files, Sarah goes to court to obtain a preliminary injunction—an order from the judge—that will prevent Ann from engaging in any of the prohibited activities set forth in the agreement until the case is over. Because Sarah does business in Illinois and the noncompete agreement is governed by Illinois law, she brings the lawsuit in a court in Chicago. Since Illinois courts are quite willing to enforce properly drafted noncompete agreements, enforcing the agreement does not turn out to be a problem. The judge orders Ann to stop using information she gathered while in Sarah's employ, refrain from soliciting Sarah's employees or customers and, if she wants to continue to run her business, to do so in a distant city.

As this example illustrates, a noncompete agreement can be a very useful tool in protecting your business. However, there are some strict rules you must comply with before a court will enforce one against a former worker. As you read this book, keep in mind that courts are heavily biased in favor of free competition and the unrestrained ability to earn a livelihood when they decide whether or not to enforce a noncompete agreement against a former worker. And some states, such as California, have decided that these rights are so important that noncompete agreements should only be enforced in extreme

circumstances. We discuss the requirements for creating an enforceable noncompete agreement in Chapter 1, and the specific state rules in Chapter 2, Section B.

⚠️ **This book deals only with noncompete agreements for employees and independent contractors.** *Consult an attorney if you need a noncompete agreement for a person from whom you're buying a business or for a co-owner who's leaving your partnership, limited liability company (LLC) or limited liability partnership (LLP).*

Is a Written Agreement Really Necessary?

Like many employers, you may have an amicable, trusting relationship with your key workers, and may even be good friends with them. You may wonder whether a written agreement is necessary if the worker assures you she won't use your information, compete with you or solicit your customers when she leaves. Although a verbal assurance may theoretically bind a worker, don't rely on it. With nothing in writing, it will be your word against the worker's if you ended up in court trying to enforce the oral promise. (For information on your legal rights without a written noncompete agreement, see Chapter 7, Section A.)

In business, it's often better to be respected than loved. *Many small business owners like to be perceived as a friend to employees and contractors. After all, many small business owners are former employees themselves and understand the resentment many workers may feel at being shackled. If you're torn between your desire to be liked and your fear of competition, keep in mind that your workers may be concerned more with lucre than love. Even if it seems to conflict with your friendly management style, creating an equitable noncompete agreement with reasonable restrictions is a good way to protect your business, your investors and the livelihood of all of your employees.*

How to Use This Book

This book gives you the information and forms you'll need to create a fair and enforceable agreement—one that will protect your business and, if necessary, pass muster with a judge.

For your convenience, we have included examples of noncompete agreements—one for employees, and one for independent contractors—in Appendix 3 in the back of the book. All of the forms are included on the accompanying CD-ROM. This CD-ROM can be used with both Windows and Macintosh computers. The files are in standard file formats that can be opened, completed, printed and saved using a word processor. For specific instructions on using the CD-ROM, see Appendix 2.

The best way to ensure that your noncompete agreement will hold up in court is to make yourself familiar with the array of rules surrounding noncompete law. Read this entire book before you put your agreement together. But if you're looking for information on a specific topic before getting started, these cross-references below may help.

- For information on using noncompete agreements for employees, see Chapter 3.
- For information on using noncompete agreements with independent contractors, read Chapter 5.
- For instructions on filling out a noncompete agreement, see Chapter 4 (employees) and Chapter 6 (independent contractors).
- For information about steps to take when a worker who has signed a noncompete agreement leaves your company, read Chapter 7.
- For information on getting legal help preparing or enforcing a noncompete agreement, see Chapter 8.

Notes and Icons

 Tip *A commonsense tip to help you understand or comply with legal requirements.*

 Warning *A caution to slow down and consider potential problems.*

 Cross Reference *This icon refers you to further discussion of this topic elsewhere in the book.*

 See an Expert *A suggestion to seek the advice of an attorney or tax expert.*

Fast Track *An indication that you may be able to skip some material that may not be relevant to your situation.*

Other Resources *A reference to a book, website or other resource that may help you with a particular issue.*

Form on CD-ROM *A reference to a form included on the CD-ROM at the back of the book.*

■

1

What's In a Noncompete Agreement?

A noncompete agreement is a contract between a company and an employee or independent contractor, usually signed at the commencement of employment or services. It commonly includes three types of restrictions on what the employee or contractor can do after ceasing to work for you: a noncompetition clause, a nondisclosure clause and a nonsolicitation clause. Each of these clauses accomplishes a slightly different task, but the goal of each clause is the same: to protect your business from a former worker who tries to use your confidential information to compete against you. In this chapter, we'll explain the workings of these three clauses in more detail and explain how to create an agreement that will stand up in court.

A. Making an Enforceable Agreement

Throughout this book, you'll hear us talking about the importance of making an "enforceable" or "valid" agreement. You might wonder why we're concerned with these words. After all, if your company signs the agreement and the worker signs the agreement, doesn't that make it a valid contract? And if it is a valid contract, why would the company end up in court?

If your worker abides by the agreement, you may never end up in court—and your agreement will never be reviewed by a judge. But what if the worker

violates the agreement, by disclosing your secrets, luring customers away or opening-up a competing business a block away— what do you do? If friendly persuasion, lawyer's letters and mediation attempts don't do the trick, you'll probably head for court to ask a judge to enforce the agreement.

The judge will measure your agreement against your state's laws governing how these agreements should be written. If the agreement doesn't comply with the rules, the judge will not enforce it. Now and then a judge will rewrite an invalid agreement, but the agreement could be tossed out and your ex-worker would be free to compete, solicit or disclose as if you never signed the agreement in the first place.

On the other hand, if the judge determines that your agreement follows your state's rules, the judge will let your case proceed. In other words, only after the judge has reached this conclusion will she decide whether the former worker has violated the agreement and whether the worker's behavior (for example, working for a competitor) should be stopped.

In the following sections we take you, step by step, through the rules you need to know before you create your agreement. Please read this chapter in full before you use any of the forms in this book, so that you do not unintentionally create an invalid, unenforceable agreement.

B. Noncompetition Provisions

In a noncompetition clause, an employee or contractor agrees not to compete with the company for a short period of time after leaving (for example, by taking a similar position with a competitor). This will prevent the former worker from using your trade secrets or confidential information while working for, or running, a competing business.

 Some states will not enforce a noncompetition clause. *As explained in the Introduction, a few states flatly refuse to enforce them; others enforce them in limited circumstances. See Chapter 2, Section B, for a list of these states—and an explanation of how nonsolicitation and nondisclosure agreements can fill the void if noncompetition is off-limits for you. If your state will not uphold a noncompetition clause, you can skip this section and read the rest of the chapter, which will explain how and when you can protect your business with alternative agreements which contain enforceable nondisclosure and nonsolicitation clauses.*

States that enforce noncompetition clauses will do so only if the clause is reasonable, which will depend on:
- how long the restriction lasts
- how large the geographic scope of the restriction is

- how many activities the former worker is prevented from participating in, and
- whether the restriction places too much hardship on the former worker or the public.

To pass muster under these rules, your noncompete clause must not last too long, should cover the smallest possible territory, should restrict the fewest possible activities and should not cause too much hardship to the worker or the public. Now, we realize that we aren't much closer to explaining "reasonableness"—but the discussions below will explain each of these requirements in more depth.

1. Length of Time

If you're concerned about the effect of a worker competing against you, you'll naturally want that person sidelined for as long as possible—or at least as long as you think you'll need to grow your market share, train a replacement, launch a new product, or where competition from this person won't make a difference for some reason. At the same time, the period of time a former worker can't work for a competitor or start a similar business (we'll call that the "noncompetition period") can't be so long as to make it unreasonably difficult for the worker to make a living at his trade or occupation.

Several states have developed guidelines for appropriate noncompetition periods. For example, in Florida a six-month period is presumed to be reasonable, which means that it will pass muster unless the former worker can convince a judge it isn't warranted. A period that's longer than two years is presumed *un*reasonable—this means that a judge won't enforce it unless *you* prove that the time period is reasonable under the circumstances. And, if you ask a judge to enforce a one-year noncompetition period, she will look at all the circumstances—how long your business needs to prevent competition and how adversely this would affect the worker—without presuming that the length of time is either reasonable or unreasonable. You'll still have to prove to the judge that it's reasonable—but at least you won't start off at a disadvantage, laboring under a presumption that it's too long.

In other states, such as Louisiana and South Dakota, any noncompetition period that lasts longer than two years is presumed to be unreasonable. In New York—judging from the decisions courts have made recently—noncompetition periods ranging anywhere from one to five years may be considered reasonable.

The reasonableness of the length of your noncompetition clause will also depend on the nature of your industry or occupation. If techniques and strategies change rapidly in your line of business, you have less need for a long noncompete period than if the area is stable. For example, a federal court in New York decided that a one-year restriction on competition by a former employee of an Internet advertising firm was unreasonable because, given the dynamic nature of the industry, the useful life of the employee's information was much shorter than a year. (See *EarthWeb, Inc. v. Schlack*, 71 F. Supp. 2d 299 (S.D. N.Y. 1999).)

What does all this add up to? Unless you can point to specific reasons why a longer duration is necessary, make your noncompetition period last from six months to two years. Beyond that, courts tend to say no.

EXAMPLE: When you hire Siobhan, a software programmer, she signs an agreement with a noncompetition clause. The agreement says that, after Siobhan leaves your company, she cannot take a software or programming job with one of your competitors, or start her own competing company, for at least one year. After Siobhan has worked for your company for five years, your archrival offers her a programming job that would double her salary. But because Siobhan signed the agreement, she can't take the offer—at least not for one year after leaving your company.

If you want to impose a longer noncompetition period, consider paying the worker for it. *If you are determined to restrict a former worker from competing for more than two years, consider paying the worker for the entire duration—as you would with a severance agreement (see Chapter 3, Section D, and Chapter 5, Section C). Courts are more likely to enforce a longer noncompetition clause if the worker is compensated while prohibited from working in a chosen field. If you're interested in pursuing this route, see an experienced employment attorney.*

2. Geographic Scope

Besides thinking about your noncompetition clause's duration, you must consider its geographic scope—the area in which you want to prevent the worker from competing against you. Agreements that prevent a former worker from working in areas where you are not doing business, or in a wide geographic area (such as the western United States) are too broad and probably not necessary anyway. Overly broad agreements make it too difficult for your ex-workers to earn a living—for this reason, judges tend not to enforce them.

The agreements in this book give you a choice on how to set the geographic scope. The first alternative defines the area of noncompetition as the area where you conduct business. This should adequately protect you, whether you do business in a small town or in several regions of the country.

EXAMPLE: When Erik took a job at a Houston hair salon, Shears, he signs an agreement promising that, for six months after he leaves the salon, he will not work in another salon located in the area in which Shears does business. The next year, Erik leaves to open up his own salon two blocks away. The owner of Shears takes Erik's noncompete agreement to court and asks the judge for a preliminary injunction—to stop Erik from competing against her. The judge looks at the geographic scope of the agreement and determines that Shears has not been overbroad in setting it (such as demanding that Erik not cut hair anywhere in the United States). The judge also finds that Erik is indeed working in the area in which Shears does business—two blocks away—and grants Shears the preliminary injunction.

Our second alternative allows you to define a specific geographic area where competition will not be allowed. If you choose this alternative, consider a number of factors when defining the area, such as where your company maintains its business and where its business contacts, customers and clients are located. For instance, if you run a national ad agency with employees, customers, clients and large competitors located throughout the United States, it might be reasonable for you to keep a key worker from competing in the entire country for a short period of time.

 Balance your agreement to make it fair. *As a good rule of thumb, the bigger the geographic area you set, the shorter the duration of the noncompetition clause should be—and vice versa. Shorten the noncompetition period to six months or one year if you're inserting a wide geographic area. Conversely, if the geographic area in which you prohibit competition is small, such as the town square, you can probably get away with a longer noncompetition period.*

If you choose to limit where your worker plies his trade by where he cannot work instead of where you conduct business, be careful that you don't push the boundaries too far. If you are a local business, with a local customer base and local employees (such as a laser eye clinic with six branches in southern New York), restricting an employee from working for a competitor outside this immediate area is probably unreasonable.

 Louisiana businesses must specify a parish or municipality in which a worker cannot compete. *Louisiana state law requires an employer to specify the parishes or municipalities in which a worker cannot compete. If you don't specify a parish or municipality in Louisiana, your agreement may not be enforceable. To be on the safe side, list the parishes or municipalities in which you don't want the worker to compete. We remind you to do this in Chapter 4, Section C, when you are filling out the form.*

For some companies, such as Internet businesses that provide services or products to people throughout the country and perhaps the world, specifying the geographic area of noncompetition can be tricky. That's because it's often difficult to define exactly where an Internet company does business. Is it the geographic region of the headquarters, or where its competitors are, or where its customers are? There is no answer to this question—yet. For Internet companies whose business crosses state and sometimes international lines, using the first alternative in our agreements—to simply prevent a worker from working in geographic areas where you do business—is probably your best bet. (Note, however, that if you do business internationally, enforcing a noncompete agreement outside of the United States will be difficult, given the expense and varying international laws.)

We realize we're answering the question "Where do you do business?" by creating a noncompetition boundary of "Where you do business." Since there isn't an answer to this question right now, you may have to leave it up to a judge—or a former worker who's willing to comply with your agreement.

3. Limitation on Activities

In addition to having a limited geographic scope, a noncompetition clause cannot restrict a worker from engaging in any and all business activities—no matter how short the duration of the noncompetition period or how limited the geographic area. Such a broad restriction would make it too difficult for a worker to earn a living.

A reasonable noncompetition clause should restrict a former worker from performing only those activities that compete with your business or that might require the disclosure of your confidential information. A noncompetition clause that prevents a former worker from taking a job with a competitor in a different capacity probably won't be enforced by a judge.

> **Example:** Beth works in the accounting department at a large publishing company, but her secret dream is to become an editor. Unable to convince her boss to transfer her to the editorial department, she interviews for and receives an offer to become a junior editor at her employer's major rival. Although Beth is definitely taking a job with a competitor, it's unlikely that a court would enforce a noncompete agreement against Beth in this situation, since she won't be working in an accounting capacity.

The noncompete agreements in this book contain a list of competitive activities in which the ex-worker may not engage (such as owning stock in a competitive company or working for them as a freelancer). If a former employee proposes to take a position at a competing company that's similar to the job done for you, the agreement will prevent this by disallowing duties or responsibilities similar to those performed for you. Nor can the former employee start a competing company. Likewise, our independent contractor agreements prevent a former contractor from performing services that are similar to the services performed at your company and from starting a competing company.

4. Hardship on the Worker and Violation of Public Policy

Even if a noncompete agreement satisfies all of the conditions we discussed above, a court may still refuse to enforce it if doing so would place too great a burden on the worker or harm the public.

For example, some courts will refuse to enforce noncompete agreements that effectively prohibit workers from practicing their trade anywhere within a reasonable distance of their residence. This is particularly true if it's the only trade or profession the worker has ever had—tool and die making, for example—and the worker does not have an adequate education to make a transition to another type of employment or another industry.

EXAMPLE 1: Ever since Ron graduated from high school 30 years ago, he's been a widget riveter at Gadgets R Us. Ron is the best riveter at Gadgets R Us—he's fast and efficient, so much so that over the years he has single-handedly boosted the company's widget production by as much as 10%. Gadgets R Us would suffer if Ron left. The company would like Ron to sign a noncompete agreement to prevent him from taking his skills to a competitor within a 100-mile radius of Gadgets R Us's factory, for two years after he leaves. But riveting widgets is highly specialized work (it's completely different than riveting work in other industries), and it's the only job Ron knows how to do. If Ron can't work as a widget riveter, Ron probably isn't going to be able to support himself or his family. This is what courts call "undue hardship"—the inability to earn a living—and many courts wouldn't enforce a noncompete agreement against Ron under these circumstances.

Example 2: Heather is a market researcher for a company that manufactures a famous line of popular children's dolls and accessories. Because the toy industry is so competitive, her company asks her to sign an agreement in which she agrees not to perform market research for any other U.S. company that produces a competing product for a period of six months after she leaves. Before Heather went to work for her current employer, she conducted market research for a company that manufactured ice cream, and before that, for a company that manufactured microwave popcorn and canned soup. Because it's clear that in Heather's line of work she can get another job conducting market research for a company that doesn't compete with her old employer, a judge would probably enforce this noncompete agreement (as long as it's reasonable in other ways, of course). In this case, enforcing a noncompete agreement wouldn't keep Heather out of the workforce or prevent her from earning a living while the noncompete agreement was in effect.

Noncompete agreements that violate public policy—by injuring the public in some ways, not just the ex-employee—may fare no better. For instance, suppose a noncompete agreement prohibits a surgical nurse from practicing in a rural area with limited medical services. To protect the public's access to the nurse's services, a court might refuse to enforce the noncompete agreement.

Separate Rules for Professionals and Business Partners

Some professionals—most often doctors and lawyers—are subject to special rules limiting the reach of noncompetition agreements. For instance, in Colorado a physician may compete against a former employer or partners even if the physician signed a noncompete agreement. (However, a doctor in Colorado *can* be required to pay a former employer or partners financial compensation if the doctor competes in violation of a noncompete agreement.) A few other states that enforce noncompete agreements for most professions do not permit doctors to enter into them at all.

As for attorneys and accountants, many law and accounting firms are organized as partnerships, limited liability companies (LLCs) or limited liability partnerships (LLPs). These business entities are often subject to special rules governing noncompete agreements. For example, many states that don't enforce noncompete agreements against employees or contractors will enforce them against partners who leave partnerships or against business owners who sell their interest in a business. Check your state's business laws for these rules. (Often, these exceptions are listed right after the general prohibition against noncompete agreements, as in California, Montana and a few other states.)

To further confuse matters, lawyers are often governed by separate rules of professional conduct, which specifically prohibit attorneys from entering into agreements not to compete.

If short, if you want to use a noncompete agreement for a professional, a partner who might leave a partnership or a business owner who's selling a business, consult an attorney.

■ Imposing financial penalties for competing. *Instead of prohibiting competition by workers outright, some companies create agreements that impose financial penalties on workers who compete against the company. For instance, an employer might force an employee who competes against the company to forfeit lucrative stock options or a large bonus; or might require the employee to fork over any profits made from former customers of the employer. We don't include financial penalties in our agreements because there are so many ways to design them. More importantly, it's unclear whether a judge would enforce them at all. If you're interested in creating an agreement with penalty provisions, talk to an employment lawyer.*

Blue-Penciling: Judges Take Agreements Into Their Own Hands

If a judge concludes that a particular clause of a noncompete agreement is unenforceable, in some states the judge may rewrite it to make it more reasonable, rather than throwing out the clause (or the entire agreement). For instance, suppose a noncompete agreement provides that an employee can't compete with a former employer for a period of two years after leaving the company. If a judge thinks this duration is too long to satisfy the reasonableness requirement, she may rewrite the provision and substitute a shorter period of time. Or, if deleting certain language can solve the problem, a judge may do so while leaving other words or provisions intact, so that the clause as a whole becomes reasonable. (Fixing clauses by deleting the problematic parts is called "blue penciling.")

You can't count on a judge to rewrite or blue-pencil an unreasonable provision. Your chances are greater if the bulk of your agreement is fair and the problematic parts are just a little too broad, long or wide. But if you've seriously overreached, don't count on any judicial editing. In many situations, the judge will simply invalidate the entire clause (or worse, the entire agreement) instead. To avoid these dire results, make sure that all the components of your noncompetition clauses (duration, scope of activities, geographic limitations and their impact on the worker and the public) are reasonable.

C. Nondisclosure Provisions

In the nondisclosure provision in our agreements, the employee or contractor agrees not to use, or disclose to anyone else, your company's confidential information and trade secrets. (We'll refer to this clause as an "NDA.") The NDA goes hand in hand with the noncompetition clause. The nondisclosure clause prevents the former worker from using your information, while the noncompetition clause removes much of the motivation and temptation for her to do so (if the former worker is not competing against you, she won't have any reason to use your secrets).

If you live in a state that will not enforce a noncompete clause, you won't be able to take the "belt and suspenders" approach of using a noncompete plus nondisclosure clause. You do, however, have a good way to protect confidential business information by using the nondisclosure clause by itself. This section shows you how to craft an effective, legal clause for your agreement.

Limited State Law Protection for Your Secrets

Your state's laws governing unfair business practices and trade secrets may give you some protection when it comes to stopping the use of your business secrets by former workers. For example, many states have laws that prevent workers from using or disclosing trade secrets (which we explain in Section C3, below) and also have unfair competition laws, which prevent employees and former employees from engaging in certain unfair business practices, like bad-mouthing your business to customers. But you'll be much better protected if you beef up any protection afforded by your state with one of our noncompetition agreements.

---

1. Using a Nondisclosure Clause by Itself

Even if your state will enforce a noncompete clause, you may choose not to use one. For example, you might use an NDA alone for independent contractors or non-critical employees who have access to your confidential information. In these situations, you aren't concerned about where the non-critical employees will next work; you just want their lips sealed. In addition, you can use an NDA to obtain confidentiality from people who have not worked for you, but who know your crucial secrets. For instance, if you've disclosed sensitive business information to potential investors but don't want them blabbing your trade secrets to anyone else, you can present them with an NDA. See Section C2, below, for more information on creating a simple NDA with our agreements.

But for important employees who have access to a lot of your information and/or are essential to your business's success, if you can, it's without a doubt safer to write an agreement using both noncompete and nondisclosure clauses. Having both agreements in place will cut down on the monitoring you'll have to do once that employee leaves. For instance, when employees who have signed only an NDA take a new job, you may have to check into whether they are disclosing your secrets at the new company. If a former worker is doing so, you'll have to sue to stop the disclosures. That's a substantial burden, and even if you win, the cat will be out of the bag since some trade secrets at least will have already been disclosed.

With a noncompete agreement coupled with an NDA, you don't have to worry about whether an ex-employee will disclose secrets at a new job, because the employee is prohibited from taking a job that would utilize those secrets. This can give you peace of mind and save you the hassle of monitoring former workers to see if they've violated an NDA.

2. Properly Defining What Your Worker Can't Disclose

Like noncompetition clauses, a nondisclosure clause must be reasonable to be enforceable. A reasonable nondisclosure clause is limited to protecting company information that qualifies as trade secrets—confidential information that provides value to your business because it is not generally known (see Section 3, below, for an explanation of what qualifies as a trade secret).

Accordingly, it's not wise to try to classify everything the employee or independent contractor learns in the course of employment as trade secrets. Instead, take the time (after reading about trade secrets, just below) to distinguish between true trade secrets and everything else, such as public information and general skills and knowledge the employee or contractor learns on the job.

Carefully limiting the extent of your nondisclosure clause can be very important if your worker violates it. If you have to go to court to enforce the clause, you'll be in a precarious position if you've tried to protect information that isn't a trade secret. If you're lucky, the judge will rewrite the clause for you to protect only your trade secrets. If you're unlucky or you live in a state in which judges aren't allowed to rewrite contracts, the judge may refuse to enforce the entire clause. That's why drafting your nondisclosure clause sensibly is so important.

Each of our agreements sets out a definition of trade secrets that should cover the information that a specific type of employee or contractor has access to. The agreement gives you a place to add information about your company's secrets if our definition doesn't cover the bases. But to avoid problems, we also encourage you to delete any information that doesn't apply to your business or that doesn't qualify as a trade secret in your business. Our goal is to help you create a nondisclosure clause that defines your trade secrets but doesn't try to classify all of your business information as trade secrets.

➡ **In the following section, we explain the basics of trade secret law, including how trade secrets are defined, created and protected.** *If you are familiar with trade secret law skip to Section F to learn about nonsolicitation clauses. If you are not familiar with trade secrets, we recommend that you read this section.*

3. Trade Secrets

Every business has secret information that gives the business a competitive edge—an advantage that would be lost if others had access to the information. Fortunately, your business has the right to stop others from improperly using, stealing or disclosing ("misappropriating," in legalese) this confidential information—called trade secrets—unless there is a legal justification or it is done with the trade secret owner's consent. But in order to take advantage of these protections, you must be able to prove the information qualifies as a trade secret. Only then can you protect the information with a noncompete agreement.

Trade Secrets and Confidential Information

Throughout this book we use the terms confidential information and trade secrets interchangeably. Technically, not all confidential information is a trade secret. In other words, a business may consider certain information confidential, but a court, reviewing the same information, might not consider it to be a trade secret. We discuss this gray area in subsection c, below. Keep in mind, however, that it doesn't matter which term you use to describe your valuable business data. What matters is that you follow the rules in this chapter and treat all such important business data as if it were a trade secret.

a. What Is a Trade Secret?

Broadly speaking, a trade secret is secret information owned or developed by your company that gives it a competitive advantage in its industry.

Most states have adopted a version of the Uniform Trade Secrets Act (UTSA), a standardized set of laws that define and protect trade secrets. Fortunately, all states, even those that have not adopted the UTSA, share a common understanding of the definition of trade secrets. A trade secret is information that:

- is known only to one person or company
- gives the company an economic advantage over its competitors because it isn't known to them and can't be easily discovered, and
- is kept secret by means of reasonable steps undertaken by the company.

Trade Secrets Defined by UTSA

The UTSA defines a trade secret as "information, including a formula, pattern, compilation, program, device, method, technique or process that: (i) derives independent economic value, actual or potential, from not being generally known to, and not being readily ascertainable by proper means by, other persons who can obtain economic value from its disclosure or use, and (ii) is the subject of efforts that are reasonable under the circumstances to maintain its secrecy." (Uniform Trade Secrets Act § 1(4) (1985).)

If you are called upon to defend your noncompete agreement—if an ex-employee threatens to disclose a secret formula, for example, and you need to go to court to stop him—it will be up to you, the trade secret owner, to prove that information qualifies as a trade secret. That means you must be able to prove that the information:

- is not generally known or can't be discovered using legal methods, such as a customer list with private information that is not found in phone book or other public records

- gives you a competitive advantage or has economic value to you, such as the formula for Coca-Cola, and
- is the subject of your reasonable efforts to keep it secret, such as by routinely asking employees with access to the information to sign noncompete or nondisclosure agreements.

Examples of Trade Secrets

Here are examples of information that courts have protected as trade secrets. This list isn't exhaustive, but hopefully it will give you an idea of the wide range of information that can be protected:

- special manufacturing processes (such as the process for manufacturing skis)
- product formulas (such as the formula for a famous soft drink)
- hard-to-obtain customer information (such as special customer needs or even the types of customers that might be interested in a certain product)
- business strategies, such as business and marketing plans (for instance, market research about the target demographics for a highly competitive product, such as a fruit drink), and
- product pricing information.

Even the knowledge that a certain process or formula *doesn't* work can qualify as a trade secret—courts call this "negative know-how." For instance, say an unscrupulous former employee steals plans for a manufacturing process for one of your products. By mistake, the employee takes plans that your company discarded because they didn't work (she's stolen plans your company isn't using). When she uses the plans at the new job, she'll quickly discover that they are no good—and she'll move on to other research and development. Although she never had the plans for your actual manufacturing process, she (or whomever she gives the plans to) will still have gained a competitive advantage over you, because she never wasted time developing a process that didn't work.

b. How to Tell Whether Information Is a Trade Secret

It's one thing to say that a trade secret must be information that's not widely known, gives you a competitive advantage and is held under wraps at your company. It's another thing to accurately determine whether a particular piece of information would qualify. The questions that follow are used by judges when they're called upon to rule on the question. You, too, can use them to help you know whether you've accurately classified a process or know-how. The more you can answer "Yes" to these questions, the more likely it is that you're dealing with a true trade secret.

- **Is the information not known to people in your industry?** If the information is generally known in your field, it's not a secret and, therefore, not entitled to legal protection.
- **Are only a few people within your company privy to the information?** If the phone operator, the dishwasher or the mailroom guy knows it, it's probably not a secret worthy of legal protection.
- **Is the information valuable to you and your competitors?** Unless information is important to the success of your business, and your competitors would reap a benefit if they got their hands on it, it probably doesn't qualify for legal protection.
- **Has your company spent considerable money or efforts creating or compiling the information?** The longer you've been amassing or collecting the information, or the more time and money you've spent coming up with the idea or process, the more likely it qualifies as a trade secrets.
- **Would it be difficult for someone else to independently create or duplicate the information?** If someone else can easily recreate the information, your chances of protecting it are slim. The opposite is also true—the harder it would be for someone else to develop the information independently, the more likely it is that the information is a trade secret.
- **Would it be difficult to discover or figure out this information by analyzing public information?** For instance, if you sell dental equipment, you would have a tough time claiming that your customer list of dentists is a secret, since most dentists in a particular area are listed in the phone book.
- **Did you follow a few simple precautions to keep the information confidential?** If you want information to be protected as a trade secret, you shouldn't routinely leave documentation lying around unprotected areas of your workplace (such as the company kitchen), post it on the Internet or reveal it to third parties without using a noncompete/nondisclosure agreement.

EXAMPLE: A manufacturer of class rings developed a computerized process for creating ring molds that gave it an advantage over its competitors (most still made molds by hand). The employee who developed the process left to work for a competitor and implemented the same process at the competitor. The former employer sued, arguing that the computerized ring mold creation process was a trade secret. The court disagreed, finding that when the company (who was initially interested in licensing the system to other ring manufacturers) made a presentation about the process to other experts in the ring manufacturing field, the information lost whatever trade secret status it might have had. Further, the company didn't tell the employee the information was a secret or require him to keep it confidential. Finally, none of the employees who worked with the technology were required to sign confidentiality agreements, and none of the documents were marked "Confidential." Because of this, the employee wasn't liable for misappropriation of a trade secret. *Jostens, Inc. v. National Computer Systems, Inc.*, 5318 N.W. 2d 691 (Minn. 1982).

c. Secrets That Aren't Trade Secrets After All

If you've run through the questions listed above in subsection b and come up with a few "No's," your information or process may not qualify as a trade secret. But even if you have a straight string of "Yes" answers, you'll need to consider a second set of questions, posed below. These are questions that are typically asked *after* your "secret" has been talked about by

your former worker or has shown up on a rival company's shop floor. Again, you're looking for "Yes" answers. Unless you have a long string of positive answers to these questions, you probably won't be able to stop someone from using or disclosing your information.

- **Can you prove that the information was not legitimately acquired from another source?** For instance, if two companies have independently developed the same formula for a new drug, each has the right to use it because they've both developed it on their own. Even if you took every precaution to safeguard your secret, you can't claim it as your own if someone else was independently hard at work developing the same information.

- **Can you show that your former worker did not develop the information independently?** For example, if a worker is a software programmer who developed a new software program on his own time before he started working for you, he has the right to use and disclose it, even if it's the same (or substantially similar) to a software program your company is developing.

- **Can you show that the information wasn't acquired by taking apart your product (as long as it isn't stolen) or analyzing your process?** Working backward in this way is called reverse engineering. If a clever soul has done this to your secret, he'll escape liability as a trade secret thief as long as he can prove that he actually reverse engineered the secret.

> **EXAMPLE:** Bob, a chemist, analyzes the secret formula for a popular lemon-lime soft drink and figures out its ingredients and their proportions. As long as Bob can prove that he learned the secret after long hours of work in his laboratory (that is, without violating an agreement or stealing information), he is free to use and disclose it.

d. Customer Lists, Collections of Data and Employee Know-How

By using the questions in subsections b and c, above, you can go a long way towards answering your questions about the status—protected, or not—of your business secrets. Unfortunately, there may still be some uncertainty when you're dealing with three types of confidential information: customer lists, collections of data and employee know-how. If you're looking to protect this type of information with a nondisclosure agreement, read the discussions below carefully.

i. Customer Lists

One of the most hotly contested issues in noncompete/nondisclosure agreement disputes is whether a customer or client list

can be protected as a trade secret. When deciding whether a customer list deserves protection as a trade secret, ask yourself the following questions (again, you're hoping for "Yes" answers).

- **Is the information in the list not readily available from another source (for example, in telephone books or trade publications)?** If you've painstakingly developed a client base pulled from various quarters (for example, you operate a commercial laundry and supply fastidious customers in a wide array of trades), it will be impossible for someone to replicate your list by doing research. On the other hand, if all someone has to do is look in the phone book to determine who your customers are, then your customer list is probably not a trade secret.

- **Does the list include more than names and addresses?** A list with idiosyncratic information tagged to every customer is more likely to be protected than a simple listing of names and contact information. For example, a customer list that includes pricing and special customer needs is more likely to be protected because this information has economic value to your company and it isn't easy for someone else to discover.

- **Was there a substantial amount of effort required to assemble the list?** The more time and effort went into creating the list, the more likely it will qualify as a trade secret, and

- **Is the customer list long standing or exclusive?** If a company can prove that a customer list is special to its business and has been used for a long period of time (some courts call these customer relationships "near-permanent" relationships), the list is more likely to be protected.

In sum, a customer list that contains information beyond names, addresses and telephone numbers is more likely to be protected. If a list doesn't contain detailed information such as a customer's key contacts, pricing schemes and volume of business, it is less likely to receive protection as a trade secret.

> **EXAMPLE 1:** A salesman worked for an insurance company selling credit life insurance to automobile dealers. He switched jobs to work for a competing insurance company and took his customer list and contacted the customers at his new job. A court ruled that the customer list was not a trade secret because the names of the automobile dealers were easily ascertainable by other means and because the salesman contributed to the creation of the list. *Lincoln Towers Ins. Agency v. Farrell*, 99 Ill. App. 3d 353 (1981).

> **EXAMPLE 2:** Former employees of a temporary employee service business took a client list and used it to solicit those clients. The former employees argued that the list wasn't a trade secret, since the information could be obtained through other means. A court disagreed and prevented the ex-employees from using the list because the former employees could not show, using public information, which companies were likely to use temporary employees; and because the list also included such hard-to-find information as the volume of the customer's business, specific customer requirements, key managerial customer contacts and billing rates. *Courtesy Temporary Serv., Inc. v. Camacho*, 222 Cal. App. 3d 1278 (1990).

Pair your nondisclosure agreement with a nonsolicitation provision to help protect your customer lists. *Discussed in Section F below, a nonsolicitation provision can prohibit an employee from soliciting your clients or customers for a period of time. Coupling your nondisclosure agreement with a nonsolicitation provision (as do the agreements in this book) will show a judge that you are serious about protecting the information, making it more likely the information will get trade secret status.*

ii. Collections of Data

Collections of data, such as credit reports, sales figures or marketing statistics, may also qualify as trade secrets. Like customer lists, databases are less likely to be protected if the data is readily obtainable from other sources. For example, in one case a judge decided that data related to a casino's profit margin and community contributions was not a trade secret because anyone could obtain the information by visiting the casino, reading newspaper articles and talking to agencies that received mandatory community service contributions from the casino.

A database is more likely to be protected if the data can't by figured out by someone else without a lot of hard work. For instance, in another case an insurance company successfully claimed that its collection of data—including expiration dates and gross revenues from insurance policies—was a trade secret because this information was not public and was very valuable to the company's business.

iii. Employee Skills and Know-How

Finally, employee skills and know-how may or may not qualify as trade secrets, depending on the circumstances. When training employees, you often teach them certain skills and know-how they didn't bring to the job but that are essential to your business. This employee knowledge or skill will qualify as a trade secret if it is a specialized skill known only to your business, rather than a general skill used by most employees in the field.

For example, if you operate a jewelry business, you cannot claim that your jewelry designer's general skills and knowledge in designing jewelry are trade secrets. However, that employee's know-how can qualify as a trade secret if it consists of a secret process used only by employees in your business. Suppose you train that jewelry designer in a special process that prevents stones from falling out of the settings (and no other jewelry designer or manufacturer knows this technique nor could figure it out without a lot of effort and hard work). You can claim this special process as a trade secret and prevent the designer from revealing it to a third party or using it in the designer's own jewelry business.

D. Managing Your Secrets So They Stay That Way

In addition to asking key employees and contractors to sign reasonable noncompete and/or nondisclosure agreements, there are other steps you must take to protect your secrets. Proper "care and management" of your trade secrets will increase your chances that the information will qualify as a trade secret if you ever have to go to court to enforce it. In this section, we discuss a few simple procedures you can implement to help ensure that your carefully designated trade secrets remain safe and secure.

1. Tell Workers What's Secret—and What Isn't—In Your Policies

You can't expect your employees or independent contractors to keep your secrets if they don't know what information is a secret. You also need to tell them how to handle your trade secrets and confidential information. By creating a trade secret policy, you can both inform and guide your workers. Your policy should:

- **Define your trade secrets and confidential information.** For example, a publishing company might specify that all financial information, publishing plans, sales histories and projections are secret and confidential.
- **Explain how your employees must treat that information.** You need to guide your workers on how they may use your secrets. For example, you may allow them to take laptops containing sensitive business information on business trips, but forbid them from working on sensitive files at the airport or in-flight.
- **Inform employees of the steps the company will follow to protect its trade secrets.** For instance, you should tell employees that no

confidential files may be removed from the office without permission, that all visitors must sign in and wear badges and that all file cabinets or rooms with sensitive information should remain locked at all times.

If your company has an employee handbook, it should include your trade secret protection policy. Otherwise, make a copy of the policy and see that every worker receives a copy (and post it conspicuously in the workplace). If you hire independent contractors, attach a copy of the policy to your contract for services and make sure that the contract refers to it and states that the contractor has read it and agrees to abide by it.

2. Explain Your Policy to New Hires

Let every new hire know that you have a trade secret policy and that you expect the worker to follow it, regardless of whether the worker actually signs a noncompete/nondisclosure agreement. Tell your new workers that their participation in protecting your trade secrets is vital to the success of your company. Ask each new hire to sign an acknowledgment that they've received, read and understood your trade secret protection policy, whether it's part of an employee handbook or a separate document.

3. Secure Your Information

One of the best steps you can take to protect your trade secrets is to implement some relatively simple security measures. But don't worry—you don't have to turn your office into Fort Knox. Just take some commonsense precautions, as explained below.

- Use "Confidential" stamps to identify confidential documents and other materials that contain trade secrets.
- Use passwords to protect computers or parts of your computer network or folders that contain confidential data or trade secrets. Allow only workers who need the information to have access to it.
- Lock file cabinets, offices and other locations that contain confidential information and materials; and restrict access to employees and independent contractors who need to have access to the information.
- Have a receptionist or someone at the entrance to your workplace who monitors visitors. Do not allow visitors free access to your office space and make sure an employee accompanies visitors at all times. Lock all unmonitored doors and building or office entrances and keep a list of employees and others who have keys. Mark these keys "Do Not Duplicate" and don't forget to retrieve them when the employee leaves.

- Require employees and independent contractors to return all confidential information and files in their possession when they leave. (The agreements in this book contain a clause in which the employee/contractor promises to do this.)

4. Conduct Exit Interviews

When a worker leaves your employ or a contractor finishes a job, have a discussion to let them know that you expect them to keep your secrets after they leave (exit interviews are discussed further in Chapter 7, Section B). If an employee or contractor has signed a noncompete or nondisclosure agreement, also take the rest of the steps to remind the employee or contractor about her duty to abide by her agreement—such as sending a letter reminding the worker of her obligations—as outlined in Chapter 7, Section B.

5. Create a Stable Workforce

Of course, the best way to keep your trade secrets from leaving with your workers is to keep your workers from leaving in the first place. In addition to asking employees and contractors to sign noncompete agreements, keeping your employees happy is the best way to get them to stay. We can't tell you how to do this; only you know what will make your employees satisfied. But a combination of fair employment policies, decent salaries and benefits (including retirement plans and profit-sharing or other performance-based bonuses) and a pleasant work environment can go a lot further in retaining your employees than a noncompete agreement.

E. Avoid Using Others' Trade Secrets

So far in this chapter, we've concentrated on explaining the steps you can take to protect *your* secrets. But what about the possibility of inadvertently using another's trade secrets? You may one day find yourself hiring an employee or contractor who previously worked for one of your competitors. Since this worker may have had access to the former employer's or client's trade secrets, you must tread carefully and not encourage this person to break any nondisclosure contract with the competitor, disclose its trade secrets or otherwise damage the competitor.

There are some commonsense steps you can take to assure yourself that you won't end up accused of benefiting from someone else's trade secrets. A few judiciously asked questions and thoughtful management of that worker should give you peace of mind. The subsections below suggest ways to approach the situation.

1. Determine If a Prospective Hire Has Worked for a Competitor

An applicant's resume should list former employees or clients. If a prospective hire has worked for one of your competitors, ask for more information beyond the job description listed on the resume. Ask about the applicant's projects and daily responsibilities to get an idea what information that worker had access to. If necessary, double-check this information with previous managers or supervisors. The more similar the worker's previous job description to the position you are trying to fill, the more likely it is that a competitor will squawk about the applicant working for your company.

2. Find Out About Any Pre-existing Agreements

If a prospective hire has worked for one of your competitors, ask whether that person signed a noncompete agreement (or a nondisclosure/nonsolicitation agreement). If so, it could be a violation of the agreement for that worker to take a job with your company or to perform services for your company.

If the applicant claims not to be subject to any kind of noncompetition, nondisclosure or nonsolicitation agreement, get this statement in writing. (When a worker signs one of the agreements in this book, the worker promises not only not to divulge your secrets to anyone else, but also that the worker is not a party to any agreements that would be violated by working for your company.) This way, a previous employer will have a harder time claiming that you knew that a noncompete agreement existed but hired the worker anyway. If the prospective hire tells you she has signed an agreement, ask to see it before you extend an offer of employment, or at the very least, before work starts. Ask your attorney to review the agreement and advise you whether you can legally hire this person.

 Be very careful hiring someone who has signed a noncompete agreement. *An employee or independent contractor isn't the only one on the hook if she breaches a noncompete agreement by working for you. If your company knows a worker signed such an agreement and hires her anyway, you could find yourself at the receiving end of a lawsuit for tortious interference with a contract, as well as a claim for trade secret misappropriation.*

3. Managing New Hires From a Competitor

If you hire an employee or independent contractor who has worked for a competitor, resist the temptation to ask your new hire to use, or tell you about, the previous employer's trade secrets—even if that worker did not sign any agreements with the competitor. (As explained in Section C1, former workers in some states are subject to laws that limit their ability to share a former employer's information, even if they haven't signed an agreement.) In fact, to protect yourself, you should take some active steps after you hire this person, including:

- monitoring the new hire's work, to make sure there's no use of material copied from the old employer that contains confidential information. Secure a written promise that all materials containing confidential information were returned to the former employer. (The agreements in this book require the worker to promise this.)

- giving the new worker duties or projects that won't involve the former employer's trade secrets, at least for a short period of time. If the valuable life of the competitor's secrets is relatively short, this can be a good way of avoiding any inadvertent use or disclosure of your competitor's trade secrets.

- telling the worker not to solicit employees or independent contractors who work for the former employer or client. You can advertise for new positions you need to fill, but don't directly contact prospective hires at your worker's previous employer.

(Soliciting a competitor's employees or contractors on the basis of information provided to you by your new worker can expose you to a lawsuit for unfair competition.) To be safe, ask the new hire to promise in writing not to solicit employees or contractors who work for the former employer. (The agreements in this book require the worker to promise this.)

F. Nonsolicitation Provisions

A nonsolicitation clause, the third and final type of restriction included in our agreements, prevents a former worker from raiding:

- your clients or customers. The worker must not solicit the business of former customers and clients— that is, encourage any of your customers or clients to leave your company and take their business elsewhere, and
- your employees. The worker must not solicit other employees to leave and work for the worker's new company.

Like noncompetition and nondisclosure clauses, a nonsolicitation clause must be reasonable. The duration of a nonsolicitation clause cannot be too long, and the nonsolicitation provision can't make it too difficult for a worker to earn a living—or unfairly limit a competitor's ability to obtain customers or hire workers through legitimate means. The subsections below explain these rules in more detail.

1. Length of Time

A good rule of thumb is to keep your nonsolicitation period no longer than the amount of time you've specified for the agreement not to compete, such as six months or a year. As with a noncompetition clause, if you try to make the time during which a former employee or independent contractor can't contact or solicit customers too long (say, five years), you'll likely run into trouble if you need to ask a judge to enforce it. (See Section B1, above, for a discussion of what constitutes a reasonable length of time in noncompetition clauses.)

There may be situations when it makes sense to make your nonsolicitation clause last longer than your noncompetition clause. For instance, you might want the noncompetition clause to last only three months because, in your fast-evolving industry, your trade secrets won't be valuable to a competitor after that time has passed. But you might want the nonsolicitation clause to last six months, in order to prevent the former worker from stealing your customers while you train a new worker and allow time to establish solid relationships with your customers.

2. Range of Customers

To qualify as a reasonable restriction on your former worker, a nonsolicitation clause must not restrict the person from contacting too broad a range of customers. For instance, if you try to prevent a worker from soliciting all of your current clients plus any possible future clients, you've probably gone too far—and if the worker violates the agreement, a court might find you are overreaching and refuse to enforce it.

> **EXAMPLE:** Bitsy sells makeup door-to-door for Glowing Goddesses, Inc. She is responsible for a specific territory in and around Dallas, Texas. Glowing Goddesses is just starting out and doesn't have a list of existing customers. Instead, the company sends Bitsy out with some marketing data about her neighborhood and wishes her luck. Before Bitsy starts, Glowing Goddesses asks her to sign an agreement not to solicit any of its existing customers when she leaves. They don't ask her not to solicit "potential" customers because the range of potential customers is too broad (basically, everyone is a potential customer), and Glowing Goddesses hasn't developed or given Bitsy any special information to identify these potential customers anyway. This is a reasonable nonsolicitation clause.

Limiting potential customer solicitation is tricky because your ability to do it depends on how much information about potential customers you've developed and shared with your ex-worker. If you've done extensive market research and have targeted a particular group (and your worker knows about your plans), you may be able to rule this population off-limits in a nonsolicitation provision. Put another way, you'll be on shaky ground if you use a nonsolicitation clause that prevents a worker from soliciting clients and customers whom your worker did not learn about while in your employ. It's hardly fair, after all, to prohibit a former worker from engaging in legitimate competition with your business if the worker is simply approaching the same undefined pool of customers as you are.

> **EXAMPLE:** Fred takes a job as an insurance agent for EZ Insurance, a company that provides various types of insurance—life, disability, homeowner's and auto—to its customers. EZ gives Fred a list of EZ's current clients and tells him to call them and make sure they are happy with their existing policies. EZ also gives Fred a list of *potential* customers that EZ has put together through various marketing resources and asks him to contact these people to "determine their insurance needs." Before it hires Fred, EZ asks Fred to sign an agreement promising that, for one year after he leaves

EZ's employ, he will not solicit any of EZ's existing customers or potential customers who Fred learns about through EZ. This is probably a reasonable nonsolicitation clause.

3. Special Relationships With Customers and Clients

In states that take a dim view towards nonsolicitation clauses, employers are allowed to limit a worker from soliciting clients and customers only when the worker had a personal relationship with these people. All other clients and customers— the ones who dealt with your worker at arms' length—are fair game. In theory, if the worker didn't have personal contact with the customer, the worker has less sway over the customer than if the employee was the customer's main contact (the employer's hope is that the main contact, who has stayed behind, will keep the customer in the fold).

> **EXAMPLE:** Olympic Paper Company sells disposable paper products to restaurants. Reddy worked for Olympic in various capacities over the years and was eventually promoted to sales representative. At his promotion, he was required to sign an employment agreement that contained noncompetition and nonsolicitation provisions. The agreement prevented Reddy from contacting and performing services for

any Olympic account within a 150-mile radius, for a full year.

Olympic fired Reddy, who took a job with Olympic's direct competitor, Dublin Paper. Ignoring his agreement with his former employer, Reddy began contacting his former Olympic customers and soliciting their business. Olympic sued him and Dublin, and the judge ruled in favor of Olympic. However, the judge modified ("blue-penciled") the nonsolicitation clause, by limiting the Olympic customers Reddy could contact to those with whom he'd had a working relationship, rather than all of Olympic's customers in a certain geographic area. (*Olympic Paper Co. v. Dublin Paper Co.*, No. 4384, (Court of Common Pleas, Philadelphia County, Pennsylvania 2000).).

Depending on your circumstances, it might make sense to limit the range of customers to those with whom the worker had actual contact, rather than just those the worker learns about by working for you. But as long as you don't try to prohibit honest, legitimate competition, you should be fine.

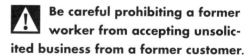 **Be careful prohibiting a former worker from accepting unsolicited business from a former customer.** *If a customer wants to voluntarily take its business to the former worker's new company (and the former worker has scrupu-*

lously avoided soliciting the client's business), you probably won't be able to stop them. In most circumstances, a court will only prevent a former worker from encouraging customers to switch to the new company. If they want to go on their own, there's probably not much you can do.

4. Enticing Your Remaining Employees to Leave

A nonsolicitation clause can prevent workers from wooing remaining employees to join them at a new place of employment, but the clause can't keep your employees from voluntarily joining the departing worker or prevent your competitors from hiring your other employees legitimately. For instance, let's say one of your employees, who has signed a nonsolicitation agreement, leaves and joins a competitor. The competitor needs to hire more employees and posts several job openings on its website and elsewhere. Some of your other employees answer these ads, interview and receive job offers from the competitor. As long as your former employee

didn't encourage your workers to leave, you probably can't prevent these employees from taking these jobs.

⚠️ **If your business is located in a state that doesn't enforce noncompetition clauses, follow the above rules carefully.** *States like California don't enforce noncompetition clauses, but do enforce nonsolicitation clauses and nondisclosure clauses—if they're reasonable. If your nonsolicitation clauses and nondisclosure clauses are so strict they effectively prevent a former worker from competing against you, and your state doesn't enforce noncompetition clauses, a court in your state probably won't enforce them.*

Finally, even though although an employee or independent contractor may have agreed not to solicit your clients and customers, she is generally free to inform them that she will no longer be working for you, and give them her new business information, as long as the communication does not actively solicit their business. ∎

2

When to Use a Noncompete Agreement

As you know from reading the Introduction to this book, there are many good reasons to use a noncompete agreement. It will help you protect your trade secrets, cut down on competition from former workers and retain your employees. While all of these factors will influence your decision to ask an employee or contractor to sign a noncompete agreement, never use these agreements indiscriminately, handing them out to every worker. Instead, use them only if doing so is necessary for your business interests. This chapter explains the situations that call for noncompetition agreements—and cautions you against using them in certain others. In addition, several states have special rules, which we explain.

 Never ask an employee to sign a noncompete agreement to intimidate or scare the worker into staying with your company. *If you try to do this, or try to prevent a worker from getting another job, as punishment for quitting or to avoid legitimate competition, a court will likely toss out the agreement.*

A. Who Should Sign a Noncompete Agreement

Before you ask a worker to sign a noncompete agreement, take a moment to think about it. Does the receptionist or the guy who delivers the mail really need to sign a noncompete agreement? Sure, they probably know some information about your business that you wouldn't want disclosed, but is the information they know a trade secret? Plus, how likely are they to try to sell themselves to competitors? In this section, we'll give you guidelines on how to identify the right employees and contractors for your noncompetition agreements—key people who have:

- special skills
- relationships with customers, or
- access to your trade secrets.

 Noncompete agreements can dampen your workforce morale. *When you limit your workers' choices— their freedom to move from job to job, to talk about what they know and to encourage coworkers and customers to join them—you may find that there's resentment. No matter how valid your reasons for wanting to restrict workers, be prepared for some negative fall-out—another reason to use these agreements sparingly.*

1. Key Employees

A key employee is someone who is essential to the success of your business. These persons are likely candidates for noncompetition agreements. You can usually identify a key employee as someone who fits one, some or all of the following characteristics:

- has access to your confidential information or trade secrets
- manages a manufacturing, production or sales department

- possesses valuable skills and knowledge unique to your business or industry
- develops or researches new products
- has enough information about your business to create a competing business
- creates sales, promotional and marketing tools or plans
- has intimate knowledge about maintaining your products or services
- designs, drafts or engineers key products, or
- maintains close relationships with your clients and customers.

EXAMPLE: You may remember Sarah, who operates her own public relations firm in Chicago, from the Introduction. After working by herself for several years, Sarah hires Ann. Although Ann has little P.R. experience, she quickly learns the business from Sarah and soon has unrestricted access to Sarah's client database (which contains all kinds of juicy tidbits—and hard-earned information—about the clients). Ann also has frequent contact with Sarah's clients. As Sarah's business grows, she hires more employees but only Ann, her trusted assistant, has full access to the confidential client database. One day, Ann announces she's quitting to form her own public relations firm and she is taking several of Sarah's clients and employees with her.

In the example, above, Ann is a key employee with intimate knowledge of

Sarah's business information and clients. This makes Ann an excellent candidate for a noncompete agreement, because, as you can see, Ann is in a position to do serious harm to Sarah's business if she wants to. If Sarah had required Ann to sign a noncompete agreement at the time she hired Ann, it is less likely that Sarah would have lost clients and employees to her.

 Be consistent when requiring employees to sign noncompete agreements. *If you're consistent as to the level and type of employee whom you ask to sign a noncompete agreement, a judge will be more inclined to enforce a particular agreement. By contrast, if you are inconsistent in your choice (for example, by requiring only one of several high-level employees to sign one) a judge will likely question your commitment to protecting your trade secrets and will be less likely to enforce any of them.*

While non-key employees are not appropriate candidates for full-blown noncompete agreements, you might consider requiring them to sign simple nondisclosure agreements. For instance, more easily replaceable employees who nonetheless have access to vital, secret information (such as the CEO's assistant, or someone in payroll) should probably sign simple nondisclosure agreements. You may not mind if these people work for a competitor, but you don't want them blabbing your secrets after they leave. (And remember, one of the best ways to show a court that something is a trade secret is by routinely protecting it with nondisclosure agreements.) In Chapter 4 (employees) and Chapter 6 (independent contractors), we show you how to remove the noncompetition and nonsolicitation clauses from the agreements in this book, leaving the nondisclosure clause as the centerpiece of the agreement.

 For more detailed nondisclosure agreements, see Nondisclosure Agreements: Protect Your Trade Secrets & More, *by Richard Stim and Stephen Fishman (Nolo).*

2. Noncompete Agreements for Particular Key Employees

All of our employee noncompete agreements are similar, but the details vary depending on the type of employee signing the agreement. That's because each employee will have access to different information and will have different customer relationships. We've tailored the agreements in this book to fit several key employee categories, including:

- "information technology" (IT) specialists, Web engineers and software programmers, who may have access to a great deal of technical information (software source code, for example)
- high-level executives, who may be privy to considerable amounts of other proprietary information, such as corporate marketing strategies or product pricing schemes

- salespeople with significant client contact or access to customer lists and confidential client information
- business development or marketing managers with access to important marketing strategies, new product and/or product pricing information, and
- employees involved in research and development, who have access to formulas, manufacturing processes or proprietary product design information.

Depending on the type of employee you're dealing with, one of our agreements should provide you with the appropriate protection you need in light of the employee's duties. If an employee doesn't fit into one of these categories, don't worry. We provide a general noncompete agreement for all employees, which should work for most other employees and which you can easily adapt to your employee's specific situation.

All of these agreements are discussed in more detail, section by section, in Chapter 4, along with instructions for filling them out. The forms themselves are included in the CD-ROM at the back of this book.

3. Key Independent Contractors

As with employees, ask only key independent contractors to sign agreements with noncompetition clauses. A key independent contractor is someone who possesses enough information about your business to create a successful competing business—for example, a contractor who has valuable skills and knowledge unique to your business and/or maintains close relationships with your clients and customers. But keep in mind our mantra throughout this book—restrict a worker's ability to compete only when it is necessary to protect your business interests. Without a valid reason for preventing an independent contractor from working for a competitor or soliciting your customers, a judge may not enforce your agreement.

You also have to decide which noncompete provisions (noncompetition, nonsolicitation and/or nondisclosure) are appropriate to put in an agreement with your independent contractor. Your decision will depend on the contractor's importance to your company, the information the contractor has access to, your bargaining position and the type of services the contractor performs. Our advice is to:

- use full-blown noncompete agreements (containing noncompetition, nondisclosure and nonsolicitation provisions) with key contractors only, and
- use simple nondisclosure agreements (without noncompetition and nonsolicitation clauses) with all other contractors.

In addition, as we discuss in Chapter 5, it will probably take some negotiation on your part to get any contractor to sign a restrictive agreement, especially if it contains a noncompetition clause. For this reason alone, consider asking contractors to sign agreements containing only nonsolicitation and nondisclosure clauses.

4. Noncompete Agreements for Particular Key Independent Contractors

The details necessary in an independent contractor agreement will vary depending on the contractor's profession or skills. In order to assist you with some of the more common contractor situations, we have prepared specific noncompete agreements for the following types of contractors:

- Web engineers/designers who may have access to marketing strategies, proprietary design information and business methods
- software engineers/beta testers who may have access to a great deal of technical information (software source code, for example)
- salespeople with significant client contact or access to customer lists, confidential client information and product pricing information
- brokers/agents who have significant client contact or access to customer lists, confidential client information, product pricing information and business plans or strategies
- marketing/market research consultants with access to important marketing strategies, sales projections, new product and/or product pricing information, and
- consultants or contractors who conduct new or existing product research and development who have access to formulas, manufacturing processes or proprietary product design information.

Depending on the type of contractor you're dealing with, one of our agreements should provide you with the appropriate protection you need given the services the contractor provides. If a contractor doesn't fit into one of these categories, don't worry. We provide a general noncompete agreement for all contractors, which you can easily adapt to your contractor's specific situation.

All of these agreements are discussed in more detail, section by section, in Chapter 6, along with instructions for filling them out. The forms themselves are included in the CD-ROM at the back of this book.

B. States That Restrict Noncompetition Clauses

As mentioned in the Introduction, some states refuse to enforce, or they at least put limits on, noncompetition clauses in agreements with workers. But even in states in which noncompetition clauses aren't enforced, you can create agreements containing nondisclosure and nonsolicitation provisions to protect your trade secrets, customers and employees. In Section 3, below, we give you instructions on what to do if your business is located in one of the states listed below.

1. State Rules for Agreements With Employees

Several states have rules covering noncompetition clauses for employees. These states restrict the types of employees whom you may restrict, as well as the situations in which you may use them. This section explains restrictions in the following states.

- California, Montana, North Dakota and Oklahoma have enacted laws that severely restrict the enforcement of noncompetition clauses for employees (see subsections a and b).
- Florida, Oregon and Texas have laws that define specific situations in which a noncompetition clause will be enforceable against an employee (see subsections c and e).
- Alabama and Colorado have laws that limit the types of employees against whom noncompetition clauses can be enforced (see subsection d), and
- Florida, Louisiana and South Dakota have laws that limit the duration of noncompetition clauses for employees (see subsection f).

The rules are summarized in "State Laws on Employee Agreements Not to Compete," below. If your business is located in one of these states, make sure you read this section to determine whether or not you can use a noncompetition clause in your agreement and to be aware of other rules governing your employees.

If your business is not located in one of these states, you can skip this section and go straight to Chapter 3.

State Laws on Employee Agreements Not to Compete*

State	Code Section	Allows Noncompetition Clauses	Special Time Limits
Alabama	Ala. Code § 8-1-1	Yes, but not for all occupations; consult an Alabama employment law expert.	No
California	Cal. Bus. & Prof. Code §§ 16600-16602	No	N/A
Colorado	Colo. Rev. Stat. § 8-2-113	Yes, but only for executive and managerial employees and their assistants or to protect trade secrets. Not enforceable against physicians. Consult a Colorado employment law expert.	No
Florida	Fla. Stat. Ann. § 542.33, 542.335	Yes, but only to protect trade secrets, customer lists and a few other business interests.	Six months to two years is a considered "reasonable" duration.
Louisiana	La. Rev. Stat. Ann. § 23.921	Yes	Two-year maximum
Montana	Mont. Rev. Code Ann. § 28-2-703	Probably not, but it's unclear. Consult a Montana employment law expert.	No
North Dakota	N.D. Cent. Code § 9-08-66	Probably not, but it's unclear. Consult a North Dakota employment law expert.	No
Oklahoma	Okla. Stat. Tit. 15, §§ 217-219A	Maybe. Consult an Oklahoma employment law expert.	No
Oregon	Or. Rev. Stat. § 653.295	Yes, but only if entered into when the employee is hired or promoted. Allows a "bonus restriction agreement"—an agreement in which the employee forfeits some money or bonus if she competes—however, at other times.	No
South Dakota	S.D. Codified Laws Ann. §§ 53-9-8 to -11	Yes	Two-year maximum
Texas	Tex. Bus. & Com. Code Ann. §§15.03, 15.05	Yes, but only for employees who are under employment contracts. Consult a Texas employment law expert.	No

*You can find the full text of these statues in Appendix 2.

a. California

Like those maverick early California settlers, California bucks the national trend and refuses to enforce agreements containing noncompetition clauses between employers and employees. While California courts *will* enforce noncompetition clauses in connection with the sale of a business or the dissolution of a partnership or an LLC (limited liability company), they almost pride themselves on their refusal to enforce agreements containing noncompetition clauses for employees.

Hapless employers who have tried to enforce such agreements in California have run smack into California Business & Professions Code § 16600, which reads: "Except as provided in this chapter, every contract by which anyone is restrained from engaging in a lawful profession, trade or business of any kind is to that extent void." And, although California courts have given lip service to enforcing noncompete agreements that are written to protect trade secrets, the reality is that this is rarely, if ever, a basis for enforcement of a noncompete agreement in California.

This doesn't mean California employers have to stand helplessly by while former employees steal trade secrets and solicit customers and employees. California courts *will* enforce properly drafted nondisclosure and nonsolicitation agreements, as long as they don't impede a former employee's ability to make a living. So if your business is located in California, don't despair—the forms in this book can be adapted to include only nondisclosure and nonsolicitation clauses—see Section 3, below, for more information.

It Doesn't Pay to Use Noncompetition Clauses in California

If your business is located in California, you might be tempted to ask an employee to sign an agreement containing a noncompetition clause even though it's not enforceable. You might reason that although *you* know it wouldn't be enforced, the employee doesn't, and it can't hurt if it deters an employee from going to work for a competitor, right?

Wrong! Aetna, one of the country's largest insurance companies, found out the hard way that this isn't a good idea. Aetna had a policy of requiring all of its employees above a certain level nationwide—including those in California—to sign noncompete agreements. Aetna told employees who refused to sign the agreement that it would try to "relocate" them to jobs within the company that didn't require noncompete agreements, but employees who didn't sign noncompete agreements were eventually fired.

One of Aetna's California employees, Anita Walia, refused to sign the noncompete agreement. Anita had done some research and discovered that noncompete agreements were invalid in California. Although she told her employer that she didn't think the agreement was enforceable in California and refused to sign it, she and 25 other California employees were fired for refusing to sign the agreement.

Walia sued Aetna, claiming she was terminated in violation of public policy, because California Business and Professions Code § 16600 prohibits noncompete agreements in the employer/employee context. The jury returned a $1.2 million verdict against Aetna. (Not long after this, Aetna decided to stop asking its California employees to sign noncompete agreements.)

The moral of this story? If you are a California employer who is tempted to fire an employee who doesn't want to sign a noncompete agreement, don't—it could end up costing you.

 California employers may be able to prevent unfair business practices (such as interference with existing business contracts or misappropriation of trade secrets) without an agreement under existing laws that prevent unfair competition. See Chapter 7, Section A3.

b. Montana, North Dakota and Oklahoma

Montana, North Dakota and Oklahoma have laws that appear to prohibit employee agreements that contain noncompetition clauses. However, unlike California, some courts in these states have indicated that such agreements might be enforceable against employees in spite of what the law says. For instance, in Montana, the Montana Supreme Court has said that post-employment restrictions that meet a "reasonableness" test might be upheld. If your business is located in one of these states, we recommend that you seek the help of an expert if you want to create an enforceable agreement that includes a noncompetition clause.

Oklahoma recently amended its existing prohibition on noncompetition clauses for employees. The amended law specifically permits former employees—even those who sign noncompete agreements—to work in the same or similar industry as a former employer's as long as the former employee doesn't "directly solicit the sale of goods, services or a combination of goods and services from the established customers of the former employer." This means that the employee cannot solicit your customers but will be allowed to compete with you. Oklahoma courts will probably enforce an employer's agreement containing nonsolicitation and nondisclosure clauses (but not noncompetition clauses). However, since this law is so new and hasn't been tested yet, we recommend that you seek the advice of an experienced Oklahoma employment lawyer before you ask an employee to sign a noncompete agreement.

Employers in these states may be able to prevent unfair business practices (such as interference with existing business contracts or misappropriation of trade secrets) without an agreement under existing unfair competition laws. See Chapter 7, Section A3, for more information.

c. Florida and Oregon

A few states have laws that allow agreements containing noncompetition clauses, but they put certain limitations on their use. In Florida and Oregon, such agreements are enforceable, but only if they comply with specific rules.

Florida takes the unusual step of laying out in detail the circumstances under which a noncompete agreement will be enforceable. In Florida, a noncompete agreement can be used only to protect trade secrets; valuable, confidential business or professional information; relationships with specific prospective or existing customers, patients or clients; or extraordinary or specialized training. As long as you are using a noncompetition clause to protect your trade secrets or customer lists, as we discussed in Chapter 1, Section A, you shouldn't have a problem in Florida.

In Oregon, agreements containing noncompetition clauses are enforceable as long as they're signed when employees are hired or promoted. But Oregon law allows employees and employers to enter into another type of noncompete agreement, called a "bonus restriction agreement," that can be made at any time during employment. A bonus restriction agreement forces an employee to forfeit any profit-sharing or bonus compensation if the employee competes against the employer after the employee leaves the company. See an Oregon lawyer if you are interested in this type of agreement.

d. Alabama and Colorado

Alabama allows noncompetition clauses in general, but prohibits "professionals," such as doctors, lawyers, accountants and vet-

erinarians, from entering into them. Since the Alabama state courts have had a tough time assessing what qualifies as a "profession," as a opposed to a trade or business, we recommend that you seek the help of an expert if you want to create an enforceable noncompete agreement in Alabama.

Colorado law also permits their use with any type of employee. However, Colorado courts are not partial to agreements not to compete, and you'll probably have a tough time convincing a judge that an agreement with a noncompetition clause is truly necessary to protect your trade secrets. A judge is more likely to think that a simple nondisclosure clause would do the trick. If you're interested in using a noncompete agreement to protect your trade secrets in Colorado, it would be wise to consult a Colorado employment expert.

Colorado law will also enforce agreements containing such a clause only for "executive and management personnel and officers," as well as "employees who constitute professional staff to executive and management personnel." However, any type of employee in Colorado can sign an alternative noncompete agreement—one that provides only for the recovery of educational and training expenses if the employee works for the employer for less than two years.

Colorado law also prohibits doctors from entering into traditional noncompete agreements, but it allows them agree to pay damages (financial compensation) to their former employers or co-owners if they compete after they leave their firm. That means that a physician's former employer (or a former co-owner of the physician's practice group) can get damages from the doctor, but a court won't issue an injunction (a court order) preventing the physician from working for a competitor.

e. Texas

Texas, like California, has blazed another unusual trail through noncompetition law. In Texas, state courts have decided that they will enforce noncompetition clauses against only those employees who receive a benefit over and above a job in exchange for signing an agreement containing a noncompetition clause. In legal terms, the employee must receive more than "at-will employment" in return for signing such an agreement. (At-will employment means that, with certain exceptions, you can fire an employee at any time for any reason, and the employee can quit at any time for any reason. See Chapter 3, Section B, for more information on at-will employment.)

A benefit that counts as more than at-will employment can be anything from simply giving the employee access to trade secrets or promising (and providing) the employee a 14-day notice period before the employee is terminated, to giving the employee a fixed-term employment contract. Because coming up with an adequate benefit under Texas law can be a tricky business, if you want to create a noncompete agreement for an at-will employee in Texas, consult a Texas employment law expert.

f. Florida, Louisiana and South Dakota

The courts of Florida, South Dakota and Louisiana will enforce employee agreements containing noncompetition clauses, but they put limits on how long an employee can be kept from competing with a former employer. South Dakota and Louisiana law don't allow such agreements to last more than two years after an employee leaves the company.

Florida law provides that such agreements with employees are presumed to be reasonable if they last from six months to two years, unless the agreement is entered into to protect trade secrets, in which case five years is presumed to be reasonable. Because it's difficult to predict which time limit will apply to your situation, it's probably best to seek the advice of a Florida employment law expert before you ask an employee to sign a noncompete agreement that lasts longer than two years.

You can look up the law yourself.
If you live in one of the states we've just talked about and want to find out more about how your state law works, you can do it yourself. It's easier to research the law than you think—Nolo's website, http://www.nolo.com, has links to all state statutes (laws) as well as lots of helpful information on how to do your own legal research. Each state's noncompetition law is listed in the table above and the full text is provided in Appendix 2. Simply record the number of the law and search for it.

2. State Rules for Agreements With Independent Contractors

Several states will also limit how you restrict independent contractors—those who are not your employees but who may have access to your secrets and plans, making them potentially dangerous competitors. Here is a brief summary of special state rules that apply to contractors:

- Alabama, California, Montana, North Dakota and Oklahoma have enacted laws that severely restrict the enforcement of noncompetition clauses for independent contractors.

- Florida, Oregon and Texas have laws that define specific situations in which a noncompetition clause will be enforceable against a contractor.

- Florida, Louisiana and South Dakota have laws that limit the duration of noncompetition clauses for contractors.

If your business is located in one of these states, make sure you read this section to determine whether you can use a noncompetition clause in your agreement and to be aware of other rules governing your employees.

If your business is not located in one of these states, you can skip this section and go straight to Chapter 5.

State Laws on Contractor Agreements Not to Compete*

State	Code Section	Allows Noncompetition Clauses for Independent Contractors	Special Time Limits
Alabama	Ala. Code § 8-1-1	No	No
California	Cal. Bus. & Prof. Code §§ 16600-16602	No	N/A
Colorado	Colo. Rev. Stat. § 8-2-113	Maybe	No
Florida	Fla. Stat. Ann. §§ 542.33; 542.335	Yes, but only to protect trade secrets, customer lists and a few other business interests.	Six months to two years is a considered "reasonable" duration
Louisiana	La. Rev. Stat. Ann. § 23.921	Yes	Two-year maximum
Montana	Mont. Rev. Code Ann. § 28-2-703	Probably not, but it's unclear. Consult a Montana employment law expert.	No
North Dakota	N.D. Cent. Code § 9-08-66	Probably not, but it's unclear. Consult a North Dakota employment law expert.	No
Oklahoma	Okla. Stat. Tit. 15, §§ 217-219A	Maybe. Consult an Oklahoma employment law expert.	No
Oregon	Or. Rev. Stat. § 653.295	Probably not	No
South Dakota	S.D. Codified Laws Ann. §§ 53-9-8 to-11	Yes	Two-year maximum
Texas	Tex. Bus. & Com. Code Ann. §§15.03, 15.05	Yes, but at-will employment is not sufficient consideration to support enforcement of agreement. Consult a Texas employment law expert.	No

*You can find the full text of these statues in Appendix 2.

a. California

California has the toughest stance in the entire country on noncompetition clauses. Section 16600 of the California Business and Professions Code effectively bans the use of noncompetition clauses against employees *and* independent contractors. Noncompetition clauses in connection with the sale of a business or the departure of an owner from a partnership or LLC (limited liability company) are the only exceptions to this rule.

California courts *will* enforce properly drafted nondisclosure and nonsolicitation agreements, as long as they don't impede a former contractor's ability to make a living. These provisions will prevent a contractor from revealing trade secrets and from stealing clients and customers. So if your business is located in California, don't despair—the forms in this book can be adapted for you to include only nondisclosure and nonsolicitation clauses. See Section 3, below, for more information.

b. Montana, North Dakota and Oklahoma

Montana, North Dakota and Oklahoma have laws passed by the legislatures that appear to prohibit the use of noncompetition clauses for independent contractors. However, the *courts* in these states have interpreted these laws to mean that possibly—just possibly—noncompetition clauses will still be enforced. In a few cases in which these courts have considered the validity of nondisclosure and nonsolicitation clauses (which they generally consider to be valid), the courts have stated that at some point in the future, they might enforce a reasonable agreement not to compete, if all the facts and circumstances were right.

Unfortunately, you can't count on these hints becoming a reality. Because the law in these states is so iffy, contact an attorney if you're interested in creating an agreement that prevents an independent contractor from competing with you.

Oklahoma recently amended its existing prohibition on noncompetition clauses for workers. The amended law specifically permits former workers who sign a noncompete agreement to work in the same or similar industry as a former employer's as long as the former worker doesn't "directly solicit the sale of goods, services or a combination of goods and services from the established customers of the former employer." Basically, this means that, regardless of whether the contractor entered into an agreement not to compete, a former contractor cannot solicit your customers but will be allowed to compete with you. Oklahoma courts will probably now enforce agreements containing nonsolicitation and nondisclosure clauses (though not noncompetition clauses), but since this law is so new and hasn't been tested yet, we recommend that you seek the advice of an experienced Oklahoma employment lawyer before you ask a contractor to sign a noncompete agreement.

Regardless of whether courts in these states prohibit noncompetition clauses, they will enforce nondisclosure and nonsolicitation restrictions, as long as these provisions don't impede a contractor's ability to make a living. For more on how to do this, see Section 3, below.

c. Alabama

Alabama does not allow noncompetition clauses to be enforced against independent contractors. Oddly, Alabama does allow them to be used against employees. This is a strange quirk in the law, and may eventually be changed. But until then, independent contractors cannot be bound by noncompetition clauses. However, Alabama employers can enter into and enforce reasonable nondisclosure and nonsolicitation agreements with independent contractors. For more on how to accomplish this, see Section 3, below.

If you insist on having an Alabama contractor agree not to compete, consider making her an employee. *If you can afford it and the contractor is willing, there's no reason you can't hire the contractor as an employee and ask her to sign an agreement containing a noncompetition clause as a condition of employment.*

d. Colorado and Oregon

Colorado law permits the use of agreements containing a noncompetition clause with an independent contractor if it is for the purpose of protecting trade secrets. However, Colorado courts are not partial to noncompetition clauses; for this reason, if you're interested in using noncompetition clauses to protect your trade secrets in Colorado, we advise consulting a Colorado employment expert. You *can* enter into nondisclosure and nonsolicitation agreements with independent contractors in Colorado, as long as they are reasonably tailored to meet your needs and aren't so restrictive that they amount to an agreement with a noncompetition clause.

Oregon law doesn't address whether agreements containing noncompetition clauses are valid for independent contractors. If you are interested in entering into a agreement not to compete with an independent contractor, consult an Oregon attorney who is familiar with Oregon employment law.

e. Texas

Texas courts will enforce noncompetition clauses against independent contractors in most situations. Unlike employees, these clauses are enforceable without offering anything more than you otherwise would to an independent contractor. That's because Texas courts assume that independent contractors have stronger bargaining positions and can negotiate additional benefits if they want them in return for agreeing not to compete. So you really don't have to provide additional consideration to an independent contractor—the job is enough.

Here's why: Unlike an at-will employee, when you hire an independent contractor, whether you have an agreement or not, usually the contractor is guaranteed the job until the term of the contract is up or the contractor has completed the project for which you hired her—in other words, you do not have the right to terminate the contractor whenever you feel like it, for any reason. Usually, there are two circumstances under which your relationship with a contractor ends: either the term of the agreement expires or you terminate the contractor because she is not holding up her end of the bargain.

Our agreements provide that the employer/contractor relationship ends only when the job is done or when the contractor ceases to perform her contractual duties. Since, under our agreements, you will not be able to terminate a contractor at any time you want to, the contractor is receiving enough of a benefit in exchange for her agreement not to compete. As a result, as long as you don't want or need the right to terminate a contractor at any time for any reason, you can safely use the agreements in this book for contractors in Texas.

However, some employers do want to hire independent contractors but still be able to fire them at any time for any reason. In such cases, the independent contractor agreement would include a clause that states that either party is free to terminate the relationship at any time, for any reason. If you're interested in hiring an independent contractor on this basis and you want her to sign a noncompete agreement, consult a Texas employment law expert, because you may not be able to enforce a noncompete agreement against an independent contractor in these circumstances.

⚠ **Be careful hiring independent contractors who you can fire at any time, for any reason.** *The IRS tends to think that independent contractors who can be fired any time, for any reason at all, without cause, look an awful lot like employees. If you are not 100% sure a worker qualifies as an independent contractor, talk to an employment law expert before you hire an independent contractor on this basis.*

f. Florida, Louisiana and South Dakota

Louisiana law specifically allows noncompetition clauses to be enforced against independent contractors, as long as they don't keep the contractor from competing against the employer for more than two years.

Florida courts will enforce agreements with independent contractors that contain noncompetition clauses as long as the noncompetition period is between six months and two years as long as the purpose of the agreement is to protect trade secrets. Anything longer than that will probably be considered to be unreasonable and won't be enforced.

South Dakota law also allows independent contractors to enter into agreements containing noncompetition clauses with employers, but doesn't allow such agreements to last more than two years after a contractor's work is done.

3. What to Do in States That May Not Enforce Noncompetition Clauses

If your business is located in one of the states mentioned in Sections B1 or B2, above, where noncompetition clauses may not be enforced, all is not lost. You can still limit a worker's ability to disclose confidential information and trade secrets or to solicit your employees and customers. You can do this by asking a worker to sign a shortened agreement that includes a nondisclosure clause and a nonsolicitation clause, but not a noncompetition clause.

A nondisclosure clause (discussed in Chapter 1, Section C) will prohibit a worker from disclosing trade secrets to outsiders, and a nonsolicitation clause (discussed in Chapter 1, Section F) will prevent a worker from soliciting clients, customers and co-workers to leave your company.

The form instructions in Chapter 4 (employees) and Chapter 6 (independent contractors) show you how to accomplish this.

⚠ Don't include a noncompetition clause in your agreement if it's not enforceable. *You might think that it can't hurt to include a noncompetition clause in your agreement if your business is located in one of the states we've mentioned above. After all, the contractor might not know it isn't enforceable and abide by it. The problem with this approach is that in the event that a dispute arises, a judge will view your approach as being in "bad faith." Instead of simply invalidating the noncompetition provision, the judge may invalidate the whole agreement. In that event, the contractor would not be prevented from disclosing your trade secrets or soliciting your customers.* ∎

3

Using Noncompete Agreements for Employees

Now that you know what's in a noncompete agreement and when to use one, it's time to learn when, and how, to get your employees to sign them. There are just a few simple rules to follow here, but they're very important, so make sure to read this chapter carefully. For example, the date that an employee signs a noncompete agreement—before work starts or after—can affect its enforceability.

The sections that follow also give you tips on how to convince new, existing and departing employees to sign noncompete agreements and how to negotiate with reluctant employees. We also cover your options in the event an employee balks at signing an agreement.

A. The Cost of Your Noncompete Agreement

You already know that a noncompete agreement will give you substantial benefits, including the preservation of your trade secrets and retention of your customers and workforce. It may surprise you to learn, however, that these benefits aren't free—your agreements won't be enforceable unless your employees, too, receive something of value from you for signing them. This section explains why this is so and how you can make sure your agreements are enforceable.

Bear with us for a moment while we explain a legal principle that underlies our discussion. Your noncompete agreement is a contract. Every legal contract involves the exchange of value—for example, in exchange for your money, which is valuable, Nolo will send you a book, which is also valuable. In legal terms, the things of value—such as money, goods, services or benefits or the promise to supply them—that each party agrees to give the other is called "consideration." Unless each party to a contract receives some consideration from the deal, a court will not enforce it.

Because a noncompetition agreement is a contract, the requirement of consideration applies here. You must give the employee something of value—benefits, money or services—in exchange for his agreement to give up the ability to work where he chooses, use information from your company as he likes or convince customers and employees to join him at his new job (all of which are or could be valuable activities to him). This rule applies to full-blown noncompetition agreements and to agreements that involve only nondisclosure and nonsolicitation agreements. Moreover, the consideration you provide must be something of *real* value—attempting to secure a noncompetition agreement for one dollar won't work.

How you provide adequate consideration to your employee will depend on whether the employee is a prospective hire, an existing employee or is departing for greener pastures. In the following sections, we discuss how to handle each of these situations so that you create a contract that is supported by the right kind of consideration.

B. New Employees

Every new hire who you decide merits a noncompete agreement should sign the agreement before starting work. In fact, signing a noncompete agreement should be a condition of employment. This policy has an obvious advantage: The agreement is more likely to get signed. An applicant who wants a job is likely to sign the agreement if doing so furthers the chances of being hired. In other words, you will have more bargaining power *before* you offer the applicant a job. Once someone is on board, your leverage has disappeared.

There's another tactical reason to tie the job offer to the agreement. In every state but Texas, the job itself will supply the consideration you need to make the agreement enforceable. (As explained above, you must give something of value in order to make the agreement enforceable.) Even if you hire employees and do not provide them with an employment contract (which is the case with the overwhelming majority of your employees), in most states the job offer itself will do the trick, as explained in Section 1, below. If you do give an employee a contract, as you might do with a top-level hire, you'll definitely be providing enough consideration, as explained in Section 2, below.

1. Employees Who Won't Have Employment Contracts

Most of your employees have been hired with the understanding that you may terminate their employment for any reason (except a discriminatory or illegal reason). The legal term for this understanding is "at-will" employment. These employees have no written or oral guarantee of a job—and they are free to quit when they want, too. In short, both of you can walk away from the relationship at any time.

In every state except Texas, the offer itself of at-will employment is enough of a benefit to create consideration for signing a noncompete agreement. Since you probably offer at-will employment to most of your new hires, you shouldn't have to change your hiring practices to create enforceable noncompete agreements. A prospective hire may try to negotiate for a higher salary or other perk in return for signing the agreement, but whether you agree to this is up to you—and the economy. If an applicant needs the job badly enough, you may not have provide anything extra. In states that enforce noncompete agreements, the job will provide the necessary consideration to make your noncompete agreement enforceable.

EXAMPLE: Ellis applies for a job as a systems analyst at Mega Corp. He has good experience and Mega Corp. offers him the job, but conditions it on signing a noncompete agreement. Ellis asks what he will receive in exchange for signing the agreement. The human resources director tells him it is a condition of employment and that he will receive a job in exchange for signing the agreement. She also hints that hundreds of other qualified people applied for the position, and Mega Corp. does not feel it needs to offer any additional perks in exchange for signing noncompete agreements. If he wants the job, he will have to sign it. Ellis is reluctant to limit his future employment without getting something more in return and continues to negotiate. Mega Corp. eventually withdraws the job offer and gives the job to another applicant, who accepts on the spot and signs the noncompete agreement. Ellis continues his job hunt.

In Texas, however, just offering at-will employment probably does not satisfy the requirement for consideration. If you are a Texas employer, you will need to offer the employee something more than just a job in order to secure an enforceable noncompetition agreement. See Chapter 2, Section B1e, for more information on providing a sufficient benefit if your business is located in Texas.

The agreements in this book are intended for use with at-will employees—and while they bind the employee to the terms of the noncompetition agreement, they don't change that worker's status as an at-will employee.

Finally, always get the employee's signature on the agreement before work begins—a delay of even a few weeks can hurt your chances of enforcement. Once the employee has started the job, you'll have to provide something beyond employment to make it enforceable.

EXAMPLE: Janie starts her new job as a programmer at Software Express on March 15th. Six months later, Janie's boss asks her to sign a noncompete agreement, and she agrees. However, Janie doesn't receive anything in exchange for signing the agreement, such as a raise, a bonus or a promotion. Software Exchange might not be able to enforce the noncompete agreement against Janie, since it didn't provide an additional benefit (something more than continued employment) to Janie in exchange for signing the agreement.

When—And Why—You Fire an Employee May Affect Your Agreement

If you need to go to court to enforce your noncompetition agreement, the circumstances surrounding your employee's departure—why you terminated the worker, and when—may affect the outcome. Firing an employee very soon after work started means that your worker enjoyed the benefit he got from signing the agreement—his job—for a very short time. A judge may think this brief period is not enough to hold him to the agreement.

Why you fired the worker is just as important. If you fire someone for a good reason—for poor productivity or insubordination—your chances of being able to enforce the agreement are fairly good. Letting a worker go for no reason—which you can do for any at-will employee—places you in a less strong position. And certainly, if you fire someone for an illegal or discriminatory reason (such as terminating someone who blows the whistle on illegal company practices), a court will probably refuse to enforce your agreement.

 If you want to fire an employee who has signed a noncompete agreement, make sure you have a justifiable, legitimate reason for the termination—one that will pass muster with a judge. To learn more about how to avoid legal problems when firing employees, see Dealing With Problem Employees: A Legal Guide, *by Amy DelPo and Lisa Guerin (Nolo).*

2. Employees Who Have Contracts

The alternative to at-will employment is to hire a worker for a definite or fixed term. Usually, employers do this with a written employment contract, in which the employee promises to do certain work in exchange for a promise of continued employment. Employees with contracts can still be fired—if they fail to follow through on their job responsibilities, break company rules or do something seriously illegal, for example—but they can't be let go without reason, as can at-will employees.

Fixed-term employment relationships are usually reserved for top company executives and professional athletes. Still, you may want or need to create a fixed-term agreement with a prospective employee. If you give an employee a promise of continued employment with a contract, that promise alone provides the consideration you need to support a noncompetition agreement.

Employment contracts for a specific time period are rare in the United States, and we don't recommend you use one lightly, since it ties your hands when it comes to managing your workforce. There are practical considerations, too, that argue against coupling noncompetition agreements with fixed-term employment contracts: If the noncompete provision is incorporated in the employment contract but your employee continues to work beyond the end of the employment period—becoming an at-will employee—the restraints included in the noncompetition provisions may not roll over. You'll need to renew the noncompete agreement, with fresh signatures, when the employment contract ends—and go through the negotiation process all over again.

> **EXAMPLE:** In 1995, Dr. Fine hired Dr. Burke and entered into a two-year fixed-term employment agreement that contained a two-year post-employment noncompetition provision. When the contract expired in 1997, Dr. Fine didn't ask Dr. Burke to renew the agreement, even though Dr. Burke continued to work for him until 1999. After Dr. Burke left, Dr. Fine attempted to enforce the noncompetition agreement. A Minnesota court decided that, along with the employment agreement, the noncompetition clause expired in 1997

because neither the clause, nor the contract, contained a statement that the noncompetition clause would survive the expiration of the agreement. However, Dr. Fine could have enforced the noncompetition provisions if he had renewed the employment agreement. *Burke v. Fine,* 608 N.W. 2d 909, 2000 Minn. App. LEXIS 346 (2000).

Because the area of fixed-term employment has so many potential minefields, we suggest that fixed-term employment agreements containing noncompetition provisions be reviewed by an attorney specializing in employment law.

 For more information on fixed-term employment contracts, see The Employer's Legal Handbook, *by Fred S. Steingold (Nolo).*

3. Convincing a Reluctant New Hire to Sign

A prospective employee may balk at signing a noncompete agreement. Employees worry about their ability to make a living after leaving your company, especially since most won't have the job security associated with a fixed-term employment contract. If a potential employee is reluctant to sign a noncompete agreement, and you are sure that no other applicant could fill the position, consider the following negotiating points:

- Can you "sweeten the pot" for the prospective hire by offering more money or other perks in exchange for signing the noncompete agreement? Often, a new hire will be willing to accept some additional benefits in exchange for her agreement not to compete. This can range from a company car to promising the employee you'll continue to pay her salary during the noncompetition period. There are no rules here—it's whatever you and the employee can agree on.
- Can you offer job security to the new hire? For example, could you promise fixed-term employment, such as two years, rather than "at-will" employment (which means that the employee can be fired at any time)?

If, after negotiations, the prospective employee still refuses to sign the noncompete agreement, weigh the following factors:

- How badly do you want or need the employee? Think about what will happen to your business if you don't make the hire. Will you be able to find another suitable candidate? Will your business plan fall apart if you don't fill the position with this particular employee? Will you lose a lucrative contract if this person doesn't come on board? If the answer to any of these questions is

"Yes," hiring the employee might be more important than getting a noncompete agreement signed.

- Assuming the new hire will be successful at your company, can you estimate the damage to your business if the employee were to later compete with you or solicit your customers or clients? For instance, if you are hiring this person to manage the launch of a new product, she may have access to marketing plans, pricing strategies and product formulas. If you are in a highly competitive business, your business could suffer if she takes this information to a competitor. In other words, if you're going to lose more by her competition than you would lose by not hiring her, move on and find another candidate.
- Have you had problems with ex-employees competing with you or soliciting customers? If you have been burned by former employees before, you may decide it's worth your while to hold out for an employee who's willing to sign a noncompete agreement.
- What other legal options are available to protect your business interests? If there are any, will they adequately protect your business? Although a noncompete agreement is the best way to protect your business and its secrets, the law provides

a few remedies for businesses whose employees steal trade secrets or engage in other sleazy behavior. (See Chapter 7, Section A, for more information.)

Since we don't know your business, we cannot tell you how much importance you should attach to these issues. If you are primarily worried about the potential for competition and loss of customers, it is in your best interest to obtain a signed noncompete agreement, even if it means you don't get to hire your first choice for the job.

 Recommend that employees take your noncompetition agreement to a lawyer for review. *By doing so, you'll not only build trust with the employee, you'll also be in a strong position should the employee later challenge the agreement. An employee who signs an agreement after consulting a lawyer, presumably getting a complete understanding of its consequences, will have a difficult time convincing a judge that the agreement shouldn't be enforced.*

C. Existing Employees

If you ask an employee who is already working for you to sign a noncompete agreement, you have to be careful to provide enough of a benefit to the employee in order to create a valid contract. In this section, we discuss the practicalities of asking existing employees—both at-will and fixed-term—to sign noncompete agreements, including your options if an employee refuses to sign on the dotted line.

1. Creating a Benefit for Existing At-Will Employees

An "at-will" employee is someone who does not work for you under the terms of a written or oral fixed-term employment contract—an employee whom you can fire at any time for any legal reason. (See Section B1, above, for more information on at-will employment.) When you hire an at-will employee in all states except Texas, you need not offer anything beyond the job itself if you want to create an enforceable noncompetition agreement at the time of hiring. But what about asking for this promise *after* the employee is on board?

In most states, refraining from exercising your right to terminate the employee at will is benefit enough to the employee to support an enforceable noncompete agreement. Of course, signing a noncompete agreement with you doesn't give that employee any job security or curtail your ability to fire at will in the future. The benefit that the employee receives is your willingness not to end the employment relationship then and there, when you ask for the signature—small benefit for the employee, but it satisfies the judges.

Courts in a few states (such as North Carolina) take a slightly different approach. They recognize that merely agreeing to continue to employ a worker in exchange for signing a noncompete agreement is not enough of a benefit to justify enforcing the agreement—in other words, these courts don't accept the idea that the employee benefits from the employer refraining to exercise its right to terminate the employee at will. In these states, employers must give an existing employee some real benefit—such as a pay raise or promotion—to create a valid contract.

It's difficult even for experts to know how state courts will approach the issue—that is, whether your momentary willingness to continue to offer employment will be enough of a benefit to create an enforceable noncompetition agreement. Accordingly, it's prudent to provide any existing, at-will employee with an additional benefit—over and above keeping her job—in return for signing a noncompete agreement.

The most common way to provide an additional benefit is to give the employee a promotion and/or an accompanying raise. To guarantee the enforceability of your noncompete agreement, this promotion and raise should not be the kind you would periodically grant to that type of employee. In other words, if your company has a policy of lock-step promotions or raises for certain jobs, it's not a good idea to tie signing the noncompete agree-

ment to these raises or promotions. You need to give the employee a meaningful promotion to a position with more responsibility and/or a raise that's larger than the employee would receive according to your normal advancement policy. Or, you could give the employee a different benefit, such as stock, stock options, an unexpected bonus check or an otherwise unanticipated perk.

> **EXAMPLE:** Rusty works for an ad agency and has been Audrey's assistant for two years. Rusty has done such a great job for Audrey that when a slot opens up for a new advertising executive, she recommends him for the position. Rusty gets a big new office, a substantial raise and a major increase in responsibility. As part of this package, the ad agency asks him to sign a noncompete agreement, since he'll be in a position of trust and confidence with the agency's clients and will have access to a lot more confidential information, such as client databases and marketing strategies. Rusty wants the promotion, so he signs the agreement. The ad agency has provided Rusty, an existing employee, with enough of a benefit to satisfy the sufficient benefit requirement.

Obtaining an existing employee's signature on a noncompete agreement can be harder than getting a new hire to sign an agreement. With a new hire, if the applicant wants the job, the odds are in your favor that she'll agree to sign a noncompete agreement. That's not the case with an existing employee, since that person has less incentive to agree to what you're asking. One option—threatening to fire an employee who balks at signing the agreement—is not a great idea, as explained in Section 3, below. On the other hand, if you make signing the noncompete agreement a condition of receiving a real raise or a good promotion, this will make the agreement more attractive to your employee. If you do run into problems or suspect that you will, read Section 3, "If an Existing Employee Refuses to Sign," below.

2. Creating a Benefit for Existing Fixed-Term Employees

Although it's unlikely your business has any employees with fixed-term employment contracts, if it does, you will have to provide a reward or additional benefit to the employee when you ask the employee to agree to noncompete provisions. As with at-will employees, you can often provide a sufficient benefit by giving the employee a raise (a *real* raise, not just a normal, yearly pay increase mandated by the employment contract or the company), a significant promotion, corporate stock, a grant of stock options or an unexpected cash bonus.

If you make receiving a raise, promotion or other benefit a condition of agreeing to noncompete provisions, the employee may be more willing to agree to them. But if your employee is reluctant or you suspect he will be, read "If an Existing Employee Refuses to Sign," below.

If your employee agrees to noncompete provisions, you will have to add noncompetition, nondisclosure and nonsolicitation clauses to the employment contract. You'll do this by filling out a detailed amendment to the contract that spells out the noncompetition, nondisclosure and nonsolicitation terms and the new consideration (such as the raise or promotion). Because amending a fixed-term employment agreement can be tricky, we recommend you seek the help of an experienced employment lawyer if you're interested in doing this.

 Remember to renew the employee's contract. *If you add noncompete provisions to an employee's contract, make sure that you renew or renegotiate the amended agreement before it expires. If the employee continues working beyond the expiration of the contract, a court might find that the noncompete provisions have expired as well and aren't part of the new at-will employment relationship.*

3. If an Existing Employee Refuses to Sign

How you handle an existing employee who refuses to sign a noncompete agreement will depend to a large extent on whether the employee is at-will or has a fixed-term employment contract.

a. At-Will Employees

If an existing at-will employee refuses to sign a noncompete agreement, you could decide to risk the potential disclosure of your trade secrets and let the employee stay (see Section B1, above, for factors to consider when making this decision). If you forego the noncompetition agreement, you can limit the employee's access to confidential information or to your customers and clients. If you need to, you might be able to accomplish this with a demotion, without risking an employee lawsuit. But taking adverse employment actions against employees is an area of the law that can be treacherous for employers. Before taking any containment actions, consult an attorney knowledgeable in employment law.

Your second alternative is to fire (or threaten to fire) the employee for refusing to sign a noncompete agreement. This is a risky approach and exposes you to a lawsuit. An at-will employee who's been fired and is angry about it may decide to sue you for wrongful termination—a catch-all phrase that describes the various ways em-

ployers can violate the law when firing workers—whether the claim is valid or not. Even if you win such a lawsuit, the experience will not be pleasant and is guaranteed to be expensive.

 If your business is located in a state that doesn't enforce (or severely restricts) agreements not to compete, don't threaten termination if your employee refuses to sign. *In these states, which are hostile to the idea of noncompetes to begin with, the employee's chances of winning are higher than elsewhere. You may end up having to pay back pay, future pay and even punitive damages (damages that punish you for being unfair).*

However you decide to handle an at-will employee who refuses to sign a noncompete agreement—by retaining the employee or choosing to terminate—do it carefully, by consulting an employment law attorney to minimize your chances of being sued. The more tactfully and peacefully you handle the termination of an at-will employee, the less likely you are to end up in court.

 For more information on safely firing or demoting an employee, see Dealing With Problem Employees: A Legal Guide, *by Amy DelPo and Lisa Guerin (Nolo).*

b. Fixed-Term Employees

If an employee with a written employment contract refuses to sign a noncompete agreement, you'll have to retain the employee unless that worker does something that merits dismissal. Remember, fixed-term employment contracts generally specify the circumstances or conduct that that will result in the employee's termination before the end of the contract (usually called "good cause"). Refusing to agree to noncompete provisions may not qualify as good cause under your contract or under your state's common law or statutory definition of good cause.

If you terminate a fixed-term employee who refuses to sign a noncompete agreement, the consequences can be dire. The employee will probably have the right to sue you for breaching the employment contract and might be able to obtain money damages from you. Although it's unlikely that a court would agree that the employee was somehow obligated to sign the amended agreement, stranger things have happened in the legal world, and you don't want to be the test case.

The alternative to firing the employee—placing him in a position where he won't have access to confidential information or customers and clients, thereby lowering the risk of trade secret disclosure—is no better, unfortunately. Marginalizing or demoting a fixed-term employee, or significantly changing the worker's job duties,

might expose you again to a lawsuit for breach of contract, especially if job duties and title are spelled out in detail in the contract.

No matter what you decide to do, consult an employment lawyer before you take any adverse employment action against a fixed-term employee.

D. Departing Employees

You may be reading this book with a certain amount of anxiety, knowing that a key employee who never signed a noncompete agreement has announced she is leaving. Or worse, you're preparing to terminate an employee who never signed a noncompete agreement and are concerned that she's going to work for a competitor or start a competitive business to spite you. Your best hope to prevent competition in these situations is to ask the employee to sign a noncompetition agreement before departure—but be prepared to pay for it.

In these situations, employers usually agree to continue to pay the employee's salary (and sometimes even benefits) for a period of time, such as six months or a year, after departure. In return, during the noncompetition period the employee promises to refrain from engaging in competitive business activities, disclosing your trade secrets and confidential information and soliciting your customers and other employees to leave too.

1. Noncompetition Agreements and Severance

The amount of money or other benefits you'll have to pony up will depend on the relative bargaining strengths of you and your soon-to-be ex-worker. Someone who had access to vital, valuable information, is easily employable and a magnet for customers or your remaining employees can naturally demand more than a worker who had limited access and faces few job opportunities. Your calculations boil down to balancing the cost to your company without the signed agreement versus the cost to obtain it. (See "Negotiating With a Departing Employee," below.)

An out-the-door noncompetition agreement is often referred to as a severance agreement—in fact, we do so in this book, in Appendix 3. It's important to understand that severance—money or other benefits, such as continued health coverage, which you give a departing worker—may be something you *already* have to pay this worker. No law requires you to offer severance—but if you regularly give departing employees a "severance package," you have to do so for all employees, including the one whom you'd like to sign a noncompetition agreement. You cannot condition the severance for a particular employee on his signing a noncompete agreement. In order to secure a valid

noncompete agreement, you'll have to offer something more than the usual package—more money, benefits or so on. On the other hand, if your company has no policy of regularly giving severance, you may condition the receipt of severance on a signed noncompete agreement.

Don't confuse a noncompetition agreement signed at the end of employment with a "release," or promise by the employee not to sue you for any employment-related claims. A release is an entirely different promise, and—you guessed it—you'll have to pay separately for this one, too. Our noncompetition agreements in this book do *not* include releases—your employee will remain free to sue you over any claims, such as unpaid wages or discrimination, that the worker wants to make the subject of a lawsuit. If you and your employee are parting in anger—you're terminating because the worker has sexually harassed a coworker, for example—you'll need a release to prevent future lawsuits from this worker. Consult an attorney for help drafting a release.

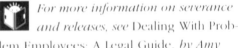 *For more information on severance and releases, see* Dealing With Problem Employees: A Legal Guide, *by Amy DelPo and Lisa Guerin (Nolo).*

2. Negotiating With a Departing Employee

A departing employee who already has a job lined up may not be eager to sign a severance agreement. Without the need for your "quiet money," the worker may decide it's more important to retain flexibility and freedom than some extra cash. On the other hand, you might convince a job-hunting employee to view the noncompetition period as a paid six-month, or yearlong, search period or vacation.

But be prepared—a savvy employee who thinks you're worried about where she will work next is likely to push for more money or other perks in return for not competing with you. Unlike the start of the employment relationship, when an employer typically has more leverage, you're not in a strong bargaining position with a departing employee. You may have to adjust your expectations (and your bargaining stance) accordingly—be willing to shorten the period of noncompetition or pay the employee more severance money.

Pay the employee over time instead of all at once. *Paying in increments gives the worker a reason to continue to abide by the agreement. And if your former employee violates the severance agreement by going to work for a competitor or disclosing your trade secrets, at least you'll be out less money than if you'd paid it in one lump sum.*

If a departing employee refuses to sign a severance agreement, there's not much you can do except keep a watchful eye on the worker and the new employer to make sure they are not using your trade secrets or confidential information. As explained in "Limited State Law Protection If Your Employee Won't Sign," below, state laws will give you some help when it comes to protecting your trade secrets (but state laws will not prevent competition). For more tips on preventative steps to take when an employee leaves, see Chapter 7, Section B.

If you live in a state that doesn't enforce noncompetition clauses when they're entered into at the time of hiring or during employment, you'll want to be careful not to hand that worker an out-the-door severance agreement that contains the offending clause. In these states (California, Montana, North Dakota and Oklahoma), you can use our severance agreement as long as you remove the noncompetition clause. This will leave you with a valid severance agreement that will prevent a departing employee from disclosing your trade secrets and soliciting your employees or customers. The form instructions in Chapter 4, Section C, explain how to do this.

Limited State Law Protection If Your Employee Won't Sign

Your current employees have a "duty of loyalty" to you, which applies to them even if they haven't signed any noncompetition, nondisclosure or nonsolicitation agreements. This duty means that they can't compete with you or reveal your trade secrets while they're working for your company. However, the duty of loyalty lasts only as long as the worker is in your employ. Former employees have a much more limited version of this obligation to guard trade secrets; and without a noncompete agreement, a former employee is generally free to compete against you.

Under laws in most states, employees are also prohibited from openly disparaging your business with untrue statements or interfering with your business contracts (for instance, by trying to convince a customer or client to break a contract with you).

In rare cases, a judge might prevent a former employee from competing against you if you can prove that it's practically impossible for the worker to take a particular job *without* disclosing your trade secrets. This "doctrine of inevitable disclosure" boils down to convincing a judge that ruling a job off-limits is the only way you can enjoy your right, under state law, to have your trade secrets kept that way. As you might imagine, it's hard to get a judge to make such an order. Far better to spend your time and money convincing a reluctant employee to sign a comprehensive noncompetition agreement.

Creating a Noncompete Agreement for an Employee

n this chapter, we'll help you create an employee noncompete agreement. One by one, we'll take you through the clauses in our noncompete agreements and explain their meaning and importance. Along with each explanation, we provide instructions on how to fill it out and an example of what the clause will look like when it's completed.

The clauses in our noncompetition agreements are numbered and naturally fall into several groups, or clusters:

- introductory clauses, reciting the introduction and purpose (Clauses 1 and 2)
- a clause describing the work relationship (Clause 3)
- the "noncompete" clauses, including the noncompetition, nondisclosure and nonsolicitation clauses (Clauses 4 through 8)
- clauses that appear only in the severance agreement, which are used when an employee signs the agreement upon leaving your company (Clauses 8 through 12), and
- "boilerplate" clauses, which are standard clauses that protect your basic contract rights, found in most contracts (Clauses 9 through 16).

We have designed one general form (Form EMPL-6) that you can use for any employee. But because your needs will vary depending on whom you ask to sign an agreement— trade secret descriptions for technical workers, for example, are dif-

ferent than those for sales people—we provide you with specialized forms, too, which are appropriate for certain types of workers. When you're ready to start creating an agreement, choose the agreement that's appropriate for your employee's position, according to the following list:

- Form EMPL-1: Information technology (IT) specialists, including Web engineers and software programmers
- Form EMPL-2: High-level executives
- Form EMPL-3: Salespeople
- Form EMPL-4: Business development or marketing managers
- Form EMPL-5: Research and development employees
- Form EMPL-6: General noncompete agreement (use for any employees who don't fit into one of the categories above).

All of the above forms are appropriate for new hires *or* employees who are already working for you. Keep in mind that you must give something to existing employees, such as a bonus or a promotion, in order to know for sure that you've created an enforceable agreement (see Chapter 3, Section C). The instructions for filling out forms in Sections A through F refer to any of these forms (the basic version or the specialized ones). In Section G, we provide special instructions for the amendment page.

If you would like to obtain a noncompete promise from an employee who is leaving your company, use Form EMPL-7, which is a severance agreement. (Note that the severance agreement is organized slightly differently than the rest of our employee forms, with alternative descriptions of employee duties to choose from instead of separate forms for different kinds of employees.) If your company regularly gives severance to departing employees, you'll have to add benefits to your standard package (see Chapter 3, Section D, for an explanation of severance). Form EMPL-8 is an amendment form, which you can use if you need to modify your noncompete agreement in the future.

 All of the forms discussed in this chapter are on the CD-ROM at the back of the book. The forms may be filled out directly on your computer. For detailed information on using your word processor to fill out these forms, see Appendix 1.

 Have a blank form in front of you as you read these instructions. *The instructions will be clearer if you refer to one of the blank noncompete forms as you go along. Open the form you want to use in your word processor and follow along or print out a hard copy and use it as a rough draft.*

A. The Introductory Clauses

These clauses appear at the beginning of all of our agreements. They introduce the names of the parties (the worker and the employer) and provide background for the agreement.

1. Introduction

The introduction clause states the names of the parties to the agreement (the worker's name and the name of your company) and provides the date the agreement was entered into.

Fill in the date (month, day and year) the agreement is being entered into, the employee's name and the name of your company. Just make sure a new employee signs the agreement *before* she starts work (and if you're promoting an existing employee, make sure she signs the agreement before she starts her new job).

In the last blank in this paragraph, fill in the state in which your company was formed and its type of legal structure—for example, "a *California corporation*." Below you'll see an example (the underlined portions are the blanks you will complete in your own agreement):

> This Agreement ("Agreement") is made and entered into as of *December 9, 2001,* between *Ralph Dooley* ("Employee") and *Acme Internet Solutions,* a*n Illinois corporation* ("Company").

2. Purpose

The purpose clause (sometimes called the "recitals" or "whereas" portion) explains why the parties are entering into the agreement.

In the first blank, describe your company's business—for example, "Company is in the business of _manufacturing and designing widgets, which are key components of gadgets._"

Then, choose one of the two alternatives that come next. Depending on whether the employee is new or is already working for you, choose the one for new employees or the one for current (pre-existing) employees. Delete the alternative you do not use. Then follow these instructions:

a. Alternative # 1: New Employee

In the first blank of alternative 1, list the employee's formal title, such as _Web designer._ In the second blank, fill in a very general description of the employee's duties. For instance, "Employee's duties will include _updating, maintaining and designing Company's website._" You can include a lengthier job description if you wish, as shown in the example below.

[ ] Alternative # 1: New Employees

Company would like to employ Employee as its _Manager of Information Systems._ Employee's duties shall include:

(a) taking charge of Company's network infrastructure

(b) purchasing and tracking of hardware and software inventory

(c) supervising vendor interactions, servers, email platform, user-management software, telecommunications infrastructure and contracts, and

(d) overseeing and managing office systems contracts and maintenance.

In exchange for Company employing Employee, and for other good and valuable consideration, the receipt and sufficiency of which is hereby acknowledged, Company and Employee agree as follows:

---

b. Alternative # 2: Existing Employee

If you are promoting an existing employee, choose Alternative #2a. In the first and second blanks, list the employee's previous title (for instance, _QA Tester_) and the employee's new title (for instance, _Senior Applications Developer_). In the third blank, fill in a very general description of employee's new duties, such as "Employee's duties will include _developing and testing_

Company's software applications." In the last blank, repeat the employee's new title.

[ ] Alternative # 2a: Promotion

Employee is currently employed by Company as its *Information Systems Technician*. Company would like to employ Employee as its *Manager of Information Systems*, a more responsible position at a higher rate of pay. Employee's duties will include:

(a) taking charge of Company's network infrastructure

(b) purchasing and tracking of hardware and software inventory

(c) supervising vendor interactions, servers, email platform, user-management software, telecommunications infrastructure and contracts, and

(d) overseeing and managing office systems contracts and maintenance.

In this new position, employee will have greater responsibility and access to Company's Confidential Information, as defined in this Agreement. In exchange for Company's employing Employee as its *Manager of Information Systems*, and for other good and valuable consideration, the receipt and sufficiency of which is hereby acknowledged, Company and Employee agree as follows:

Note that the last paragraph states that the employee will have greater responsibility and access to your confidential information—this demonstrates the need for the agreement and also reiterates that the employee is being asked to sign a noncompete agreement because she's getting a promotion.

If you are not promoting the employee, but are providing the employee with some other incentive to sign the noncompete agreement, choose Alternative #2b, "Other benefit." In the space provided, describe the benefit you are providing to the employee.

[ ] Alternative #2b: Other benefit

In exchange for Employee's obligations under this Agreement, and for other good and valuable consideration, the receipt and sufficiency of which is hereby acknowledged, Company will provide Employee with the following: *beginning December 9, 2001, Employee's yearly salary shall increase to $75,000 per year*. Company and Employee therefore agree as follows:

Delete the alternative you do not use. Remember, in most states you need to provide an existing employee with a raise and/or a promotion—or some other kind of new benefit—to create an enforceable agreement. See Chapter 3 for more information.

In our severance agreement, you'll notice that the purpose clause is worded slightly differently and instead states that the purpose of the agreement is to terminate the employee's employment with the company. In the severance agreement, you'll choose alternatives depending on whether the employee had an employment contract or was at-will.

⚠ Oregon law allows employees to sign noncompete agreements only when they are hired or promoted. *(See Chapter 2, Section B3c.) If you want to ask an existing employee to sign a noncompete agreement without a promotion, see an Oregon employment lawyer.*

B. Description of the Work Relationship

The introductory clauses are followed by a clause entitled "Acknowledgment of At-Will Employment," which defines the relationship between the employer and the employee as "at-will." At-will employment means that the employee can quit at any time and you can terminate employment, as long as you don't do so for an illegal reason. (See Chapter 3, Section B1, for a fuller explanation of at-will employment.) This clause does not appear in the severance agreement, since the work relationship is ending and does not need to be defined.

Including a provision that confirms the working relationship as "at will" makes it difficult for the employee to later argue that you promised her a job for a specific period of time. You don't need to add anything to the clause.

> Employee acknowledges that his or her employment with Company is at will and that Company may terminate Employee's employment with Company at any time for any reason, and Employee may terminate his employment with Company at any time for any reason.

C. The Noncompete Clauses

The clauses we discuss in this section are the heart of your agreement. These are the clauses that protect your business, your trade secrets, your workforce and customers.

You may notice that the nondisclosure clause comes before the noncompetition and nonsolicitation clauses. It appears first because it describes the main reason you want to prevent the employee from competing against your company—to protect your trade secrets. The other two clauses (noncompetition and nonsolicitation) exist to protect the confidential information you describe in the nondisclosure clause.

1. Nondisclosure of Confidential Information

The nondisclosure clause is the place for you to define your trade secrets (subsection a) and specify how your employee must treat them—what the employee can and cannot do (subsection b).

a. Defining Your Trade Secrets

Subsection a contains a broad definition of confidential information that will be appropriate for most employers. The specialized forms contain a definition that will be appropriate to that industry or position and the severance form gives you several alternative definitions from which to choose. If anything contained in this description of confidential information isn't relevant to the employee's job or duties or doesn't describe information the employee will have access to, delete it. Remember, your goal is to be as reasonable as possible about the information you're trying to protect. An over-inclusive description of confidential information may be met with skepticism by a judge.

If there's particular, sensitive information that you would like to include in the definition of confidential information, enter that information in the blank space provided. For example, if your employee will conduct quality assurance testing on your company's new video game, you might want to add: "*any and all information, data, source code, ideas, processes, musical or literary works relating to*

Company's video game product titled "Blubber Man IV…"" Or, if you are using this agreement for a new chef at your restaurant, you may want to insert the names of proprietary recipes, such as your world-famous crab bisque (but don't include the actual recipe; that should remain a secret). Otherwise, just delete this blank.

The sample below shows how trade secrets are defined in the information technology form. The language in the agreement you draft will depend on your choice of forms and the nature of your business and the employee's duties.

---

a. Company may need to disclose to Employee or give Employee access to Confidential Information so that Employee may properly fulfill his or her duties to Company. "Confidential Information" means Company's trade secrets, including, but not limited to, technology; equipment research, design and development; database, website or network specifications or contents; product pricing information, research, design or development; contemplated new products or services; engineering processes or methods; any titles, themes, stories, treatments, ideas, art work, computer hardware or software; *any and all information, data, source code, ideas or processes relating to Company's e-commerce product titled "eSolution"*; or any other information which is not generally known and from which the Company derives an economic benefit. The Confidential Information may be written, such as computer source code, programs, hardware and software, tapes, disks, documents, drawings, data or product specifications; or unwritten, such as unwritten knowledge, ideas, processes, practices or know-how. Confidential Information does not include information that is in the public domain, information that is generally known in Company's industry or information that Employee acquired completely independently of his or her services for Company.

Our severance agreement provides several alternative definitions of confidential information. *Our severance agreement is set up a little differently than the sample above, which is taken from an agreement for a new or continuing employee. Because our severance agreement can be used for an employee in any position, it provides several different definitions of confidential information (and will also be in the past tense, since you've already disclosed the information to the employee). You'll need to choose the best description of the confidential information among the alternatives provided.*

b. Limits on the Employee's Use

In the next paragraph, subsection b, the worker agrees not to use this confidential information or reveal it to any one else.

b. For as long as the Confidential Information is not generally known and Company derives an economic benefit from the Confidential Information, Employee shall not use or disclose to any other person or entity any Confidential Information or any copy or summary of any Confidential Information unless Employee is required to do so to perform Employee's duties to Company or as required by law.

As an added measure of protection, in subsection c, the worker also agrees not to make unauthorized copies of this information, for herself or anyone else (a worker who can't reproduce your information will be less likely to use it if she goes to work for a competitor).

c. While Employee is employed by Company and afterward, Employee shall not remove or copy any Confidential Information or participate in any way in the removal or copying of any Confidential Information without Company's written consent. Employee shall immediately return to Company all Confidential Information when Employee's employment with the Company terminates, or any time Company requires such Confidential Information to be returned.

The worker also promises to refrain from getting access to your confidential information for any reason other than to do her job. This helps limit the amount of confidential information the employee knows (and the less confidential information the employee knows, the less information she can take with her to a new employer or disclose to a competitor).

> d. Employee will not obtain or attempt to obtain any Confidential Information for any purpose whatsoever except as required by Company to enable Employee to perform his or her job duties.

Subsection d does not appear in the nondisclosure clause of our severance agreement because the employee will no longer be performing any duties for the employer.

c. Prior Employers' Secrets

If you're hiring an employee who has worked for one of your direct competitors, or if you suspect the employee may have had access to a competitor's trade secrets at a previous job, it's very important to make sure that these secrets won't be revealed at your company. (If you receive trade secrets of a worker's previous employer, you may be on the hook for trade secret theft.) Subsection e of this clause requires the employee to promise not to reveal any of the previous employer's trade secrets to your company. This clause puts the employee on notice that you aren't willing to accept any trade secrets from a previous employer, and it will help protect you if your new hire reveals them inadvertently.

Fill in the name of the employee's previous employer in all three blanks. If sub-

section e does not apply to the employee's situation, delete it.

> e. Employee will not disclose to Company or misuse any third party's trade secrets, including any trade secret information of Employee's former employer, _Achtung Solutions_, nor will Employee solicit any former employees or consultants of _Achtung Solutions_ on Company's behalf. Employee represents and warrants that he or she has returned all trade secret materials to _Achtung Solutions_ and that the execution of this Agreement by Employee will not violate or conflict with the terms of any other agreement to which Employee is a party.

 This subsection does not appear in the noncompetition clause of our severance agreements. _With the employee no longer working for you, you won't be concerned about her revealing prior employer's trade secrets._

2. Noncompetition

The noncompetition clause prevents employees from competing directly with your company when they leave to join a competitor or start their own competitive ventures. As explained in the Introduction and Chapter 2, Section B, some states will not enforce (or will restrict) noncompetition provisions. After consulting the table "State Restrictions on Noncompete Provisions," below, proceed to the instructions.

State Restrictions on Noncompete Provisions

Locate your state in the chart below, then follow the directions for completing this form.

Location of your business	Restrictions on noncompetition agreements	Your next step
California	Will not enforce any noncompetition agreements	Remove Section 5, "Noncompetition," in its entirety from the agreement and renumber the remaining sections accordingly. (See Chapter 2, Section B1a, for more information.)
Montana, North Dakota or Oklahoma	May not enforce this part of the agreement	Consult an employment law expert to determine whether or not you should include Section 5 in the agreement. (See Chapter 2, Section B1b, for more information.)
Alabama, Colorado or Texas	Enforceable depending on the type of employee or employment status (at-will or contractual) of the employee	Consult an employment law expert. (See Chapter 2, Sections B1d and B1e, for more information.)

Even if your state enforces noncompetition clauses, you may have reason to create an agreement without one (for instance, for an employee who refuses to sign an agreement with a noncompetition clause but doesn't have a problem with nondisclosure and nonsolicitation clauses). It's easy to modify any of our agreements to include only nondisclosure and nonsolicitation clauses. Simply remove the section titled "Noncompetition" in its entirety from the agreement and renumber the remaining sections accordingly. Similarly, if you wish to have a worker sign an agreement containing only a nondisclosure clause, remove the section titled "Nonsolicitation" in its entirety and renumber the remaining sections.

a. Length of Time

The first part of this clause sets out the period of time (the noncompetition period) that the worker will not be allowed to compete with you after leaving your company. In the blank, fill in a reasonable amount of time—and be careful to avoid an unnecessarily long period (see Chapter 1, Section B1, for advice). Specify whether the number you choose refers to months or years. For instance, your agreement should read, "and for a period of _6 months_ thereafter...."

> Employee agrees that in order to protect the Confidential Information described above, while Employee is employed by Company, and for a period of _one year_ thereafter (collectively, the "Term"), Employee shall not:....

 In our severance agreement, the period of noncompetition appears in a different section of the agreement. _If you are creating a severance agreement, the period of noncompetition will be the amount of time you agree to pay the employee after she leaves. This amount of time will be entered into the "Severance Payments" section (see Section D2, below)._

b. Owning or Working for a Competing Company

Next, the clause states that during the noncompetition period, the former worker is prevented from taking part in the ownership of a competing company.

> a. plan for, acquire any financial interest in or perform services for (as an employee, consultant, officer, director, independent contractor, principal, agent or otherwise) any business located in the Territory that would require Employee to use or disclose any Confidential Information, or ...

In addition, the employee is prohibited from taking a position at a competing company that's similar to the position she held at your company.

> b. perform services (as an employee, consultant, officer, director, independent contractor, principal, agent or otherwise) that are similar to Employee's current duties or responsibilities for any person or entity that, during the Term, engages in any business activity in which Company is then engaged or proposes to be engaged and that conducts its business in the Territory.

c. Geographic Area

Next, the geographic area ("Territory") in which the employee will be prohibited from competing against you is defined. There are two alternatives. The first alternative defines the geographic area as any area in which you do business.

Territory means

[ ] Alternative #1: General Territory

any geographic area in which Company conducts its business during the Term.

The second alternative allows you to insert a specific geographic area in which the employee may not compete against you (we recommend you do this if your business is located in Louisiana).

[ ] Alternative #2: Specific Territory

the city limits of the city of Chicago, Illinois.

Choose one of the alternatives and delete the other. If you choose the second alternative, please refer to Chapter 1, Section B2, for a discussion of choosing a reasonable geographic area.

3. Nonsolicitation

Each agreement in this book also contains a nonsolicitation clause, which prevents the employee from soliciting your customers, clients and other employees on her own behalf (if she leaves to start a competitive business) or on her new employer's behalf (if she leaves to join a competitor).

Like the noncompetition clause, this clause specifies exactly how long the

worker can't solicit your customers and employees. Fill in a reasonable amount of time (refer to Chapter 1, Section F1, for more information). Remember to specify whether the number you choose refers to months or years.

While Employee is employed by Company, and for a period of _one year_ thereafter, Employee shall not:

a. employ, attempt to employ or solicit for employment by any other person or entity, any Company employees;

b. encourage any consultant, independent contractor or any other person or entity to end their relationship or stop doing business with Company, or help any person or entity to do so or attempt to do so; or

c. solicit or attempt to solicit or obtain business or trade from any of Company's current customers or clients or help any person or entity do so or attempt to do so.

 In our severance agreement, the period of nonsolicitation appears in a different section of the agreement. _If you are creating a severance agreement, the period of nonsolicitation will be the amount of time you agree to pay the employee after she leaves. This amount of time will be entered into the "Severance Payments" section (see Section D2, below)._

4. Right to an Injunction

An injunction is an order by a judge that requires someone to do something (such as return company property) or not do something (such as work for a competitor). When former employees break non-competition agreements, employers generally go to court and ask for an injunction directed at the employee, to stop the competition, disclosures or solicitations as soon as possible. It takes very little time to get an injunction—sometimes only a few days or a week—but they're only temporary. Normally, they're followed by a full-blown trial that will determine whether the judge's order should stick. In the meantime, however, the employer is protected against further disclosures or competition.

It's in your best interests to seek an immediate injunction against a former worker who violates your agreement, to stop the offending behavior while final determination of your suit is being decided, since lawsuits can drag on for years. Money damages—financial compensation a worker will have to pay to repair harm done to your company—often don't get awarded for years, and are often very hard to measure. Far better to stop the former employee from using your trade secrets in the first place.

Unfortunately, injunctions are often difficult to get. Your chances will improve if the worker has agreed in writing that you should be entitled to one if she violates the agreement. In the "right to an injunction" clause in our agreements, your employee does just that. You don't have to add anything to this clause.

Employee acknowledges that his or her services to Company are special and unique and that, while performing these services, Employee will have access to and Company may disclose to Employee the Confidential Information described above. Employee also acknowledges that his or her position in Company will place him or her in a position of confidence and trust with employees, clients and customers of Company.

If Employee breaches or threatens to breach any of the provisions of Sections 4, 5 or 6 of this Agreement, Company will sustain irreparable harm. Company shall be entitled to an injunction to stop any breach or threatened breach of this Agreement, including the provisions of Sections 4, 5 or 6. Employee acknowledges and agrees that monetary damages would not adequately compensate Company for any breach or threatened breach of these sections and that if Company seeks injunctive relief to put an immediate halt to the offending conduct, Employee shall not claim that monetary damages would be an adequate remedy.

5. Reasonable Restrictions and Survivability

In this clause, the worker acknowledges that the restrictions in the agreement (the nondisclosure, noncompetition and nonsolicitation provisions) are reasonable and necessary. This helps you defend against a future claim by the worker that the restrictions are unreasonable and aren't really necessary to protect your business.

This section also provides that the worker's obligations—not to compete against your company, solicit your customers or employees or talk about your trade secrets—continue to be enforceable ("survive") after the worker has left your company. We include this so that your former employee can't argue that, because the employment has terminated, the employee's obligations have terminated too. You don't need to add anything to this clause.

Employee acknowledges that the restrictions set forth in Sections 4, 5 and 6 of the Agreement are reasonable and necessary for the protection of Company, its business and its Confidential Information. The provisions of Sections 4, 5, 6 and 7 of this Agreement shall survive the termination, for any reason, of Employee's employment with Company.

If you are creating an agreement for a new or continuing employee, skip ahead to Section E, "Boilerplate Clauses," below.

D. Additional Clauses for the Severance Agreement

If you are asking a departing employee to sign a noncompetition agreement, you'll need to pay for it—typically, by providing cash or benefits for a period of time after the employee leaves the company. You can use a severance agreement to accomplish this exchange. Because of these added twists, our severance agreement contains a few clauses that aren't in the noncompete agreements for new and existing employees.

See a lawyer if you need to create a severance agreement with a noncompetition clause in Oregon. *See Chapter 2, Section B1c, for an explanation of that state's unique requirements.*

1. Termination of Employment

Here, you and the employee agree on the date the worker's employment or services will end. This makes it clear that even though you're going to make severance payments to the worker, the worker will no longer be employed by you and can't enter into contracts on behalf of the company or otherwise hold herself out as an employee of your company for any purpose.

Fill in the date (month, day and year) of the last day the employee will work for your company.

Employee's employment with Company shall terminate as of _December 31_, _2001_ ("Termination Date"). On Termination Date, Employee shall cease to be either an employee or an agent of Company and Employee shall not make any representation to any third party that he or she is an employee or agent of Company or has the authority to bind Company to any agreement.

remain trade secrets, which could be either shorter or longer than the "Term."

In the first blank, fill in the day on which you'll pay the severance amount each month. Next, fill in the amount of the severance payment, first written out longhand and then numerically, the way you fill out a check—for example, "_Six Thousand_ Dollars ($_6,000_). Then fill in the term of the agreement—the dates (month, day and year) on which the agreement will begin and end; for example, beginning on _December 31_, _2001_, and ending on _May 31_, _2002_ (the "Term").

> ⚠ **Don't make the term too long.**
> _See Chapter 1, Section B1, for a discussion of how long it is reasonable to keep a former employee from competing against you._

2. Severance Payments

This clause describes the severance payments you will make to the worker, including the date they will begin and the date they'll end. This period of time, called the "Term," is also the period of time during which the employee won't be permitted to compete against you or solicit your clients, customers or employees. It doesn't apply to the amount of time an employee can't use or disclose your trade secrets (the nondisclosure clause), however, because the employee won't be allowed to disclose your secrets for as long as they

In consideration of Employee's promises in this Agreement, Company shall pay Employee a severance allowance, payable monthly on the _1st_ day of each month, of _Five Thousand_ Dollars ($_5,000_), beginning on _December 1_, _2001_, and ending on _May 1_, _2002_ (the "Term").

In Company's sole discretion, this severance allowance may be subject to Company's normal withholding and payroll practices, including but not limited to the withholding of state and federal income taxes.

⚠️ **Severance payments may be "wages," subject to withholding.** *As you know, you have to withhold taxes on any income that counts as wages. What about severance? Unfortunately, the IRS position is unclear. If you don't withhold and the IRS decides you should have, you may be slapped with fines and penalties. We suggest that you consult an attorney for advice.*

If you determine that you do not need to withhold income or employment taxes from severance payments, provide the worker with a Form 1099-MISC on which you summarize the worker's severance payments. You must report the severance amounts to the IRS.

3. Continuation of Benefits

If you want to provide certain benefits to the employee as part of the severance compensation, this is where you list them. If applicable, list of all the benefits the employee will continue to receive during the term of the agreement, such as health, dental, life and long-term disability insurance.

If your company doesn't provide any benefits, or you will only be providing the departing employee with cash, insert "none."

During the Term, Employee shall continue to be eligible for and Company shall continue to provide the following benefits to Employee: *health, dental, life and long-term disability insurance*. In addition, Company shall make available to Employee all benefits for which Employee is eligible under the Consolidated Omnibus Budget Reconciliation Act ("COBRA").

Your COBRA Obligations

Whether you provide additional benefits or not to your departing employee, you must comply with the Consolidated Omnibus Budget Reconciliation Act, or "COBRA," if your company:

- has more than 20 employees, and
- provides health insurance to your employees via a group medical plan.

COBRA requires you to give an employee whose employment is terminated for any reason (except gross misconduct) the right to continue her health coverage. You don't have to pay the premiums—the employee does—but COBRA gives the employee the right to stay on your medical plan for a period of time that's specified under federal law.

For more information on the employer's obligations under CO-BRA, see The Employer's Legal Handbook, *by Fred S. Steingold (Nolo).*

4. Termination of Obligations

This clause states that if the worker violates the agreement, you don't have to continue to pay the severance and the employee must return to you any money you've already paid out. Since money is the standard way most employers provide consideration for a former employee's promise not to compete, the former employee should have to repay you for these amounts if she breaches the contract. If you provided some other form of consideration, you may want to modify this paragraph to require the return or reimbursement of that benefit (for instance, if you paid for a job placement service as part of the employee's consideration, you might want to require the employee to refund those amounts as well).

This clause protects you if the worker competes against you, discloses your trade secrets or violates any other provision of the agreement. Nothing needs to be inserted here.

> If Employee breaches any of Employee's obligations under Sections 4, 5 or 6 of this Agreement, Company's obligations under this Agreement will immediately terminate and Employee will immediately refund to Company the full amount of any severance payments made to Employee pursuant to Section 9.

5. Confidentiality

It's important to prevent remaining workers from assuming that all employees are entitled to some sort of severance payment when they leave or, worse, from thinking that they can hold you hostage for money by threatening to reveal your trade secrets. To dispel this assumption, we have included a provision in our severance agreement that requires the employee to keep the terms of the contract confidential. This clause prevents other employees from learning about the terms of your agreement. Nothing needs to be inserted here.

> Employee shall not directly or indirectly disclose either the existence of this Agreement or any of the terms of this Agreement other than to Employee's attorney, except to the extent that disclosing such terms is required by law.

6. Notice

After the employee's departure, you may need to contact her. Since you and the departing worker will no longer be seeing each other frequently, it makes sense to exchange mailing addresses. This clause states how correspondence should be sent and provides a space to add the name and address of your company and your former worker, as well as your attorneys (if necessary).

Fill in the employee's name and address and your company's name and address. If you or the employee is represented by an attorney, you can list their address here so that copies of any correspondence will be sent to them. If not, you can leave these spaces blank or delete these lines.

All notices, requests, demands and other communications hereunder must be in writing and shall be considered properly given if delivered by hand or mailed within the continental United States by first-class, registered mail, return receipt requested, postage and registry fees paid, to the applicable party and addressed as follows:

To Company:
  Bayside Web Design
  1858 Circle Drive
  Hayward, CA 95555
  Attention: Emily Rodriguez

---

with a copy to Company's attorney:

  Dewey, Cheatum & Howe
  444 First Street
  Oakland, CA 94444
  Attention: Donald J. Freidkin, Esq.

To Employee:
  Alexandra Stewart
  455 Walnut Street
  San Francisco, CA 94115

E. Boilerplate Clauses

Now that you understand the core clauses of the agreement and how they work together to protect your business, several important technicalities remain. The clauses we discuss below appear in almost every business contract you'll see because, over time, lawyers have realized that failing to include them can cause problems later. You won't have to modify these clauses and will need to add very little information.

➡ **If you're already familiar with general contract law, you can browse this section quickly.** *However, be sure to follow the instructions below for inserting information in the "Applicable Law" clause and the "Jurisdiction" clauses. You don't need to insert any information in the other boilerplate clauses.*

1. Severability

If you need to go to court to enforce your agreement against a worker who has violated it, there's a slight chance that the judge may find some part of the agreement void or unenforceable. In that case, you'll want the court to remove ("sever") the unenforceable part of the contract and leave the remaining, enforceable provisions intact. Without a "severability" clause, there's a greater risk that a judge will invalidate the entire agreement if she finds something wrong with it.

EXAMPLE: On the day she is hired, Anna willingly signs an agreement containing noncompetition, nondisclosure and nonsolicitation clauses. The next year, Anna leaves your company and violates the agreement by encouraging some of your key employees to go to work for the new company she is starting. You file suit against Anna for violating the nonsolicitation clause in your agreement, and the judge asks to review the entire agreement.

Although the noncompetition clause in your agreement is not at the center of the lawsuit, the judge finds that it is unenforceable because it lasts for five years after the employee leaves your company. However, because the agreement contains a severability clause, the judge agrees to disregard the noncompetition clause and enforce only the nonsolicitation

clause, which is perfectly valid. Without the severability clause, the judge might have thrown out the entire agreement.

> If a court determines that any provision of this Agreement is invalid or unenforceable, any invalidity or unenforceability will affect only that provision and shall not make any other provision of this Agreement invalid or unenforceable. Instead, such provision shall be modified, amended or limited to the extent necessary to render it valid and enforceable.

2. Applicable Law

This clause allows you to specify which state's law will govern your agreement. If you need to go to court to enforce it, a judge will probably use the laws of that state to enforce (or not enforce) the agreement.

Since every state has different laws regarding noncompete agreements, choosing which state's law will govern the agreement is important. There are also some practical considerations—it's usually advantageous to have the laws of your home state govern your agreement, since this is the law that you and your attorney will probably be most familiar with. If you decide to choose a different state, consult an attorney first—unfortunately, legal rules limit your choices.

It's important to understand that your choice of which state's law will govern your agreement is not the same as choosing the state in which a lawsuit will be tried. It's perfectly legal for someone to file a lawsuit in a state that's different than the state whose governing law controls the agreement. You'll specify *where* the lawsuit must be filed (as opposed to which law will be used to interpret the agreement) in another clause, called "Jurisdiction."

Take advantage of your choices. *If you and your employee are located in different states and the employee's state enforces agreements not to compete but yours does not, you might be able to choose that state's law to apply to your agreement. Although it's often perfectly legal to this, you should do so only with the guidance of an attorney.*

Usually, your business location and your employee's residence will be in the same state. Fill in that state. If you and the employee are located in different states, choose the state in which your business is located. (California employers—and non-California employers with California employees—should see "Special Rules for California Employers & Employees," below.) Below is an example of the brief, but important, "applicable law" clause.

> This Agreement shall be governed by and construed in accordance with the laws of the State of _California_.

Special Rules for California Employers & Employees

If you're a California employer—or if your business is located outside of California and you have California employees—you know by now that California will not enforce a noncompete clause. You may be wondering whether you can choose a different state's law to apply to your agreement, add a noncompetition clause to the agreement and get around California's prohibition. Whether you can do this depends on your situation. Here's a brief summary of the reasons you might choose the law of a different state, and how it's likely to hold up in court.

- A California employer with California employees can't insert the law of a different state and expect a California court to apply it to avoid California's stringent noncompete rules. California judges frown on blatant attempts to flout California law like this.

- A California employer who has employees outside of California should insert the law of the state in which the employee lives or performs services for you while she's your employee. As long as the employee lives and works there, the California employer has a legitimate reason for applying the law of a different state to an employee. More than likely, a California judge will uphold this choice of law if you or the employee sues over the agreement.

- A non-California employer whose employee works and lives in California will have a tough time convincing a California judge to apply the law of another state, even his own. California judges are very protective of their citizens' rights to choose where they will work, and will apply California law unless an out of state employer has some very good reasons why they shouldn't. In one case, a Maryland employer tried to enforce a noncompete agreement against a former employee in California by claiming that Maryland law (which allows noncompete agreements) should apply. The California court disagreed and decided that since the Maryland employer had "significant contacts" in California, and since the former employee was trying to take a job with a California company, California had a greater interest in applying its law than Maryland did. *Application Group, Inc. v. Hunter Group, Inc.,* 61 Cal. App. 4th 881 (1998).

The bottom line is that getting a California court to apply the law of another state is tricky at best. Out-of-state employers should not attempt it without the help of an experienced attorney.

3. Jurisdiction

The jurisdiction clause in our agreements refers to the physical place (county and state) where you will bring a lawsuit to enforce your agreement, if necessary. It also governs where your employee may sue. Most of the time, you and your employee will be in the same county, which is the one you'll choose for this clause. But if you and your employee are located in different counties or states, you'll need to give some thought to where you'd want to litigate. Most of the time, practicality will be your guide.

For instance, let's say your business is located in Arizona and your employee works in New Mexico. If the two of you get into a dispute over the agreement and your employee sues you (perhaps to ask a judge to declare your agreement unenforceable), it's going to be a lot more convenient for you if the employee files the lawsuit in Arizona, in the county in which your business is located. Just imagine if your employee filed a lawsuit against you in New Mexico—you'd have to hire New Mexico lawyers and probably incur lots of costs and expenses traveling back and forth to New Mexico during the course of the litigation. For you, it makes much more sense to require the employee to bring the lawsuit in Arizona so you can avoid this potential expense and inconvenience.

Similarly, if you and your employee are located far away from each other in the same state (for instance, your business is located in San Diego and your employee works and lives in San Francisco), you might want to specify that the jurisdiction in which either of you can file a lawsuit is San Diego County.

Most of the time, the state you choose for your jurisdiction clause will be the same as the law of the state you choose to govern your agreement (in the "applicable law" clause). Insert the county and state in which you want any lawsuits to be filed.

> Employee and Company consent to the exclusive jurisdiction and venue of the federal and state courts located in _San Diego County, California_, in any action arising out of or relating to this Agreement. Employee and Company waive any other venue to which either party might be entitled by domicile or otherwise.

 Some states do not allow employees to agree to go to court in another state. _Almost all states allow a resident of one state to agree in writing to be sued in another state (this is called "waiving personal jurisdiction"). However, Idaho, Montana and Alabama do not. If your business is in one of these states, choose the state where your business is located._

4. Entire Agreement

Sometimes, you and the employee will discuss certain ideas or issues that aren't recorded in your written agreement. To reduce the risk that the employee will claim that something you talked about—but didn't include in the written agreement—is part of your contract, we've included this "entire agreement" clause. This provision (in legalese, called an "integration clause") says that only what is written in this agreement, and nothing else you may have discussed, is part of the contract between you and the worker. Nothing needs to be inserted here.

> This is the entire agreement between the parties. It supersedes and replaces any and all prior oral or written agreements between Company and Employee that relate to the matters covered by this Agreement.

5. Assignment and Binding Effect

This clause simply means that if you sell your company or merge your company into another, the new company will gain your rights and protections under the contract—without having to get the employee's permission. Nothing needs to be inserted here.

> This Agreement shall bind the Company's successors and assigns, and Company may assign this Agreement to any party at any time, in its sole discretion, without Employee's consent. This Agreement shall bind Employee's heirs, successors and assignees. Employee shall not assign any of Employee's rights or obligations under this Agreement without Company's prior written consent.

6. Waiver

Having spent considerable time (and perhaps expense) drafting your agreement and getting the employee to sign it, you probably intend to see that it's followed. There may be times, however, when a violation of the agreement just isn't worth getting upset over. For instance, the information leak may not that important; or the employee who's been wooed away may be someone you're glad to see depart. However, you'll want to know that, should you need to, you can hold your ex-worker to the letter of the agreement and expect a judge to do so, too.

The legal problem you may face is called "waiver and estoppel." Having let prior violations go by, your ex-employee may claim that you've given up the noncompete protections you once had. Especially if the worker has relied on your apparent lack of concern, you may have a tough time getting a judge to enforce your agreement.

EXAMPLE: Sadie left her job as an insurance agent at Insure-We-Will to join a competitor. Because Insure-We-Will is a California company, Sadie signed a severance agreement that contained only nonsolicitation and nondisclosure clauses.

Before Sadie left the company, she solicited a couple of other Insure-We-Will employees to join her at her new employer, in violation of her agreement. The Company's CEO knew about Sadie's violation of the agreement, but decided not to take any action against her, since the agents who left with her were also poor performers.

Emboldened, Sadie managed to convince one of Insure-We-Will's top agents to move to her new company (which earned her a position in the recruitment division). This time, the CEO was furious. He immediately called a lawyer and told her to file a lawsuit against Sadie for violating the agreement. Sadie and her lawyer responded by arguing that because Insure-We-Will hadn't tried to enforce the agreement when the first few employees left, they may have waived their right to sue Sadie for soliciting the top-performing agent. They also pointed out that Sadie will lose her promotion if she can no longer recruit at her old company. Insure-We-Will had a very tough time convincing the

judge that it hadn't waived its right to enforce the nonsolicitation clause against Sadie

The waiver clause in our agreement will help prevent your former employee from claiming that you have waived your right to enforce a part of the contract even if you've ignored it for a time. However, a waiver clause is no guarantee that you can "pick your fights" at whim. It's best to be diligent about enforcing your rights under your agreement. Nothing needs to be inserted here.

> If Company waives any term or provision of this Agreement, that waiver shall only be effective in the specific instance and for the specific purpose for which Company gave the waiver. If Company fails to exercise or delays exercising any of its rights or remedies under this Agreement, Company retains the right to enforce that term or provision at a later time.

Preserve your rights while you think. *If you learn that an employee is violating your agreement but aren't ready to fire off a lawsuit (or even a stern letter from your lawyer), your best bet is to inform the worker that he is in violation and that your present stance is not a waiver of your rights. Send a letter in which you acknowledge that you are not taking immediate action, but that you will enforce your rights in the future—then do* *so! Understand that if you continue to let the violation go unchecked, a judge may decide later that you have waived your rights by inaction, no matter how many letters you might have sent.*

7. Amendment

You and your worker may have conversations about the noncompetition agreement after it's been signed. The signed document, however, should be the last (and only) word on what's been agreed to. If you both agree to change the agreement, that's fine—but put the change in writing and make it part of your agreement. This will prevent an employee from claiming that statements made orally later or in separate documents should take precedence over what's said in the agreement.

The amendment clause requires any amendments to the contract to be in writing and to be signed by both parties, so there won't be any doubt as to who agreed to what: Nothing needs to be inserted here. In Section G, we'll show you how to use the Amendment form.

> This Agreement may be modified, changed or amended only in writing, and such writing must signed by both parties.

8. Counterparts

This clause, arguably the most mundane in the entire agreement, means that you and the employee can sign the agreement on separate signature pages, but that it will still be considered to be one agreement. Nothing needs to be inserted here.

> The parties may execute this Agreement in counterparts, each of which shall be considered an original, and all of which shall constitute the same document.

Congratulations! You've made it through the form. All that's left is to learn about the signature portion of the agreement. Read Section H, "Completing Your Agreement," below, for instructions on signing, copying and amending your agreement.

F. Clauses Not Included in Our Employee Agreements

Some noncompete agreements include clauses covering how disputes will be handled, who owns the employee's work product and the amount of the employee's salary. These clauses are not in our agreements. In this section, we'll tell you exactly what we've left out, and why.

1. Disputes: Arbitration and Mediation

Arbitration and mediation are alternatives to going to court that are often cheaper, quicker and less emotionally draining than going to court.

Our agreements do not require that you and your worker take your disputes to mediation or arbitration because, although we certainly hope you don't have to go to court to enforce your agreement, that's where you're most likely to get it enforced. It certainly doesn't hurt to ask an employee to mediate or arbitrate a dispute before going to court, and we recommend that you do at least ask. Realistically, however, if a former worker is violating your agreement, your best chance of stopping the offensive behavior and enforcing the agreement is to immediately ask a judge to stop it with an injunction.

Moreover, requiring an employee to agree to an arbitration clause may not work anyway. Once again, it's a matter of enforcement—many states will uphold these clauses only under certain conditions. If you're interested in including an arbitration clause in an agreement for an employee, see an employment law expert.

2. Ownership of Employee Work Product

Some employment agreements contain a clause that states that anything the worker creates or authors while working for you will belong to your company instead of

the worker. This may be important if you're hiring someone to write source code for a software program or create content for your website.

We have not included a work product clause because state laws vary on the issue. (For example, California has strict rules regarding employee ownership of employee-created inventions.) In addition, your rights as an employer will depend on what kind of intellectual property is involved and what kinds of rights you want to retain in the property. If you're interested in including such a clause, consult an attorney.

 For more information about ownership of employee works or inventions, see License Your Invention, *by Rich Stim (Nolo), and* The Copyright Handbook, *by Stephen Fishman (Nolo).*

3. Employment Terms: Salary, Benefits or Term of Employment

You may notice that our noncompete agreements for employees don't include a description of the employee's salary, the benefits you'll provide to the employee and a description of the expected work. These terms have been left out for two reasons.

First, the agreements in this book are not "employment agreements," which set a fixed term for the length of the employ ment relationship and recite the employee's benefits or duties. In fact, as explained in Chapter 3, Section B1, we are careful to maintain your employee's at-will status. Second, as an employer, you'll probably want to retain the right to change an employee's salary or benefits at any time, and you don't want to have to amend an agreement each time. And if you were to put terms such as salary and benefits into a contract, you'd have a much more difficult time changing any of these terms without the employee's crying foul.

G. Instructions for Amendment Form

You'll use the amendment form, Form EMPL-8, if you need to amend an existing noncompete agreement. For example, let's say you've decided to give a key employee, who has already entered into a noncompete agreement, a promotion. The employee's new duties will give the employee access to confidential information that isn't defined in your prior agreement. Instead of rewriting the whole noncompete agreement to reflect the employee's new duties and new confidential information, you can amend the original agreement with a brief document describing the change in the employee's duties and the new information the employee will have access to.

1. Introduction

Fill in the date (month, day and year) the amendment is being made, the employee's name and the name of your company. In the last blank, fill in the state in which your company was formed and its type of legal structure—for example, "a _California corporation_."

2. Purpose

In the first and second blanks, insert the name of the original agreement, such as "Employee and Company are parties to a _Noncompetition, Nondisclosure and Nonsolicitation Agreement_ dated as of _September 1, 2000_ ("Original Agreement").

In the third blank, explain why you are amending the agreement. For instance, "_As a result of Employee's promotion to the position of Senior Applications Developer, Company and Employee would like to amend the Original Agreement to include certain additional agreements of Employee and Company_."

3. Amendment

Depending on whether you're changing language in the original agreement or adding or deleting a new section or paragraph, choose one of the alternatives that come next and delete the others. Then follow the instructions that go with the alternative:

[ ] Alternative # 1: Replacing a Clause

Insert the number or letter of the section(s) or paragraph(s) you are changing (in both blanks) and then insert the actual text of the amendment in the blank lines.

[ ] Alternative # 2: Deleting a Clause

Insert the number or letter of the section you are deleting.

[ ] Alternative # 3: Adding a New Clause

Insert the number or letter of the new section or paragraph you are adding (in both blanks) and then insert the actual text of the new clause in the blank lines.

 Consult a lawyer to amend a fixed-term employee's employment agreement. *While the noncompetition, nonsolicitation and nondisclosure provisions of our noncompete agreements can easily be inserted into an employment agreement, you should consult an expert if you want to amend a fixed-term employment contract.*

4. Applicable Law

This amendment will be governed by the same state law as the original agreement. Fill in the state that governed the original agreement.

If the previous agreement didn't say which state's law would apply, fill in the state in which your business and the employee are located. Usually, you and your employee will be in the same state, so fill

in that state. However, if you and the contractor are located in different states, you should choose the state in which your business is located (if you ever have to go to court to enforce your agreement, it will make your life a lot easier). Refer to Section E2, above, for more explanation.

5. Entire Agreement; No Other Change

Nothing needs to be inserted here. (See Section E4, above, for an explanation of this clause.)

6. Counterparts

Nothing needs to be inserted here. (See Section E8, above, for an explanation of this clause.)

H. Completing Your Agreement

Before you sign and date your agreement and make copies of it, read the general instructions below, which apply to all of the forms in this book.

1. Signing the Agreement

Legally, it's always important for the parties to a contract (in this case, the employee and you, the employer) to sign it correctly. First, of course, there's the obvious importance of getting each party's name right (believe it or not, parties' names are spelled incorrectly in contracts all the time).

Second, you need to make sure each party's signature is "structured" correctly to make it clear who's signing the agreement, and in what capacity. This is particularly important if an entity (such as a partnership or a corporation), rather than a person, signs the agreement. In that case the "signature block" needs to state the title of the person signing the agreement (president, general partner, for example) to show that that person has the authority to sign the contract.

The following is a summary of the correct signature blocks you should use according to how your business is organized.

a. Sole Proprietorships

If you run your business as a sole proprietorship (a one-person business that isn't registered with the state as a corporation or an LLC), you are fully liable for all business contracts and debts.

Simply sign your full name and the agreement will be binding on you and your business. If you have a fictitious business name (also called a d/b/a), and you want to be more precise, you can add "doing business as" after your name, to make it clear that you are entering into the agreement on behalf of your business. Here's an example of a sole proprietor's signature block:

By: _Clark Kent_
d/b/a The Caped Crusader

The signature blocks in our agreements look like this:

_____

_____

By:_____
[insert or print name]
Its:_____

To create a sole proprietor signature block out of the lines we provide, delete the first two lines and sign your name on the third. Type or print your name on the fourth line. If you wish to include your business name, on the last line delete the "Its" and type in "d/b/a" and the name of the business, as in the above example.

b. Limited Liability Companies

Setting up the signature blocks correctly is particularly important for business structures that offer protection from personal liability for business debts (known as "limited liability"), such as corporations and limited liability companies (LLCs). Stating a person's title and the name of the company under the signature protects the limited personal liability of the person signing the agreement and of the business's owners.

If you run your business as a limited liability company (LLC), you know that the owners of LLCs are called members and the contract that governs the members' relationship to each other is called the operating agreement. Your LLC is probably managed by the members, but it might be run by one or more properly authorized managers. In addition, especially if it's large or has investors who don't partici-pate in its management, your LLC might even have officers as in a corporation, in-cluding a president, vice president and secretary.

To protect your limited liability, you and other members, managers or officers need to make sure you sign all agreements in the proper capacity.

If your LLC is member-managed, any one member can normally sign an agree-ment and bind the LLC. On the first line of the signature block, the member should insert the name of the company (including the abbreviation LLC or L.L.C.), and on the second line, the state in which the com-pany was formed and the words "limited liability company." On the next three lines, the member should sign her name, type her name and add the word "Member."

The signature block should look like this:

Kryptonite Busters, LLC,
a Delaware limited liability company
By: *Lex Luthor*
Its: *Member*

If your LLC is manager-managed, first check your LLC operating agreement to make sure that the manager, member or officer signing the agreement on behalf of the LLC has the power to bind the LLC to contracts by herself. (Some LLC operating agreements may provide that two or more managers' or members' signatures are re-quired to bind the LLC to certain types of contracts.) If your LLC has officers, the president or other high-ranking officer can probably sign the agreement, but again, it's worth consulting your company's oper-ating agreement to be sure this officer has the authority to do this.

If your LLC is manager-managed, the agreement should probably be signed by a manager and should look like the signa-ture block that follows. (If it turns out that a member or an officer has the right to bind the LLC, then insert the appropriate title, such as "member" or "president.")

Kryptonite Busters, LLC,
a Delaware limited liability company
By: *Lex Luthor*
Its: *Manager*

 Consider having your LLC formally authorize the agree-ment if you are entering into a noncompete agreement with a key ex-ecutive as part of a formal employ-ment contract. *Although LLC members or managers normally have legal authority to sign contracts, it may make sense to have all of the members of your LLC sign a reso-lution authorizing the company's signing*

of the agreement, just to be on the safe side. For more information on LLC resolutions and recordkeeping, see Your Limited Liability Company: An Operating Manual, *by Anthony Mancuso (Nolo).*

c. Corporations

If your business is set up as a corporation, you know that the owners of a corporation are called shareholders; the people who direct the policy of the corporation are the directors; and the executive employees who run the corporation on a daily basis are the officers, usually consisting of a president, a vice president, a secretary and a treasurer. Corporate shareholders, officers and directors all enjoy limited personal liability for business debts, which means they usually can't be held personally liable to pay these amounts except in extreme circumstances.

If you are in doubt as to which corporate officers have power to sign contracts, check your company's bylaws. Usually, the president or chief executive officer (CEO) of a corporation will have the authority to sign contracts by herself on behalf of the corporation, but sometimes the corporation's bylaws or even a state law will require two officers to sign a contract entered into on the corporation's behalf. (Directors don't normally sign agreements, but they can—check your bylaws to see if they are authorized to do so.)

Corporate officers and directors need to make sure they sign all agreements in their correct capacity in order to protect their limited personal liability for business debts. The officer or director who signs the agreement on behalf of the company needs to make it clear that she is signing the agreement in her corporate, not her individual, capacity. The name of the corporation (including the abbreviation Inc. or Corp.) goes on the first line of the signature block, and the state in which the company was formed and the word "corporation" should be inserted on the second line. On the next three lines, the officer or director should sign her name, type her name and add her title.

Your corporation's signature block should look like this:

Jailbreak Specialists, Inc.,
a Delaware corporation
By: *Lex Luthor*
Its: *President and Chief Executive Officer*

Consider getting shareholder approval for the agreement when entering into noncompete agreements with high-level employees as part of a formal employment contract. *In this situation, it's common in small corporations to draft a board of directors' resolution approving the agreement, and you might want to prepare a shareholders' resolution as well. For more information* *about corporate resolutions and recordkeeping, see* The Corporate Minutes Book: The Legal Guide to Taking Care of Corporate Business, *by Anthony Mancuso (Nolo).*

d. General Partnerships

If you are a partner in a general partnership, you know that you are personally liable for all business contracts and debts. It's still important, however, to structure the signatures on a contract correctly to make it clear that the partnership is the party to the contract, not the individual partner signing the contract.

A general partner of a partnership can sign all agreements on behalf of the partnership. However, consult your partnership agreement to make sure that one general partner's signature is enough to bind the company. If in doubt, all of the general partners should sign the agreement.

The name of the partnership goes on the first line of the signature block, and the state in which the company was formed and the word "partnership" should be inserted on the second line. On the next three lines, the partner signs her name, types her name and adds her title. The signature block should look like this:

Oblivious Reporters,
a Delaware partnership
By: _____Lois Lane_____
Its: _General Partner_

For more information about creating, running and operating partnerships, see The Partnership Book, *by Denis Clifford and Ralph Warner (Nolo).*

e. Limited Partnerships

Limited partnerships have general partners, who run the business and are personally liable for business debts, but they also have limited partners, who don't manage the business and are only liable for business debts up to the amount of their investment.

The general partner(s) of a partnership must sign all agreements on behalf of the partnership (limited partners can't sign agreements because they don't have the authority to bind the partnership). Consult your partnership agreement to determine if more than one general partner's signature is necessary to bind the partnership to an agreement.

The name of the partnership goes on the first line of the signature block, and the state in which the company was formed and the word "partnership" should be inserted on the second line. On the next three lines, the partner should sign her name, type her name and add her title. The signature block should look like this:

Oblivious Reporters, L.P.,
a Delaware partnership
By: _____Lois Lane_____
Its: _General Partner_

f. Multi-Tiered Companies

Individuals aren't the only ones who can be managers of LLCs or general partners in partnerships. Another company can fill these roles, too. In that case, you should list both company names.

The name of the main company goes on the first line of the signature block, and the state in which the company was formed and its type of legal structure, such as "limited liability company" or "limited partnership," should be inserted on the second line. Then insert the name of the company that's the general partner or manager of the main company, and finally the name of the person signing the document and her title. The signature block should look like this:

> *Bumbling Assistants, L.P.,*
> *a Delaware limited partnership*
> By: *Fresh off the Farm, LLC, a Delaware*
>   *limited liability company*
> Its: *General Partner*
>   By: *Jimmy Olsen*
>   Its: *Manager*

2. Altering the Agreement Before It's Signed

You can keep your noncompete agreement on your computer and easily alter it up to the day you sign the agreement.

If for some reason you must change the agreement before it has been signed but after it has been printed (for example, you've printed out a hard copy and your computer isn't available), you can simply write the changes in by hand and cross out anything you want to remove. But it's important that both parties initial each of these changes before they sign the agreement to make sure it's clear that both parties have agreed to them. Although this is a perfectly legal way to alter an agreement, it's almost always a better idea to make the changes on your computer if you can. This reduces the chance of confusion later.

If you need to change the agreement *after* it's been signed, use EMPL-8, the amendment form for employee agreements.

3. Making Copies of the Agreement

Ideally, both you and the employee should have a signed original of the agreement for your files. To accomplish this, when you're ready to sign the agreement, prepare two copies of the agreement. Sign both of them, and then have the worker do the same. If you or your worker received the advice of an attorney before signing the noncompete agreement, you might want to provide the attorney with a signed original as well.

Don't sign in black ink. *So that you'll know which documents are copies and which are originals, it's helpful to sign contracts in blue ink. Marking originals "Original" and copies "Copy" is also useful.*

Keep the original in a safe place—the employee's personnel file is a good place. While a copy is usually enough to prove the legitimacy of a signature if someone disputes its authenticity, it's always better to have an agreement with the original signature.

4. To Fax or Not to Fax

Often, parties signing an agreement aren't in the same place at the same time. It's perfectly legal to have an employee sign the agreement and fax it back to you. But if you do this, it's best to ask the worker to also sign two duplicate originals and mail one back to you, so that you'll have an original for your files.

5. Changing the Agreement After It's Signed

Sometimes, you'll want to make changes to the agreement after it's signed. This is easy to do, but it's important to make sure that any changes to your agreement are in writing. The agreements in this book specifically require all amendments to be in writing and signed by both parties. An amendment form, EMPL-8, is included on the CD-ROM. The instructions for the amendment form are in Section G, above.

6. Naming Your Agreement

Although we provide job descriptions in our employee agreement titles to make it easier for you to find them, you should delete this job description from the title. For instance, delete "Noncompetition, Nondisclosure and Nonsolicitation Agreement for IT Professionals." The final title of your agreement should instead be "Nondisclosure, Nonsolicitation and Noncompetition Agreement." (If you don't include a noncompetition clause in your agreement, the agreement should be titled "Nondisclosure and Nonsolicitation Agreement.")

The Severance Agreement for Employees should be titled "Severance Agreement."

If you are creating an amendment to an agreement, it should be titled "Amendment to Nondisclosure, Nonsolicitation and Noncompetition Agreement." (If you didn't include a noncompetition clause in your agreement, the amendment will probably be titled "Amendment to Nondisclosure and Nonsolicitation Agreement.")

Form EMPL-8: Amendment of Employee Agreement

1.   Introduction

This Amendment ("Amendment") is made and entered into as of _____, _____,

between _____ ("Employee") and _____, a
_____ ("Company").

2.   Purpose

Employee and Company are parties to a _____, dated as of
_____, _____ ("Original Agreement").

Employee and Company desire to amend the Original Agreement on the terms and
conditions set forth herein. For good and valuable consideration, the receipt and sufficiency
of which is hereby acknowledged, the parties agree as follows:

3.   Amendment

[ ]   Alternative # 1: Replacing a Clause

Section ____ of the Original Agreement is hereby deleted in its entirety. Section ____ shall now
read in full as follows:

_____

_____

_____

[ ]   Alternative # 2: Deleting a Clause

Section ___ is hereby deleted in its entirety.

[ ]   Alternative # 3: Adding a New Clause

The following clause is hereby added to the Original Agreement as Section ___. Section ___ reads in full as follows:

_____

_____

_____

4.   Applicable Law

This Amendment shall be governed by and construed in accordance with the laws of the State of _____.

5.   Entire Agreement; No Other Change

This is the entire agreement between the parties. It supersedes and replaces any and all prior oral or written agreements between Company and Employee that relate to the matters covered by this Amendment. Except for the provisions modified by this Amendment, all the provisions of the Original Agreement shall remain in full force and effect. If there is any conflict between the provisions of this Amendment and the Original Agreement, the provisions of this Amendment will control.

6.   Counterparts

The parties may execute this Amendment in counterparts, each of which shall be considered an original, and all of which shall constitute the same document.

IN WITNESS WHEREOF, the parties have executed this Amendment as of the day and year first written above in Section 1.

"Company"

_____, a _____

By: _____

_____

[type or print name]

Its: _____

"Employee"

_____

_____

[type or print name]

5

Using Noncompete Agreements for Independent Contractors

I n this chapter, we discuss how to compensate an independent contractor for agreeing to your noncompete provisions. Paying the contractor is necessary in order to make your agreement enforceable. We also explain how to negotiate and get your agreement signed, and explain your options if a contractor refuses to sign a noncompete agreement.

But first, we help you analyze a preliminary issue—whether you've properly characterized a worker as an independent contractor, not an employee. As you will see, incorrectly classifying a worker as an independent contractor can have expensive consequences.

A few states will not enforce a noncompetition clause against an independent contractor. *If your business is located in one of these states, you can still protect your business's confidential information, employees, customers and clients by using agreements that contain nondisclosure and nonsolicitation clauses. See Chapter 2, Section B2, for more information.*

A. Identifying Independent Contractors

Before you ask a worker to sign any kind of independent contractor agreement, you need to know whether that worker is indeed an independent contractor. Distinguishing between employees and independent contractors can be tricky, but it's important to classify workers correctly. If you don't, the IRS and your state employment and tax agencies can assess fines and penalties against you. In this section we look briefly at the factors that distinguish independent contractors from employees, to help you decide how to classify a particular worker.

If you already understand how to distinguish between employees and independent contractors, you can skip ahead to Section B, below.

1. The Difference Between Employees and Contractors

Many businesspeople think it's up to them to classify workers as employees or independent contractors. In reality, however, you must classify workers according to various government guidelines, explained below. The fact alone that you have decided to treat someone as a contractor does not make that person a true contractor.

Over the years, the IRS and state agencies have developed complicated tests to help employers determine a worker's status. Some of the factors in these tests include:

- whether the worker expects to make a profit or loss from the activity. (Employees don't view their jobs as a business or typically think in terms of "profit" and "loss"—they think "paycheck.")

- whether the worker is required to work on-site or can instead work wherever she chooses. (Employees are usually required to work at a specific location; independent contractors can usually work wherever they want, depending on the type of work that needs to be done.)
- whether the worker offers her services to other businesses or performs services solely for one company. (Employees usually work for only one company; independent contractors may work for as many businesses as they like.)
- whether the worker is "at will" (can quit or be fired at any time) or has an employment contract that lasts for a specific period of time. (Employees are usually "at will"; independent contractors usually have a contract that spells out how and when their services can be terminated).
- whether the worker or the company furnishes the materials for the job. (Employers usually furnish employees with the tools of the trade; independent contractors usually supply their own.)
- how the worker is paid. (Employees are paid at regular intervals; contractors are usually paid when they

complete a project or submit an invoice.)

- the length of the worker's relationship with the business. (Employees almost always work on a continuing basis; contractors usually work on a project-by-project basis and are often transient—moving from company to company.)
- how much the worker herself has invested in her trade, including training and equipment. (Employees typically don't invest much, while an independent contractor does.)
- who pays the worker's business or traveling expenses. (Employees' expenses are typically paid by the employer; independent contractors usually pay their own and deduct them as business expenses.)
- whether the worker may quit at any time or is bound by a contract to work for a specific period of time or complete a specific project. (Employees may usually quit at any time, while independent contractors are usually contractually bound to complete a project or perform services for a specific period of time.)
- how much instruction the worker must follow from the company. (Employees must generally follow instructions of their superiors; contractors should be free to complete a task or project with minimal oversight or instruction.)

- whether the worker must perform tasks in a certain order or may complete them in the order the worker deems appropriate.
- whether the worker has received training from the employer. (Employees usually receive training from an employer, while independent contractors are expected to be experts in their field and not require training.)
- whether the worker has the right to delegate duties to other people. (Employees typically can't hand off work to others; some independent contractors routinely delegate duties to assistants working for them). Similarly, an employee's assistants are hired, screened and paid by the employer, while an independent contractor usually hires and pays her own assistants.
- whether the worker has set working hours. (Employees typically have certain hours during which they are required to work, while an independent contractor can work at any time, as long as the work is finished on time.) Similarly, employees generally work full time for one business and may not work for a competitive business, while independent contractors can usually work for whomever they choose (unless, of course, they've signed a noncompete agreement).
- whether the worker's duties are integral to the business (this suggests that the worker is an employee) or are only sporadically necessary (as is true with most contractors).
- whether the worker uses special skills on the job. (Highly skilled or specialized jobs often fall to independent contractors, while employees usually staff less specialized jobs.)

The common theme among the test factors outlined above is control. What the IRS (or any other agency who conducts an audit of your business) really wants to know is how much control you have over the worker. If all you do is tell the worker what you want as the end-product and the worker controls the means and methods of producing this result, that person is probably an independent contractor. And if the work is done offsite, with the worker's own materials, and this person works simultaneously for several different businesses, you have an even stronger argument that the worker is an independent contractor.

However, if an independent contractor works at your place of business and you provide all of the materials for the job, control the method and manner of how the job gets done and generally treat the worker like an employee (including setting working hours and making workplace rules), that person is probably an employee. Calling her (and paying her as) an independent contractor won't change that.

As long as you understand the rules, hiring and classifying independent contractors is not hard. The main thing to understand about independent contractors is that they should be just that: independent.

2. Classifying Workers As Independent Contractors

It's sometimes tempting for a business to classify workers as independent contractors even if they're really more like employees. Why? There are many savings for an employer who does business with an independent contractor rather than an employee. The employer is not required to:

- withhold federal or state income taxes
- withhold and pay its share of payroll taxes (Social Security, Medicare, federal unemployment insurance and sometimes state disability taxes)
- provide workers' compensation insurance, or
- provide healthcare, retirement and other benefits that it provides to its employees.

However, the IRS and your state tax and employment agencies are aware of the potential for abuse by businesses that classify employees as independent contractors.

These agencies spend a great deal of time and money investigating employers who misclassify workers. If these agencies reclassify any of your workers, it can cost you thousands of dollars in fines and penalties.

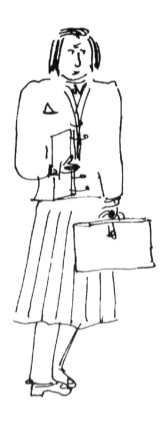

Misclassifying Workers: A Cautionary Tale

Like a lot of software companies, Microsoft hired temporary workers to edit, proofread and test its software. Microsoft did not withhold income, Social Security or Medicare taxes from their paychecks, and did not allow them to participate in any employee benefit plans. Microsoft also required each of these workers to sign an agreement stating that they were independent contractors.

The only problem was, Microsoft treated these temporary workers like employees. The temps were required to work on site, for the same hours as regular employees, and took direction from senior management, just as the regular employees did.

In 1989, the IRS audited Microsoft's employment records and determined that many of these workers were employees. Microsoft agreed, and paid the fines and penalties associated with misclassifying these workers.

However, the story didn't end there. When the workers learned of the misclassification, they sued Microsoft, alleging that as employees, they had been denied benefits that other employees received—namely, health insurance, a retirement plan and participation in Microsoft's very lucrative stock option/stock purchase plan. The employees won the suit, and a federal court of appeals affirmed a $97 million dollar verdict against Microsoft in favor of the reclassified employees.

The moral of the Microsoft story, above, is pretty clear: An independent contractor agreement, while it can help sway the IRS in a borderline situation, is not a magic wand. A taxing agency will always look at all the circumstances of a worker's employment before deciding whether a worker is in fact an independent contractor.

 You may have to pay employment taxes for certain types of contractors. *Even if your contractor meets all of the tests discussed above, the IRS might still classify her as a "statutory employee." Contractors who might qualify as* *statutory employees include corporate officers; drivers who distribute certain food products, beverages or laundry; and full-time life insurance salespeople and other salespeople. For more information about statutory employees and a more thorough*

discussion of classifying workers and correctly hiring independent contractors, see Hiring Independent Contractors: An Employer's Legal Guide, *by Stephen Fishman (Nolo), from which the preceding discussion of the IRS rules is adapted.*

3. Penalties for Misclassifying Workers

If you're audited by the IRS or your state's employment or tax agency, the way you've classified your workers will be examined. If the auditors decide you've misclassified a worker, the agency will assess penalties and fines against you. The amount you'll pay in fines and penalties will depend on whether you intentionally misclassified a worker or whether it was an honest mistake. Understandably, the penalties for intentionally misclassifying a worker are heftier than those for mistakenly misclassifying a worker.

Additionally, at least from the IRS's standpoint, the penalties you'll owe will depend on whether you provided the worker with a Form 1099 (a statement summarizing the independent contractor's wages for the tax year). The penalties are higher if you failed to provide the worker with a Form 1099.

If you provide the worker with a Form 1099 detailing the worker's pay, here's a summary of the payments you may have to make:

- 100% of the FICA (Social Security and Medicare) taxes you should have paid as the worker's employer, up to 6.2% of the employee's wages
- 20% of the FICA you should have withheld from the employee's pay (as a penalty)
- 100% of the FUTA (federal unemployment taxes) you should have paid on the employee's behalf, and
- a 1.5% penalty on all of the employee's wages for failing to withhold income taxes from the employee's pay.

If you don't provide the worker with a Form 1099, the IRS can double some of the above payments. And, if the IRS or state agency can prove that you intentionally misclassified a worker, the penalties go up even more, and can add up to an incredible 41.5% of all the compensation you've paid to the worker.

Probably most sobering thing to know about all of this is that business owners are *personally liable* for these payments. The IRS is so serious about making businesses pay this money that they will go after sole proprietors, general partners, limited liability company (LLC) owners and a corporation's shareholders to personally pay these amounts. The IRS has also pursued officers of a corporation, including the president, vice president, treasurer and secretary for these payments, even if these officers did not own stock in the business. Even bookkeepers, accountants and office managers may be personally liable for these amounts if they had any part in the business's failure to pay these taxes.

For more information about the penalties for incorrectly classifying workers, see Hiring Independent Contractors: The Employer's Legal Guide, *by Stephen Fishman (Nolo), from which the preceding discussion is adapted.*

In addition to being penalized by a federal or state government agency, the worker can sue you as well. As illustrated by the Microsoft case (see "Misclassifying Workers: A Cautionary Tale," above) the worker may be able to successfully claim that since she was an employee, she is entitled to the benefits you provide to your employees.

If you have determined that your workers are employees, not independent contractors, you don't need to read the rest of this chapter. See Chapter 3 for information on noncompete agreements for employees.

4. The Value of Written Agreements for Independent Contractors

Even if you don't ask a contractor to agree to our noncompete provisions, it's important to put your agreement with the contractor in writing. First, it will prevent con-

fusion and misunderstanding about what you and the contractor agreed to, such as job specifications and rate of pay. You may think that a quick conversation and a handshake are enough to create a good working relationship. But if you rely on oral understandings (and worse, your memory of those oral understandings), you could run into problems. Each of you might remember your conversation differently, which can lead to mistrust and disagreements about what was said. This can precipitate disputes with the contractor that you didn't anticipate and that might lead to legal problems down the road.

Once the details of your relationship are spelled out in an agreement, you and the contractor can spend more time working and less time bickering over small details, like when the contractor will get paid. A written agreement also forces the contractor to agree in writing to pay his taxes and acknowledge that he's an independent contractor, which can help if your business is ever audited by the IRS; and the agreement can define which state's law will govern your agreement (if you and the contractor are located in different states) in case of a dispute. Lastly, but most importantly for our purposes, the agreement can include nondisclosure, noncompetition and nonsolicitation provisions in the agreement right from the beginning, so you don't have to worry about these issues later.

B. Contractor Must Benefit From Signing Noncompete Agreement

First, let us explain a critical element of creating an enforceable noncompete clause: The agreement must give something worthwhile to the independent contractor who signs the contract. This is a legal concept lawyers call "consideration." As you may already know from past business dealings, no contract is valid unless this benefit, or consideration, exists.

The sufficient benefit requirement applies to any agreement your contractor signs. If a contractor signs an agreement that contains only nondisclosure and nonsolicitation clauses (for instance, because your business is located in a state like California, which won't enforce noncompetition clauses), you must still provide a benefit to your contractor before your agreement becomes enforceable.

How you provide adequate consideration to your contractor will depend on whether the contractor is someone you're beginning to do business with, an existing contractor or a person who is leaving at the end of the job. In the next section, we discuss how to handle each of these situations so that you create a contract that is supported by the right kind of consideration.

C. Noncompete Agreements for New, Existing and Departing Contractors

A noncompete agreement can stand on its own or be part of a larger independent contractor agreement (the one that describes the work and the cost) between you and the worker. Whether to use a stand-alone or integrated agreement depends largely on when you ask the contractor to agree not to compete.

- **Before starting work.** If the contractor has not started work, we recommend that you use a written independent contractor agreement that sets forth the terms of employment (such as work obligations and payment) and incorporates all or some of the noncompete provisions (see Section 1).

- **After starting work under an oral understanding.** If the contractor started working for you under an oral agreement, we recommend that you create a written independent contractor agreement that incorporates the contractor's work obligations, payment arrangements and any additional benefits, plus noncompete provisions as well (see Section 2).

- **After starting work under a written contract.** If the contractor started work under a written agreement, we recommend that you amend the original independent contractor agreement to include noncompetition clauses. Alternately, you can prepare a separate noncompete agreement that doesn't include details on the work relationship between you and the contractor (see Section 2).

- **After work has terminated.** If the contractor has left (or is planning to leave) and you wish to restrict the contractor with noncompete provisions, you will need to use a written agreement known as a termination agreement (much like a severance agreement for employees). This agreement must provide additional benefits to the contractor (see Section 3).

1. Before the Contractor Starts Work

If you are reading this book before you have hired the independent contractor, we recommend that you write a contract that spells out the details of your arrangement, such as the contractor's hourly or weekly rate and project deadlines and goals, and includes noncompete provisions right there. The independent contractor agreements in this book address all of the relevant issues of your work relationship, including:

- a description of the contractor's duties

- the term of the work relationship, whether it's a specific period of time or until the contractor completes a certain project
- how much—and how often—the contractor gets paid, and
- a statement by the contractor that she's not entitled to any of the benefits you provide your employees, and that she will pay all of the taxes associated with her compensation.

In addition, our independent contractor agreements include restrictions on competition, solicitation of customers and employees and disclosure of trade secrets. You may keep all or some of these noncompete provisions in your independent contractor agreement. See Chapter 2, Section A3, for a discussion of which provisions are appropriate for your contractor (as well as which contractors should sign agreements with restrictive provisions).

Ask an independent contractor who merits a noncompete agreement to sign the agreement prior to starting work. In fact, signing a noncompete agreement should be a condition of being hired for a job. This policy has two big benefits:

- **The agreement is more likely to get signed.** A contractor who wants to provide services for your company is likely to sign the agreement if doing so furthers his chances of getting the assignment.
- **The assignment itself is the "legal benefit," or consideration.** As ex-

plained above, you must give something of value in order to make the agreement enforceable—if you tie the agreement to the offer of work, you've satisfied this requirement. As we discuss below, once a contractor starts working for you, you have to offer him additional perks (such as a bonus or a higher hourly rate) as consideration if you ask him to sign a noncompete agreement.

If a prospective contractor is reluctant to sign your noncompete agreement, you have a few choices:

- Attempt to sweeten the deal (for instance, by providing additional payments or free equipment) to get the contractor's consent.
- Modify the agreement so that it prevents only solicitation of your customers and employees and disclosure of your trade secrets (that is, leave out the noncompetition clause).
- Modify the agreement so that it prevents only disclosure of your trade secrets (that is, leave out the noncompetition and nonsolicitation clauses).
- Offer the IC a job as an employee (if job security is an issue), or
- Don't hire the contractor.

During the negotiations, you may want to consider the following factors if the contractor is still reluctant to sign a noncompete agreement:

- How badly do you want or need the IC's services?
- If you hire the IC and she turns out to be everything you've dreamed of and more, can you estimate the extent to which your business would be damaged if she were later to compete against you or solicit your customers or clients?
- Have you previously had problems with ex-contractors competing against you or soliciting your customers?
- Can you make the deal more attractive to the IC by offering more money or other perks in exchange for agreeing not to compete against your business?
- Can you offer the IC more employment, such as an additional job or a longer contract?
- What other legal options are available to protect your interests? (See "Your Legal Rights Without a Noncompete Agreement," at the end of this chapter, for more information.)

⚠ Don't discourage a contractor from having a lawyer review the agreement. *A prospective contractor may want to have the agreement reviewed by a lawyer before signing it (whether it's an independent contractor agreement or a separate noncompete agreement). Don't discourage the review. If you ever need to go to court to enforce your agreement,* *you'll be in a much better position if you can show that the contractor had legal advice and presumably understood the consequences of the agreement before signing it.*

2. After the Contractor Starts Work

You may be working with a contractor whom you would like to put under noncompetition restrictions. Perhaps you and the worker have a written contract concerning the terms of the work, but you'd like to amend it by adding noncompete provisions. Or, you may have no written agreement at all, in which case you should put the terms of your oral understanding into a written agreement, which will also have the noncompetition provisions you want. And if you're re-hiring a contractor (for a new project, for instance), you'll want to use one agreement that combines the terms of the deal and the noncompetition provisions you've chosen. This section will help you with the mechanics of adding a noncompete agreement to an existing contract or writing a comprehensive contract that includes work details and noncompetition provisions.

Keep in mind that whatever route you take—amending an existing contract or writing a comprehensive agreement—you'll have to decide whether you want to include all three restrictions—on competition, solicitation of customers and employ-

ees and disclosure of trade secrets—or just some of them. See Chapter 2, Section A3, for help in deciding which provisions are appropriate for your contractor.

Before turning to the technicalities of creating a new agreement or amending an old one (subsections c and d), let's discuss how to adequately compensate a contractor for signing the agreement (subsection a). Remember, you must do so in order to satisfy the consideration requirement discussed in Section B, above. We also offer some tips on how to handle a contractor who is reluctant to sign (subsection b).

a. Providing an Adequate Benefit

When you ask an existing contractor sign a noncompete agreement, you have to give the contractor something of value, over and above the contractor's current rate of pay. You can satisfy this requirement if you provide the contractor with something extra such as more money, nonqualified stock options, a higher commission rate or other benefits.

> **EXAMPLE:** To put himself through chef school, Chet works nights and weekends as an independent contractor for Party Fools, Inc., which provides clowns for children's parties and other occasions. Chet is an instant hit with the kids; many customers ask for him by name and soon he's the most sought-after clown Party Fools has. Given that Chet has such an extensive

knowledge of Party Fools' client base, as well as some specific client needs that Party Fools' competitors may not be aware of, Party Fools would like to ask Chet to sign a noncompete agreement.

However, Party Fools has already entered into a written independent contractor agreement with Chet, in which they agreed to pay Chet $100 per party and let him keep any tips he receives, in return for Chet's agreement to provide his services. If Party Fools simply asks Chet to sign an amended contract that contains a noncompetition clause, the clause probably won't be enforceable because Chet isn't getting anything additional in return. To create a new benefit to support the noncompetition clause, either Party Fools' obligations or Chet's benefits will have to change in some way. The easiest way to do this is for Party Fools to agree to pay Chet more per party in return for his agreement not to compete. If the company doesn't want to give him more money, it can agree to pay for extras like his costumes and his transportation to his gigs, or they can agree to extend his contract for an additional six months.

b. Negotiating With an Independent Contractor

If, despite your offers of more money or other benefits, a contractor is reluctant to sign your noncompete agreement, review the negotiating tips in Section C1, above.

In particular, consider asking the contractor to sign an agreement that contains only nondisclosure and/or nonsolicitation provisions. This kind of agreement will restrict the disclosure of your confidential information and will demonstrate your diligence in protecting trade secrets. For information on modifying our independent contractor agreements to include only nondisclosure or nonsolicitation restrictions, see Chapter 6, Section C.

 For more information on nondisclosure agreements in general, see Nondisclosure Agreements: Protect Your Trade Secrets & More, *by Stephen Fishman and Richard Stim (Nolo).*

If a contractor is still reluctant to sign, your options are limited and not very satisfying. You could limit the contractor's access to confidential information and/or your customers and clients. However, if you significantly change your contractor's duties, especially if this reduces her work and her opportunity to bill you, she might have a claim against you for breach of her independent contractor agreement.

You might be tempted to fire the contractor for refusing to sign a noncompete agreement, but this is risky and exposes you to a lawsuit. Independent contractor agreements generally allow you to terminate a contractor's services only for very specific reasons (usually called "good cause")—such as engaging in illegal acts, sexually harassing a member of your workforce or severely failing to perform her obligations under the contract. Most likely, refusing to sign an amended agreement with noncompete provisions will not qualify as good cause. If you terminate the contractor for refusing to sign a noncompete agreement, the contractor might sue you for breaching the contract and might obtain money damages from you.

The lesson boils down to this: If you've reached an impasse with your contractor, consult an employment lawyer before you take any adverse action. You may, in the end, have to live with the risk that this contractor will compete against you, disclose your secrets or solicit your workers or customers. Chances are your next independent contractor agreement will contain noncompetition provisions from the start.

c. Adding Noncompetition Provisions to Existing Written Agreements

If you have a written independent contractor agreement with a contractor who has agreed to some or all of the three noncompete provisions, you can use our amendment form, which will add noncompetition, nondisclosure and nonsolicitation clauses to your original agreement (or change the ones that are there already).

Instructions on how to fill out the amendment form are in Chapter 6, Section G. Or, instead of amending your independent contractor agreement, you can enter into a separate noncompete agreement by using one of our full-length independent contractor agreements (instructions for these forms can also be found in Chapter 6).

d. Adding Noncompetition Agreements to Existing Oral Agreements

If you have hired an independent contractor without a written agreement and now want the contractor to agree to noncompete provisions, it's not too late to tidy things up by writing a contract that includes specifics of the job and the noncompetition provisions you want (see "The Value of Written Agreements for Independent Contractors," in Section A4, above). The written agreement—which you create by filling in one of our full-length forms—will record the details of the existing work relationship, including the contractor's work obligations and payment arrangements. It will also incorporate the noncompete provisions (nondisclosure, nonsolicitation and/or noncompetition clauses). You will have to make sure that your new agreement includes all of the components of your original oral agreement. If it doesn't, you can add the provisions in the paragraph called "Additional Agreements" in the form. We explain how to do this in the form instructions in Chapter 6, Section B8.

EXAMPLE: Roseanna begins working for Country Homes, Inc., as an interior decorator on September 1, 2000. She and the president of Country Homes orally agree that Country Homes will hire Roseanna for one year, and that she will earn 15% of any decorating fees she generates from existing clients of Country Homes and 50% of any fees she earns from new clients she finds herself.

After she commences work, the president of Country Homes is pleased with Roseanna's performance and provides Roseanna with more details about the company. The president decides to increase Roseanna's commissions to 20% and 55% respectively, and decides it would be in the best interests of the company to formalize the agreement in writing and have Roseanna agree not to compete against Country Homes or solicit its clients. On December 1, 2000, Roseanna and Country Homes sign an independent contractor agreement that contains noncompete provisions. The agreement details the terms of Roseanna's deal and specifies that the relationship will last for one year.

If you're in the process of re-hiring an independent contractor who has provided services for you in the past (for instance, the worker completed a particular project, but you'd like to retain her to complete another project), you can start from scratch with one of our complete written contractor agreements.

3. When the Contractor Stops Performing Services

If a contractor will no longer work for you and you are concerned that the contractor will perform services for a competitor or compete with you on her own, you can ask the contractor to sign a termination agreement that includes nondisclosure, nonsolicitation and/or noncompetition clauses.

 Use termination agreements without noncompete provisions in Alabama, California, Colorado, Montana, North Dakota, Oklahoma and Oregon, states that limit or prohibit the use of noncompetition clauses for independent contractors. *This will leave you with a valid termination agreement that will prevent a departing contractor from disclosing your trade secrets or soliciting your employees or customers. See Chapter 6, Section C, for detailed state-by-state instructions.*

In order for a termination agreement to be enforceable, you'll have to give the contractor some type of benefit (most often cash, in the case of a termination agreement) in exchange for the promise not to compete against you. How much, and how long, you pay the contractor is a matter of negotiation.

Pay the contractor over time instead of all at once. *Doing so gives the contractor an incentive to continue to honor the agreement. And, if you pay the money out over time rather than all at once, you'll be out less money in the unlikely event that the former contractor violates the agreement by going to work for a competitor or disclosing your trade secrets.*

If a departing contractor refuses to sign a termination agreement, all you can do is offer more money or other benefits. (Or, maybe you can convince her to view the agreement as an opportunity for a paid six-month vacation.) But a savvy contractor who thinks you're worried about where she will work next is likely to push for more money or other perks in return for not competing with you. Unlike the start of the relationship, when you have more leverage, you're not in the strongest bargaining position with a departing contractor. That means you may have to adjust your expectations (and your bargaining stance) accordingly—you should be willing to shorten the period of noncompetition and to pay the contractor more money.

As a business owner, you must weigh the payment amount against the potential for damage to your business. If a high-priced termination agreement will prevent the contractor from working for your main competitor and disclosing your trade secrets, then perhaps you should consider it. While the law provides some protection

against the disclosure of trade secrets by an ex-contractor—regardless of whether she signs a noncompete agreement—it won't keep a contractor from competing against you without a noncompete agreement.

If a departing contractor still refuses to sign a termination agreement after you've compromised, there's not much you can do except keep an eye on her and her new employer or client to make sure they are not using your trade secrets or confidential information. (For more tips on preventative steps to take when a contractor leaves, see Chapter 7, Section B.)

⚠ **Don't use this termination agreement if you and your contractor are parting in anger.** *The termination agreement in this book is designed for situations when you don't anticipate any subsequent problems with an ex-contractor. If you are ending a relationship with a contractor under unhappy or contentious circumstances (for instance, you are terminating a contractor's services before the contract is up because you are unhappy or dissatisfied with her performance), consult an employment law expert. An expert can advise you of any potential liability and can help you draft a termination agreement designed to help you avoid litigation (in these circumstances, a termination agreement is often called a "mutual release" or a "covenant not to sue"). The termination agreement in this book does not help you avoid any post-termination litigation.*

Your Legal Rights Without a Noncompete Agreement

If an independent contractor refuses to sign an agreement with noncompete provisions, you may wonder if the law alone can protect you against an independent contractor who competes against you. The answer: probably not.

Unlike employees, independent contractors do not have a duty of loyalty to a company for whom they perform services. Unless an independent contractor agrees in writing not to compete against you, she is perfectly free to perform services for your archrival and compete against you herself.

There are some limits on what the contractor can do with your information, however. Below, we summarize the laws that govern these limits and discuss their effectiveness:

Disclosure of trade secrets. Under the Uniform Trade Secrets Act (UTSA), you have the right to prevent people from stealing your trade secrets and using them to compete against you. However, you will be able to stop an independent contractor from using or disclosing your trade secrets only if that person had a confidential relationship with your company. This is hard to prove. For a variety of reasons, confidential relationships—relationships in which one party has an increased duty to maintain the other's secrets—generally only exist between employers and employees, not independent contractors and the companies they provide services for.

In rare cases, a judge might prevent a former contractor from competing against you if you can prove that it's practically impossible for the person to take a particular job *without* disclosing your trade secrets. This "doctrine of inevitable disclosure" boils down to convincing a judge that ruling a job off-limits is the only way you can enjoy your right, under state law, to have your trade secrets kept that way. Again, a judge will have to find that the contractor had a confidential relationship with your company before it will apply this theory.

Unfair competition. Under a broad umbrella of laws, collectively called "unfair competition," anyone may be prevented from using your confidential information to harm your business or acting unethically in a manner that harms your business—for instance, interfering with your business contracts or using confidential information to compete against you.

Interference with a contract. A contractor cannot induce a customer, client, supplier or employee to breach (break) a contract with your company. If a former contractor does so, you can sue for money damages.

Interference with economic or business relations. An independent contractor cannot deliberately interfere with, steal business from or try to damage your company. If this happens, you can go to court and ask for an injunction to stop the interference and can ask for money damages.

Creating an Independent Contractor Agreement

The information in this chapter will help you create an independent contractor agreement with non-compete provisions. We'll explain the meaning and importance of all of the clauses that are used in our independent contractor agreements. Along with each explanation, we provide instructions on how to fill it out and an example of what the clause will look like when it is filled out.

The clauses in our noncompetition agreements are numbered and naturally fall into several groups, or clusters:

- introductory clauses, reciting the introduction and purpose (Clauses 1 and 2)
- clauses describing the hiring firm/ independent contractor relationship (Clauses 3 through 10)
- the "noncompete" clauses, including the noncompetition, nondisclosure and nonsolicitation clauses (Clauses 11 through 15)
- clauses that appear only in the severance agreement, which are used when a contractor signs the agreement at the end of the job (Clauses 8 through 11), and
- "boilerplate" clauses, which are standard clauses that protect your basic contract rights, found in most contracts (Clauses 16 through 23).

We have designed one form that you can use for any independent contractor. We've also designed specialized forms for several contractors whom you're most likely to use. From the list below, choose the agreement that's appropriate for your contractor's work, according to the following list:

- Form IC-1: Web engineers and designers
- Form IC-2: Software engineers and beta testers
- Form IC-3: Salespeople
- Form IC-4: Brokers and agents
- Form IC-5: Marketing and market research consultants
- Form IC-6: Research and development consultants
- Form IC-7: General noncompete agreement (use for any contractors who don't fit into one of the above categories).

Independent contractor forms IC-1 through IC-7 are more than just agreements not to compete, solicit or divulge. They are full-blown work contracts, appropriate for contractors whom you are hiring for the first time. They document the details of the work relationship, including the contractor's obligations and your payment promises, as well as the noncompete provisions (nondisclosure, nonsolicitation and/or noncompetition clauses). As discussed in Chapter 2, Section B2, you can choose to include all of the clauses or just the nondisclosure and/or nonsolicitation clauses.

The type of agreement that you use with an existing independent contractor depends on whether you have an oral or written agreement with the independent contractor.

If you have been operating under an oral agreement with an independent contractor, we recommend that you create a written independent contractor agreement that records the details of the existing work relationship, including the contractor's work obligations and payment arrangements. Forms IC-1, IC-2, IC-3, IC-4, IC-5, IC-6 and IC-7 are appropriate for this purpose. These forms also incorporate the noncompete provisions (nondisclosure, nonsolicitation and/or noncompetition clauses). Keep in mind that you must provide an additional benefit to the continuing contractor in return for her agreeing to nondisclosure, nonsolicitation and/or noncompetition provisions (see Chapter 5, Section C).

If you have a written contract with a contractor who is still working for you, use form IC-9 to amend the agreement by adding nondisclosure, nonsolicitation and/or noncompetition clauses. This form spells out the benefit you're providing to the contractor in exchange for the contractor's willingness to add new provisions to an existing agreement. Form IC-9 can also be used in the future to make a minor change to an independent contractor agreement (whether you created the work agreement from this book or used another form).

If you have hired a contractor who will no longer be working for your company but whom you'd like to place under nondisclosure, nonsolicitation and noncompete restrictions, use Form IC-8, our termination agreement. You can use this termination agreement to end a relationship with a contractor for any reason—whether you and the contractor are parting ways amicably or you are terminating the contractor for cause. However, if you are terminating the contractor for cause, you might want to include a release of claims in your termination agreement, which our termination agreement does not include. If you and the contractor need to settle any potential legal claims in your termination agreement, you should consult an attorney.

 All of the forms discussed in this chapter are on the CD-ROM at the back of the book. *The forms may be filled out directly on your computer. For detailed information on using your word processor to fill out these forms, see Appendix 1.*

The instructions in Sections A through E apply to all forms except the amendment form, which you can use to add noncompete provisions to a pre-existing written contract or to make a minor change to your noncompete agreement at a later time. For instructions on using the amendment form, see Section G.

Have a blank form in front of you as you read these instructions. *The instructions will be clearer if you refer to one of the blank noncompete forms as you go along. Open the form you want to use in your word processor and follow along or print out a hard copy and use it as a rough draft.*

A. The Introductory Clauses

These clauses appear at the beginning of all of our agreements. They introduce the names of the parties (the contractor and the hiring firm) and provide background for the agreement.

1. Introduction

The introduction states the names of the parties to the agreement (the worker's name and the name of your company) and provides the date the agreement was entered into.

Fill in the date (month, day and year) you and the contractor are entering into the agreement (not the date that work will begin or did begin), the contractor's name and the name of your company. Have a new contractor sign the agreement before starting work. In the last blank in this paragraph, fill in the state in which your company was formed and its type of legal structure—for example, "*a California corporation.*" If your contractor operates her

business as a limited liability company (LLC) or a corporation, you must list the contractor that way in this paragraph; for instance, "*Enterprise Web Designs, Inc., a California corporation* ("Contractor")." The sample below shows how it's done (note that the underlined portions are the blanks you will be completing in your own agreement).

> This Agreement ("Agreement") is made and entered into as of *April 9, 2001*, between *Ralph Dooley* ("Contractor") and *Acme Internet Solutions, an Illinois corporation* ("Company").

2. Purpose

The purpose clause (sometimes called the "recitals" or "whereas" provision) explains the reason why you and the contractor are entering into the agreement.

In the first blank, describe your company's business—for example, "Company is in the business of *manufacturing and designing widgets, which are key components of gadgets.*"

Choose one of the alternatives that come next—the alternative for new contractors or the one for contractors who have been working for you under an oral agreement. Delete the alternative you do not use. Then follow the appropriate instructions.

a. Alternative # 1: New Contractor

In the blank in alternative 1, insert the contractor's title, such as _Web designer_.

Company is in the business of providing Internet consulting services.

[ ] Alternative # 1: New Contractor

Company would like to retain Contractor as a Website design consultant. In exchange for Company's retaining Contractor's services, and for other good and valuable consideration, the receipt and sufficiency of which is hereby acknowledged, Company and Contractor agree as follows:

---

b. Alternative # 2: Existing Contractor With Prior Oral Agreement

In the first and second blanks in alternative 2, list the contractor's title that you chose when you made the oral agreement, such as _Web designer_. In the third blank, insert the date (month, day and year) of the oral understanding between you and the contractor (this will probably be the date you hired the contractor).

In the last paragraph of this section, fill in the contractor's title in both blanks.

[ ] Alternative # 2: Existing Contractor With Prior Oral Agreement

Contractor has been retained by Company as a _Website design consultant_ pursuant to an oral independent contractor agreement effective on _April 1, 2001_.

Company shall continue to retain Contractor's services as a _Website design consultant_, but on the terms and conditions set forth in this Agreement.

As a _Website design consultant_ Contractor has access to Company's Confidential Information, as defined in this Agreement. In exchange for Company's retaining Contractor's services as a _Website design consultant_, and for other good and valuable consideration, the receipt and sufficiency of which is hereby acknowledged, Company and Contractor agree as follows:

 Don't forget to provide an additional benefit, such as more money. _Remember that even though you and the contractor are just now putting your agreement in writing, you must provide the contractor with an additional benefit in order for the noncompete provisions to be enforceable._

 If you are not creating a termination agreement, skip ahead to Section B.

c. Special Instructions for Purpose Clause in Termination Agreement

In the first blank, describe your company's business—for example, "Company is in the business of *manufacturing and designing widgets, which are key components of gadgets.*" Then choose one of the alternatives that come next, depending on whether the contractor was performing services under a written agreement or not, and follow these instructions (be sure to delete the alternative you do not use):

Alternative # 1: Contractor With Prior Written Agreement

If the contractor had a written independent contractor agreement, fill in the date (month, day and year) you entered into the agreement with the contractor in the first two blanks and the contractor's title in the third blank.

Alternative # 2: Contractor With Prior Oral Agreement

If the contractor did not work under a written contract, use this alternative. Fill in the contractor's title in the blank.

B. Description of the Work Relationship

The introductory clauses are followed by clauses that describe the relationship between you, the hiring firm, and the independent contractor. These provisions define the work relationship and clarify your worker's status as an independent contractor (not an employee). None of these clauses appear in the termination agreement, since the work relationship is ending and does not need to be defined.

1. Duties

Each independent contractor agreement contains a paragraph in which you spell out the contractor's duties. Describe the contractor's responsibilities in detail, including project deadlines or any delegations of authority you are granting to the contractor.

Contractor's duties will include:

(1) contacting prospective customers in Contractor's Territory (defined below), whether these prospective customers are provided by Company or developed through Contractor's own knowledge or contacts, to determine if these prospective customers are interested in Company's products, by providing detailed information to prospective customers about Company's products and answering any questions or concerns prospective customers might have about Company's products;

(2) contacting and calling on existing customers in Contractor's Territory (defined below) to determine existing customers' product needs, and

(3) providing customers with superior customer service, including responding promptly to customer requests and customer problems.

> "Contractor's Territory" means the city of Tampa, Florida.
>
> Contractor acknowledges that because Contractor is an independent contractor, Company will control only the results of the services Contractor provides to Company and not the means by which Contractor provides services.

2. Compensation

The compensation section in our agreements spells out how much, and when, you will pay the contractor. This section offers several alternatives for payment. Choose one, depending on whether you will pay the contractor a:

- flat fee for a project (Alternative 1)
- weekly or monthly fee (Alternative 2)
- hourly fee, according to invoices that the contractor submits (Alternative 3)
- salary (for sales reps, brokers and agents only) (Alternative 4)
- commission plus salary (for sales reps, brokers and agents only) (Alternative 5), or
- commission only (for sales reps, brokers and agents only) (Alternative 6).

For instance, a Web designer would probably get paid by the hour, but a sales representative or broker would probably be paid on a commission basis. Accordingly, the alternatives available in this section differ from form to form. Alternatives 1, 2 and

3 are available for Web engineers and designers, software engineers and beta testers, marketing and market research consultants and research and development consultants (Forms IC-1, -2, -5, -6 and -7). Alternatives 4, 5 and 6 are available only in the forms for salespeople and brokers/agents (Forms IC-3 and -4). Note that while it's rare for these people to receive salaries, we've included this option just in case this is what you and the contractor negotiate.

a. Alternatives for Consultants and Freelancers

Choose one of the alternatives and delete the alternatives you are not using.

Alternative # 1: Flat Fee

In the first and second blanks, fill in the contractor's fee, first described in words and then numerically—for instance, "_One Thousand_ Dollars ($_1,000_)." In the third blank, fill in when and how the contractor will receive this money. For instance, _"Contractor shall receive Five Hundred Dollars ($500) upon completion of website specifications and Five Hundred Dollars ($500) when the website is completed."_

> ### [ ] Alternative # 1: Flat Fee
>
> Company shall pay Contractor the sum of One Thousand Dollars ($1,000), payable as follows: Contractor shall receive $500 when the services described on Exhibit A are completed, and an additional $500 when the services described on Exhibit B are completed.

Alternative # 2: Weekly or Monthly Fee

In the first and second blanks, fill in the contractor's rate of pay, first described in words and then numerically—for instance, _One Hundred Fifty_ Dollars ($_150_).

Then, choose one payment interval—weekly or monthly—and delete the other. In the next blank, choose the date of the contractor's first payment; then elect whether you will continue pay these amounts each week or each month.

[ ] Alternative # 2: Weekly or Monthly Fee

Company shall pay Contractor the sum of _Four Thousand_ Dollars ($_4,000_) per month, beginning on the _30th_ day after the date of this Agreement and continuing on the same day of each month.

Alternative # 3: Hourly Fee, With Invoice

In the first and second blanks, fill in the contractor's rate of pay, first described in words and then numerically—for instance, _One Hundred Fifty_ Dollars ($_150_). If your contractor will bill you for hourly work (rather than simply collecting a check every week or month), you will probably want the contractor to submit invoices. Choose when the contractor must provide you with invoices—weekly or monthly. In

the third blank, fill in the amount of time you will take to pay the contractor, first described in words and then numerically—for instance, "within _thirty_ (_30_) days of receiving an invoice."

[ ] Alternative # 3: Hourly Fee With Invoices

Company shall pay Contractor the sum of _One Hundred Fifty_ Dollars ($_150_) per hour. Contractor shall submit invoices to Company on the _30th_ of each month detailing the hours worked and services performed and the total fee due. Company shall pay Contractor the invoiced amount within _ten_ (_10_) days of receiving an invoice.

---

b. Alternatives for Salespeople, Brokers and Agents

Choose one of the alternatives and delete the others you are not using.

Alternative #1: Salary, No Commission

In the first and second blanks, fill in the contractor's rate of pay, first described in words and then numerically—for instance, _One Hundred Fifty_ Dollars ($_150_). Then, choose one payment method—hourly, weekly or monthly. Include the date of the contractor's first payment and elect whether you will continue to pay these amounts weekly or monthly.

[ ] Alternative #1: Salary; No Commission

In exchange for the services to be rendered by Contractor under this Agreement, Company shall pay Contractor the sum of _Five Hundred Dollars_ (_$500_) per _week_, beginning on the _5th_ day after date of this Agreement and continuing on the same day of each _week_ during the Term. Contractor shall submit invoices to Company on the _1st_ of each month detailing the number of hours worked by Contractor and the services performed.

Alternative #2: Commission Plus Salary

Many salespeople, brokers and agents work on a commission basis with either a small weekly or monthly salary. For these contractors, use this alternative to set a contractor's salary and describe the commission structure and payment schedule.

In the first and second blanks, fill in the contractor's rate of pay—for instance, _One Hundred Fifty_ Dollars ($_150_). Then, choose one payment method—hourly, weekly or monthly. Include the date of the contractor's first payment and choose whether you will continue to pay these amounts weekly or monthly.

Finally, in the blank lines at the end of this alternative, fill in the contractor's commission structure, including information such as whether the commission is a percentage or flat fee, and when you will pay these amounts to the contractor.

[ ] Alternative #2: Commission Plus Salary

In exchange for the services to be rendered by Contractor under this Agreement, Company shall pay Contractor the sum of _Five Hundred Dollars_ (_$500_) per week, beginning on the _5th_ day after date of this Agreement and continuing on the same day of each _month_ during the Term. Contractor shall submit invoices to Company on the _1st_ of each _month_ detailing the number of hours worked by Contractor and the services performed.

Additionally, Contractor shall receive a commission for services Contractor performs under this Agreement, payable as follows:

Contractor shall receive a 5% commission on all completed sales made by Contractor.

Alternative #3: No Salary; Commission Only

Many salespeople, brokers and agents work on a commission basis with no salary. Use this alternative for these contractors.

In the blank lines, fill in the contractor's commission structure, including information such as whether the commission is a percentage or flat fee and when you will pay these amounts to the contractor.

3. Term of Services

Your independent contractor agreement
will set a specific period of time during
which the contractor will provide services
for you. This means that, unlike an at-will
employee, you generally won't have the
right to terminate the independent contractor whenever you want. Of course, if the
contractor fails to honor important terms
of the agreement, you may consider the
agreement at an end. The termination
clause, below, covers this in detail.

⚠ **The term of services does not set
the period of time the contractor
is not allowed to compete against you
or solicit customers or employees.** *It
merely describes how long the contractor
will work for your company. Sections 12
and 13 cover the noncompetition period.*

In this section, you have a choice as to
how to define the term of services. The
agreement can state a beginning and end
date for the period the contractor will provide services to you, or it can provide that
the term of services expires when the contractor completes a particular project.

Choose one of the alternatives and delete the others that you are not using.

a.   Alternative # 1: Fixed Term

Fill in the term of services (described in
words and then numerically) and the date
(month, day and year) the agreement will
end.

b.   Alternative # 2: Project-Based Term

If your agreement will terminate when the
contractor completes a project rather than
on a specific day, choose this alternative.

Write a detailed description of what
will trigger the termination of the contract—for instance, "This Agreement will
begin on the date set forth in Section 1
and will continue *until Contractor completes the installation of e-commerce platform for Company's website*." Note that
even with a project-based term, you still
want to give the contractor a "drop dead"
date by which the project must be finished. If you don't, the contractor could

potentially drag it out for an unreasonably long time. Insert that deadline in the second blank.

[ ] Alternative # 2: Project-Based Term

This Agreement will begin on the date set forth in Section 1 and will continue until Contractor completes the installation of Company's *Java platform* but shall not end later than *June 30, 2002.*

---

4. No Withholding or State Insurance

When you hire an independent contractor, you want to make it very clear that you will not withhold any state or federal income taxes, Social Security or Medicare taxes or state unemployment or disability insurance from the independent contractor's paycheck. You also need to state that you'll not be making workers' compensation insurance payments on the contractor's behalf.

This paragraph states that the contractor is not an employee, that the hiring firm will not withhold or make any of these payments on the contractor's behalf and that the contractor is responsible for reporting all income received from you and for paying all taxes on these amounts.

This clause is strong evidence, should you ever be challenged by the IRS or a state taxing entity, that you and the con-

tractor intend this to be an independent contractor relationship. This paragraph is set out below; you don't need to add anything to it.

Because Company is retaining Contractor as an independent contractor and not as an employee, Company will not withhold from Contractor's compensation any state or federal income taxes, and Company will not withhold or pay any Social Security, Medicare, federal unemployment insurance (FUTA), workers' compensation insurance, state unemployment or disability insurance payments on Contractor's behalf. Contractor agrees and covenants to report all income received from Company and make all required income tax and other tax payments in connection with Contractor's compensation. Company will provide Contractor with a Form 1099 summarizing Contractor's compensation for each tax year.

⚠ You may have to withhold employment taxes if the independent contractor qualifies as a "statutory employee." *See Chapter 5, Section A, for more information.*

5. No Partnership

This paragraph makes it clear that you and the contractor are not partners or involved in any type of joint venture. (The legal implications of being partners are much different, and much more onerous, than being in a hiring firm/independent contractor relationship.) Although it's unlikely that a court would ever find that you and the contractor are legally partners, it's safer to include a clause like this in your agreement so that the contractor can't later claim more rights than you meant to grant. This paragraph is shown below; nothing needs to be inserted by you.

> This Agreement does not create any partnership or joint venture between Company and Contractor or any relationship other than client and independent contractor. Except as described in Section 3, or unless Contractor obtains Company's written consent, Contractor shall not have the authority to and shall not bind the Company to any contract or agreement.

6. No Other Benefits

This clause lets the contractor know that she won't receive any benefits that are not set out in this agreement, and that she's not entitled to any of the benefits that you typically give your employees. Remember, the contractor is not an employee, so you want to make it clear that she's not going to be treated like one. Nothing needs to be added to this clause.

> Except as specifically set forth in this Agreement, Company is not responsible for providing and will not provide Contractor with any benefits, including but not limited to health insurance, pension benefits or any other benefits Company provides to its employees.

7. Termination of Services

The independent contractor agreements in this book do not state that you can terminate a contractor at will (basically, any time you feel like it), for two reasons. First, an at-will relationship with an independent contractor is a strong indicator that the worker is actually an employee rather than a contractor. Second, it's unusual for a contractor to agree to this (and it might render your contract unenforceable anyway, since the contractor isn't really receiving a benefit in exchange for his promise).

While your relationship with an independent contractor will not be at will, your agreement *can* provide some legitimate reasons for discontinuing her services before the term of the contract is up.

This paragraph spells out the circumstances under which you or the contractor can terminate the agreement. Your right to terminate the contract early will hinge on the contractor's failure to perform under the terms of the agreement. You don't need to add anything to the language of the clause.

> If either Contractor or Company violates, breaches or fails to perform any provision of this Agreement, either party shall have the right, with written notice, to immediately terminate services under this Agreement.

> Company and Contractor additionally agree that Company will reimburse Contractor for any reasonable expenses contractor incurs while performing services for Company under this Agreement.

⚠️ **Terminating an independent contractor before the agreement expires can be risky.** *Although our agreements provide that you can terminate the contractor's services before the contract is up—for one of the reasons above—use caution when doing this. If you wrongly terminate the contractor, you may get sued for breach of contract. Terminate a contractor only when the job hasn't been done or important aspects of the agreement have been disregarded (such as blowing deadlines several times in a row despite repeated reminders). You'll be less likely to get sued if you use your right to terminate the contractor only when there's no alternative.*

8. Additional Agreements

In this section, you can add additional terms or conditions. For instance, you might want to provide that your contractor will be reimbursed for her transportation and mailing expenses. If so, you can include it here.

If you're putting an existing oral agreement into writing, you may need to include elements of your original oral agreement that have not been covered in the provisions describing your work relationship (sections 3 through 9 in all of the independent contractor forms). Insert those elements here.

C. The Noncompete Clauses

The clauses we discuss in this section are the heart of your agreement. These are the clauses that protect your business, your trade secrets and your customers.

You may notice that the nondisclosure clause comes before the noncompetition and nonsolicitation clauses. It appears first because it describes the main reason you want to prevent the contractor from competing against your company—to protect your trade secrets. The other two clauses (noncompetition and nonsolicitation) exist to protect the confidential information you describe in the nondisclosure clause.

1. Nondisclosure of Confidential Information

As discussed in Chapter 1, each agreement in this book contains a nondisclosure clause, which defines your trade secrets and restricts the contractor from ever using, disclosing or duplicating this information without your authorization.

In the first subsection of the nondisclosure clause, subsection a, your confidential information is defined. If anything contained in this description of confidential information isn't relevant to the contractor's job or duties, or isn't information the contractor will have access to, delete it. Remember, your goal is to be as reasonable as possible about the information you're trying to protect. Just like specifying an overbroad geographic area of noncompetition, giving an over-inclusive description of confidential information may doom your agreement if it's challenged in court.

If there's particular, sensitive information that you would like to explicitly include in the definition of confidential information, we've provided a blank for it. For example, if your contractor will conduct quality assurance testing for your company's new video game, you'd want to add "*any and all information, data, source code, ideas, processes, musical or literary works relating to Company's video game product titled "Blubber Man IV...*"" Or, if you are using this agreement for a new

chef at your restaurant, you may want to insert the names of proprietary recipes, such as your world-famous crab bisque (but don't insert the recipe itself; that needs to stay secret). Otherwise, just delete this blank.

Below is a sample of this first subsection a. Remember that since the definition of confidential information varies depending on which agreement you choose, the language in this sample may differ from the exact language in your agreement.

a. Company may need to disclose to Contractor or give Contractor access to Confidential Information so that Contractor may properly fulfill his or her duties to Company. "Confidential Information" means Company's trade secrets, including, but not limited to, technology; equipment research, design and development; database, website or network specifications or contents; product pricing information, research, design or development; contemplated new products or services; engineering processes or methods; any titles, themes, stories, treatments, ideas, artwork, computer hardware or software; *any and all information, data, source code, ideas or processes relating to Company's e commerce product titled "eSolution"*; or any other information which is not generally known and from which the Company derives an economic benefit. The Confidential Information may be written, such as computer source code, programs, hardware and software, tapes, disks, documents, drawings, data or product specifications; or unwritten, such as unwritten knowledge, ideas, processes, practices or know-how. Confidential Information does not include information that is in the public domain, information that is generally known in Company's industry or information that Contractor acquired completely independently of his or her services for Company.

⚠ **If you're writing a termination agreement, choose the appropriate definition of confidential information.** *Our termination agreement, to be used for departing contractors, is set up a little differently than the sample above, which is taken from an agreement for a new or continuing contractor. Because our termination agreement can be used for any type of contractor, it comes with several different definitions of confidential information. Choose the most appropriate definition among the alternatives provided and delete the others.*

In the next paragraph, subsection b, the worker agrees not to use this confidential information or reveal it to anyone else.

b. For as long as the Confidential Information is not generally known and Company derives an economic benefit from the Confidential Information, Contractor shall not use or disclose to any other person or entity any Confidential Information or any copy or summary of any Confidential Information unless Contractor is required to do so to perform Contractor's duties to Company or as required by law.

As an added measure of protection, the worker also agrees not to make unauthorized copies of this information, for herself or anyone else (a worker who can't reproduce your information will be less likely to use it if she goes to work for a competitor).

c. While Contractor performs services for Company and afterward, Contractor shall not remove or copy any Confidential Information or participate in any way in the removal or copying of any Confidential Information without Company's written consent. Contractor shall immediately return to Company all Confidential Information when Contractor ceases performing services for Company, or any time Company requires such Confidential Information to be returned.

This clause also requires the worker not to get access to your confidential information for any reason other than to do the job. This helps limit the amount of confidential information the contractor knows.

> d. Contractor will not obtain or attempt to obtain any Confidential Information for any purpose whatsoever except as required by Company to enable Contractor to perform his or her services.

Lastly, if you're hiring a contractor who has worked for one of your direct competitors (or if you suspect the contractor may have had access to a competitor's trade secrets at a previous job), subsection e of this clause requires the contractor to promise not to reveal any of the previous employer's or client's trade secrets to your company. If your company were to receive another's trade secrets from a worker, you could be on the hook for trade secret theft. This clause will help protect you from legal liability if the contractor nevertheless shares protected information.

Fill in the name of the contractor's previous employer or client in all three blanks. If subsection e does not apply to the contractor's situation, delete it.

> e. Contractor will not disclose to Company or misuse any third party's trade secrets, including any trade secret information of Contractor's former employer, _Achtung Solutions_. Contractor represents and warrants that the execution of this Agreement by Contractor will not violate or conflict with the terms of any other agreement to which Contractor is a party.

2. Noncompetition

As discussed in Chapter 1, the noncompetition clause prevents the independent contractor from competing directly with your company if she leaves to either join a competitor or start her own competitive venture. Depending on where your business is located, however, and the type of contractor whom you're hiring, you may not be able to use a full-blown noncompetition clause. See "Limitations on Noncompete Clauses for Independent Contractors," below.

Limitations on Noncompete Clauses for Independent Contractors

Some states restrict a hiring firm's ability to bind a contractor to noncompetition provisions. Consult the table below before proceeding with your agreement.

Location of your business	Action to take
California or Alabama	Delete Section 12, "Noncompetition," from the agreement and renumber the remaining paragraphs accordingly. Be sure to change references within clauses, too. (See Chapter 2, Section B2, for more information.)
Montana, North Dakota or Oklahoma	Consult an employment law expert to determine whether you should include Section 12 in the agreement. (See Chapter 2, Section B2, for more information.)
Colorado or Oregon	Consult an employment law expert to ensure that your agreement complies with your state's rules regarding noncompete agreements and is appropriate for the type of contractor who will be signing the agreement. (See Chapter 2, Section B2, for more information.)

Even if your state enforces noncompetition clauses, you may want to omit the clause from your agreement. *For instance, if your contractor refuses to sign an agreement with a noncompetition clause, you may still be able to get him to agree to nondisclosure and nonsolicitation provisions. It's easy to modify any of our agreements to include only nondisclosure and nonsolicitation clauses. Simply remove the entire section entitled "Noncompetition" from the agreement and renumber the remaining sections. (Be sure to change references within clauses, too.) Similarly, if you wish to have a worker sign an agreement containing only a nondisclosure clause, also remove the section titled "Nonsolicitation" and renumber the remaining sections accordingly.*

The first part of this clause sets out the period of time (the noncompete period) that the worker will not be allowed to compete with you after stopping work for your company. In the blank, fill in the amount of time you think will be reasonable to require the contractor not to compete with you. Make sure to specify whether the number you choose refers to months or years.

If you are creating a termination agreement, the period of noncompetition will be the amount of time you agree to pay the contractor after he leaves. This amount of time will be entered into the "Termination Payments" section (see Section D2, below).

⚠ **Noncompetition periods that last too long may not be enforceable.** *Refer to Chapter 1, Section B1, for a discussion of how long a reasonable noncompetition clause should last. If your business is located in Florida, Louisiana or South Dakota, consult an employment law expert if you want your noncompete period to last longer than two years.*

Contractor agrees that in order to protect the Confidential Information described above, while Contractor is performing services for Company, and for a period of *one year* thereafter (collectively, the "Term"), Contractor shall not:

In the next paragraphs, you'll see that during the noncompetition period, the former worker may not take part in the ownership of a competing company or perform services that are similar to the work done for you.

a. plan for, acquire any financial interest in or perform services for (as an employee, consultant, officer, director, independent contractor, principal, agent or otherwise) any business that would require Contractor to use or disclose any Confidential Information, or

b. perform services (as an employee, consultant, officer, director, independent contractor, principal, agent or otherwise) that are similar to Contractor's current duties or responsibilities for any person or entity that, during the Term, engages in any business activity in which Company is then engaged or proposes to be engaged and that conducts its business in the Territory.

Next, the geographic area ("Territory") in which the contractor will be prohibited from competing against you is defined. There are two alternatives. The first alternative defines the geographic area as any area in which you do business.

---

c. "Territory" means

[ ] Alternative #1: General Territory

any geographic area in which Company conducts its business during the Term

---

The second alternative allows you to insert a specific geographic area in which the contractor may not compete against you. We recommend you do this if your business is located in Louisiana.

> **[ ] Alternative #2: Specific Territory**
>
> the city limits of the city of Chicago, Illinois.

Choose one of the alternatives and delete the other. If you choose the second alternative, refer back to Chapter 1, Section B2, for a discussion of choosing a reasonable geographic area; then insert it into the blank.

3. Nonsolicitation

Each agreement in this book also contains a nonsolicitation clause, which prevents the independent contractor from soliciting your customers, clients and other employees on her own behalf (if she leaves to start a competitive business) or on her new employer's behalf (if she leaves to join a competitor).

Like the noncompetition clause, this clause specifies exactly how long the worker can't solicit your customers and employees. Fill in a reasonable amount of time (see Chapter 1, Section B1, for more information). Make sure to specify whether the number you choose refers to months or years.

If you are creating a termination agreement, the period of nonsolicitation will be the amount of time you agree to pay the contractor after leaving your company. This amount of time will be entered into the "Termination Payments" section (see Section D2, below).

> While Contractor performs services for Company, and for a period of _one year_ thereafter, Contractor shall not:
>
> a. employ, attempt to employ or solicit for employment by any other person or entity, any Company employees;
>
> b. encourage any consultant, independent contractor or any other person or entity to end their relationship or stop doing business with Company, or help any person or entity to do so or attempt to do so; or
>
> c. solicit or attempt to solicit or obtain business or trade from any of Company's current or prospective customers or clients or help any person or entity do so or attempt to do so.

4. Right to an Injunction

An injunction is an order by a judge that requires someone to do something (such as return company property) or not do something (such as work for a competitor). When former contractors break noncompetition agreements, hiring firms generally go to court and ask for an injunction directed at the contractor, to stop the competition, disclosures or solicitations as soon as possible. It takes very little time to get a preliminary or temporary injunction—sometimes only a few days or a week—but they're only temporary. Normally, they're followed by a full-blown court hearing that will determine whether the judge's order should stick. In the meantime, however, the company is protected against further disclosures or competition.

Since lawsuits can drag on for years, it's in your best interests to seek an immediate injunction against a contractor who violates your agreement (assuming the contractor does not agree to arbitration or mediation—see Section F1, below, for more information), which will stop the offending behavior while you wait for the full court hearing. Money damages—financial compensation a contractor will have to pay to repair harm done to your company—often don't get awarded for years, and are often very hard to measure. Far better to stop the contractor from using your trade secrets in the first place.

Unfortunately, injunctions are often difficult to get. Your chances will improve if the worker has agreed in writing that you should be entitled to one if she violates the agreement. In the "right to an injunction" clause in our agreements, your contractor does just that. You don't have to add anything to this clause.

Contractor acknowledges that his or her services to Company are special and unique and that, while performing these services, Contractor will have access to and Company may disclose to Contractor the Confidential Information described above. Contractor also acknowledges that his or her position in Company will place him or her in a position of confidence and trust with employees, clients and customers of Company.

If Contractor breaches or threatens to breach any of the provisions of Sections 11, 12 or 13 of this Agreement, Company will sustain irreparable harm. Company shall be entitled to an injunction to stop any breach or threatened breach of this Agreement, including the provisions of Sections 11, 12 or 13. Contractor acknowledges and agrees that monetary damages would not adequately compensate Company for any breach or threatened breach of these sections and that if Company seeks injunctive relief to put an immediate halt to the offending conduct, Contractor shall not claim that monetary damages would be an adequate remedy.

5. Reasonable Restrictions and Survivability

In this clause, the contractor acknowledges that the restrictions in the agreement (the nondisclosure, noncompetition and nonsolicitation provisions) are reasonable and necessary. This helps you defend against a future claim that the restrictions are unreasonable and aren't really necessary to protect your business.

This section also provides that the contractor's obligations—not to compete against your company, solicit your customers or employees or talk about your trade secrets—continue to be enforceable ("survive") after the contractor has left your company. We include this so that your former contractor can't argue that, because the job is done, the contractor's obligations have terminated too. You don't need to add anything to this clause.

> Contractor acknowledges that the restrictions set forth in Sections 11, 12, 13 and 14 of the Agreement are reasonable and necessary for the protection of Company, its business and its Confidential Information. The provisions of Section 11, 12, 13 and 14 shall survive the termination, for any reason, of Contractor's services for Company.

➡️ *If you are creating an agreement for a new or continuing worker, skip ahead to Section E, "Standard Clauses."*

D. Additional Clauses for Termination Agreements

You'll want to use our termination agreement for contractors who have stopped working for you but who didn't sign noncompetition agreements when they began work. You can use this agreement when the job is finished or if you have terminated your relationship because the contractor has failed to perform under the contract. However, if the contractor has failed to perform under the contract, there may be some hard feelings—and some other legal issues—to resolve in your termination agreement. If that's the case, and you want the contractor to release any claims against you, you should not use the termination agreement in this book. Consult an attorney for help drafting a release of claims.

When a contractor has stopped providing services for your company—either because the job is done or you've ended the relationship—you will need to pay the contractor for his or her promise not to compete, divulge or solicit. Hiring firms usually agree to pay a sum of money, beyond what the contractor charged for the job. Because of this added twist, our termination agreement contains a few clauses that aren't in the noncompete agreements for new and existing contractors.

1. Termination of Services

Here, you and the contractor agree to the date that the contractor's services will end. You want to make it clear that even though you're going to make payments to the worker, the contractor will no longer be performing services for you and won't have the authority to enter into contracts on behalf of your company or otherwise hold herself out as a contractor of your company for any purpose.

Fill in the date (month, day and year) of the last day the contractor will work for your company.

Contractor shall cease performing services for Company as of _March 1, 2002_ ("Termination Date"). On Termination Date, Contractor shall cease to be either a contractor or an agent of Company and Contractor shall not make any representation to any third party that he or she is a contractor or agent of Company or has the authority to bind Company to any agreement.

2. Payments

This clause describes the payments you will make to the contractor, including the dates they will start and end. This period of time, called the "Term," is also the period of time during which the contractor won't be permitted to compete against you or solicit your clients, customers or employees. It doesn't apply to the amount of time a contractor can't use or disclose your trade secrets, however, because the contractor won't be allowed to disclose your secrets for as long as they remain trade secrets, which could be shorter or longer than the competition and solicitation period.

In the first blank, fill in the day on which you'll pay the contractor each month. Next, fill in the amount of the payment, first described in words and then numerically—for example, "_Six Thousand_ Dollars ($_6,000_)." Then fill in the term of the agreement—the dates (month, day and year) on which the agreement will begin and end.

⚠ Noncompetition and nonsolicitation periods that last too long may not be enforceable. *See Chapter 1, Section B1, for help in choosing a term that's long enough to provide the protection you need but not so long as to be unenforceable. If your business is located in Florida, Louisiana or South Dakota, consult an employment law expert if you want the term to be longer than two years.*

In consideration of Contractor's promises in this Agreement, Company shall pay Contractor certain payments, payable monthly on the _15th_ day of each month, of _One Thousand Dollars_ ($_1,000_), beginning on _September 1, 2001_, and ending on _March 1, 2002_ (the "Term").

As with all payments to independent contractors, you must report the termination payments to the IRS and provide the worker with a Form 1099-MISC, on which you summarize the monies you have paid the contractor during the year.

3. Termination of Obligations

This clause states that if the worker violates the agreement, you don't have to continue to pay under the terms of the termination agreement. In addition, the contractor will be required to return to you any money you've already paid. This clause protects you if the contractor competes against you, discloses your trade secrets or violates any other provision of the agreement. Nothing needs to be inserted here.

> If Contractor breaches any of Contractor's obligations under this Agreement, Company's obligations under this Agreement will immediately terminate and Contractor will immediately refund to Company the full amount of any payments made to Contractor pursuant to Section 9.

4. Confidentiality

We have included a provision in our termination agreement that requires the contractor to keep the fact of the agreement and its terms confidential, which will help prevent others from learning about it. It's important that your other contractors, and even workers, not assume that all of them are entitled to some sort of "quiet payment" when they leave. Worse yet, you don't want them thinking that they can hold you hostage for money by threatening to reveal your trade secrets. Nothing needs to be inserted here.

> Contractor shall not directly or indirectly disclose either the existence of this Agreement or any of the terms of this Agreement other than to Contractor's attorney, except to the extent that disclosing such terms is required by law.

5. Notice

Since you and the departing worker will no longer be seeing each other frequently, it makes sense to exchange mailing addresses. This clause specifies how correspondence will be sent and provides a space to add the name and address of your company and your former worker, as well as your attorneys (if necessary).

Fill in the contractor's name and address and your company's name and address. If you or the contractor is represented by an attorney, you can list those addresses here so that copies of any correspondence will be sent to counsel. If not, you can leave these spaces blank or delete these lines.

All notices, requests, demands and other communications hereunder must be in writing and shall be considered properly given if delivered by hand or mailed within the continental United States by first-class, registered mail, return receipt requested, postage and registry fees paid, to the applicable party and addressed as follows:

To Company:
   Bayside Web Design
   1858 Circle Drive
   Hayward, CA 95555
   Attention: Emily Rodriguez

with a copy to Company's attorney:
   Dewey, Cheatum & Howe
   444 First Street
   Oakland, CA 94444
   Attention: Donald J. Freidkin, Esq.

To Contractor:
   Alexandra Stewart
   455 Walnut Street
   San Francisco, CA 94115

E. Standard Clauses

Now that you understand the core clauses of the agreement and how they work together to protect your business, several important technicalities remain. The clauses we discuss below appear in almost every business contract you'll see because, over time, lawyers have realized that failing to include them can cause problems later. You won't have to modify these clauses and will need to add very little information.

➡ **If you're already familiar with general contract law, you can browse this section quickly.** *However, be sure to follow the instructions below for inserting information in the "Applicable Law" clause and the "Jurisdiction" clauses. You don't need to insert any information in the remaining clauses.*

1. Severability

If you need to bring your agreement to court to enforce it against a contractor who has violated it, there's a slight chance that a judge may find a part of the agreement void or unenforceable. In that case, you'll want the court to remove ("sever") the unenforceable part of the contract and leave the remaining, enforceable provisions intact. There's no guarantee that a judge will pare your agreement in this way, but with a "severability" clause, you've increased your chances. Nothing needs to be inserted here.

EXAMPLE: One of your independent contractors, Anna, willingly signs a contractor agreement containing noncompetition, nondisclosure and nonsolicitation clauses. The noncompetition clause lasts for five years. After finishing the job she was engaged to do, Anna violates the agreement by encouraging some of your key employees to go to work for the new company she is starting. You file suit against Anna for violating the nonsolicitation clause in your agreement, and the judge decides to review the entire agreement.

Although the noncompetition clause in your agreement is not at the center of your lawsuit, the judge finds that this provision is unenforceable because it lasts an unreasonably long time. However, because the agreement contains a severability clause, the judge agrees to disregard the noncompetition clause and enforce only the nonsolicitation clause, which is perfectly valid. Without the severability clause, the judge might have thrown out the entire agreement.

If a court determines that any provision of this Agreement is invalid or unenforceable, any invalidity or unenforceability will affect only that provision and shall not make any other provision of this Agreement invalid or unenforceable. Instead, such provision shall be modified, amended or limited to the extent necessary to render it valid and enforceable.

---

2. Applicable Law

This clause allows you to specify which state's law will govern your agreement. If you need to go to court to enforce it, a judge will probably use the laws of that state to enforce (or not enforce) the agreement.

Since states have different approaches to noncompete agreements, choosing which state's law will govern the agreement is important. There are also some practical considerations—it's usually advantageous to have the laws of your home state govern your agreement, since this is the law that you and your attorney will probably be most familiar with. If you decide to choose a different state, consult an attorney first—unfortunately, legal rules limit your choices.

It's important to understand that your choice of which state's law will govern your agreement is not the same as choosing the state in which a lawsuit will be tried. It's perfectly legal for someone to file a lawsuit in a state that's different than the state whose governing law controls the agreement. You'll specify *where* the lawsuit must be filed (as opposed to which law will be used to interpret the agreement) in another clause, called "Jurisdiction."

Take advantage of your choices. *If you and your contractor do business in different states and the contractor's state enforces noncompete agreements but yours does not, you might be able to choose that state's law to apply to your agreement. Although it's often perfectly legal to this, you should do so only with the guidance of an attorney.*

Usually, you and your contractor will be in the same state, so fill in that state. However, if you and the contractor are located in different states, you should choose the state in which your business is located.

> This Agreement shall be governed by and construed in accordance with the laws of the State of _California_.

Special Rules for California Hiring Firms & Contractors

If you're a California business—or your business is located outside of California and you have California contractors—you know by now that California will not enforce a noncompete clause. You may be wondering whether you can choose a different state's law to apply to your agreement, add a noncompetition clause to the agreement and get around California's prohibition. Whether you can do this depends on your situation. Here's a brief summary of the reasons you might want to choose the law of a different state, and how likely it is to hold up in court.

- A California business with California contractors can't insert the law of a different state and expect a California court to apply it to avoid California's stringent noncompete rules. California judges frown on blatant attempts to flout California law like this.

- A California business that engages contractors whose principle place of business is outside of California should insert the law of the state in which the contractor lives and works. As long as the contractor lives and works there, the California employer has a legitimate reason for applying the law of that state to any dispute over the agreement. More than likely, a California judge will uphold this choice of law if you or the contractor sue over the agreement.

- A non-California business whose contractor works and lives in California will have a tough time convincing a California judge to apply the law of another state, even that of the hiring firm. California judges are very protective of their citizens' rights to choose where they will work, and will apply California law unless an out-of-state business has some very good reasons why they shouldn't.

The bottom line is that getting a California court to apply the law of another state is tricky at best. Out-of-state businesses should not attempt it without the help of an experienced attorney.

3. Jurisdiction

The jurisdiction clause in our agreements refers to the physical place (county and state) where you will bring a lawsuit to enforce your agreement, if necessary. It also governs where your contractor may sue. Most of the time, you and your contractor will be in the same county, which is the one you'll choose for this clause. But if you and the contractor are located in different counties or states, you'll need to give some thought to where you'd want to litigate. Most of the time, practicality will be your guide.

For instance, let's say your business is located in Arizona and your contractor has a business in New Mexico. If the two of you get into a dispute over the agreement and the contractor sues you (perhaps to ask a judge to declare your agreement unenforceable), it's going to be a lot more convenient for you if the lawsuit is filed in Arizona, in the county in which your business is located. Just imagine if your contractor filed a lawsuit against you in New Mexico—you'd have to hire New Mexico lawyers and probably incur lots of costs and expenses traveling back and forth to New Mexico during the course of the litigation. For you, it makes much more sense to require the contractor to bring the lawsuit in Arizona so you can avoid this potential expense and inconvenience.

Similarly, if you and your contractor are located far away from each other in the same state (for instance, your business is located in San Diego and your employee works and lives in Modoc), you might want to specify that the jurisdiction in which either of you can file a lawsuit is San Diego County.

Most of the time, the state you choose for your jurisdiction clause will be the same as the law of the state you choose to govern your agreement (in the "applicable law" clause). Insert the county and state in which you want any lawsuits to be filed.

Contractor and Company consent to the exclusive jurisdiction and venue of the federal and state courts located in _San Francisco County, California_, in any action arising out of or relating to this Agreement. Contractor and Company waive any other venue to which either party might be entitled by domicile or otherwise.

 Some states do not allow contractors to agree to go to court in another state. _Almost all states allow a resident of one state to agree in writing to be sued in another state (this is called "waiving personal jurisdiction"). However, Idaho, Montana and Alabama do not allow a person to agree to go to court in another state. If your business is located in one of these states, choose the jurisdiction of your home state._

4. Entire Agreement; No Other Change

Sometimes, you and the contractor will discuss certain ideas or issues that aren't recorded in your written agreement. To reduce the risk that the contractor will claim that something you talked about—but didn't include in the written agreement—is part of your contract, we've included this "entire agreement" clause. This provision (in legalese, called an "integration clause") says that only what is written in this agreement, and nothing else you may have discussed, is part of the contract between you and the worker. Nothing needs to be inserted here.

> This is the entire agreement between the parties. It supersedes and replaces any and all prior oral or written agreements between Company and Contractor that relate to the matters covered by this Agreement.

5. Assignment; Binding Effect

This clause simply means that if you sell your company or merge your company into another, the new company will gain your rights and protections under the contract—without having to get the independent contractor's permission. Nothing needs to be inserted here.

> This Agreement shall bind the Company's successors and assigns, and Company may assign this Agreement to any party at any time, in its sole discretion, without Contractor's consent. This Agreement shall bind Contractor's heirs, successors and assignees. Contractor shall not assign any of Contractor's rights or obligations under this Agreement without Company's prior written consent.

6. Waiver

Having spent considerable time (and perhaps expense) drafting your agreement and getting the contractor to sign it, you probably intend to see that it's followed. There may be times, however, when a violation of the agreement just isn't worth getting upset over. For instance, an information leak may not that important; or the employee who's been wooed away may be someone you're actually glad to see go. However, you'll want to know that, should you need to, you can hold your contractor to the letter of the agreement and expect a judge to do so, too.

If you let violations of the agreement go by, the legal problem you may face later is called "waiver and estoppel." Your former contractor may claim that you've given up the noncompete protections you once had. Especially if the worker has relied on your apparent lack of concern, you may have a tough time getting a judge to enforce your agreement.

EXAMPLE: Sadie finished her contract job as an insurance agent at Insure-We-Will ("IWW") and then went to work as an employee for a competitor. She signed a termination agreement that contained noncompete, nonsolicitation and nondisclosure clauses.

In spite of her agreement, Sadie solicited a couple of Insure-We-Will employees to join her at her new company. IWW's CEO knew about Sadie's violation of the agreement, but decided not to take any action against her, since the agents who left with her were poor performers.

Emboldened, Sadie managed to convince one of IWW's top agents to move to her new company, a coup that earned Sadie a place on the recruitment team. This time, the CEO was furious. He immediately called a lawyer and told her to file a lawsuit against Sadie for violating the agreement. Sadie and her lawyer responded by arguing that because IWW hadn't tried to enforce the agreement when the first few employees left, they had waived their right to sue Sadie for soliciting the top-performing agent. IWW had a very tough time convincing the judge that it hadn't waived its right to enforce the nonsolicitation clause against Sadie, especially after Sadie pointed out that she'd lose her spot on the recruitment team if she could no longer contact employees at IWW.

The waiver clause in our agreement will help prevent your former contractor from claiming that you have waived your right to enforce a part of the contract even if you've ignored it in other instances or have waited for a while to enforce it. However, a waiver clause is no guarantee that you can "pick your fights" at whim. It's best to be diligent about enforcing your rights under your agreement. Nothing needs to be inserted here.

> If Company waives any term or provision of this Agreement, that waiver shall only be effective in the specific instance and for the specific purpose for which Company gave the waiver. If Company fails to exercise or delays exercising any of its rights or remedies under this Agreement, Company retains the right to enforce that term or provision at a later time.

Preserve your rights while you think. *If you learn that a contractor is violating your agreement but aren't ready to fire off a lawsuit (or even a stern letter from your lawyer), your best bet is to inform that person that he is in violation and that your present stance is not a waiver of your rights. Send a letter in which you acknowledge that you are not taking immediate action, but that you will enforce your rights in the future—then do so! Understand that if you continue to let the violation go unchecked, a judge may decide later that you have waived your rights by inaction, no matter how many letters you might have sent.*

7. Amendment

You and your contractor may have conversations about the noncompetition agreement after it's been signed. The signed document, however, should be the last (and only) word on what's been agreed to. If you both agree to change the agreement, that's fine—but the change should be put in writing and made part of your agreement. This will prevent a contractor from claiming that statements made orally later or in separate documents should take precedence over what's said in the agreement.

The amendment clause requires any amendments to the contract to be in writing and to be signed by both parties, so there won't be any doubt as to who agreed to what. Nothing needs to be inserted here. In Section G, we'll show you how to use the Amendment form.

> This Agreement may be modified, changed or amended only in writing, and such writing must signed by both parties.

8. Counterparts

This clause, arguably the most mundane in the entire agreement, means that you and the independent contractor can sign the agreement on separate signature pages, but that it will still be considered to be one agreement.

> The parties may execute this Agreement in counterparts, each of which shall be considered an original, and all of which shall constitute the same document.

Congratulations! You've made it through the hardest parts of the form. All that's left is to learn about the signature portion of the agreement. Read Section H, "Completing Your Agreement," below, for instructions on signing, copying and amending your agreement. To make sure you understand what's *not* covered in the form, however, take a look at the following section. And if you need to change your form, consult Section G.

F. Clauses Not Included in Our Agreements

Noncompete agreements sometimes contain additional clauses covering disputes and the ownership of the contractor's work product. Our agreements omit these clauses. In this section, we'll tell you exactly what we've left out, and why.

1. Disputes: Arbitration and Mediation

Arbitration and mediation are alternatives to going to court. They are often cheaper, quicker and less emotionally draining than going to court.

Our agreements do not require that you and your worker take your disputes to mediation or arbitration because, although we certainly hope you don't have to go to court to enforce your agreement, that's where you're most likely to get it enforced. It certainly doesn't hurt to ask a contractor to mediate or arbitrate a dispute before going to court, and we recommend that you do ask. Realistically, however, if a former worker is violating your agreement, your best chance of stopping the offensive behavior and enforcing the agreement is to immediately ask a judge to stop it with an injunction.

 If you're interested in including an arbitration clause in an agreement for an independent contractor, see Hiring Independent Contractors: An Employer's Legal Guide, *by Stephen Fishman (Nolo).*

2. Ownership of Contractor's Work Product

Some independent contractor agreements contain a clause that states that anything the worker creates or authors while working for you will belong to your company instead of the worker. This may be important if you're hiring someone to write source code for a software program or create content for your website.

We have not included a work product clause because state laws vary greatly on the issue, and in some states these clauses are not enforceable. (For example, California has very strict rules regarding worker ownership of worker-created inventions.) If you're interested in including such a clause, consult an attorney.

 For more information, see Hiring Independent Contractors: An Employer's Legal Guide, *by Stephen Fishman (Nolo), and* License Your Invention, *by Rich Stim (Nolo).*

G. Instructions for Amendment Form

You'll use the amendment form, Form IC-9, if you need to amend an existing noncompete agreement. Use it for a minor change (such as an extension of the term of the contract) or a major change (such as an addition of noncompetition, nonsolicitation and/or nondisclosure clauses to an existing written contractor agreement).

1. Minor Change

Follow these instructions if you are making a minor change to a written agreement.

a. Introduction

Fill in the date (month, day and year) of the amendment you are entering into the amendment, the contractor's name and the name of your company. In the last blank, fill in the state in which your company was formed and its type of legal structure—for example, "a *California corporation*."

If your contractor operates her business as a limited liability company (LLC) or a corporation, you must list the contractor that way in this paragraph—for instance, "_Enterprise Web Designs, Inc., a California corporation_ ("Contractor")."

b. Purpose

Under "Purpose," use Alternative #1, Minor Amendment, and delete Alternative #2. In the first and second blanks, insert the name of the original agreement, such as _Consulting Agreement_ and its date (month, day and year). Describe the nature and reason for making this amendment on the blank line.

c. Amendment

Under "Amendment," use Alternative #1, Minor Amendment and delete Alternative #2. Insert the number or letter of the section you are changing (in both blanks) and then insert the full, actual text of the new section.

d. Applicable Law

This amendment will be governed by the same state law as the original agreement. Fill in the state that governed the original agreement.

If the previous agreement didn't say which state's law would apply, fill in the state in which your business and the contractor are located—which is usually the same state. However, if you and the contractor are located in different states, you should probably choose the state in which your business is located. Read Section E2, above, for more information on choosing the agreement's applicable law.

2. Adding Noncompetition, Nonsolicitation and/or Nondisclosure Clauses

Follow these instructions if you are adding noncompetition, nonsolicitation and/or nondisclosure clauses to an existing written independent contractor agreement.

a. Purpose

Under "Purpose," use Alternative #2, Adding Noncompetition, Nonsolicitation and/or Nondisclosure Clauses to Existing Written Agreement, and delete Alternative #1. In the first and second blanks, insert the name of the Original Agreement, such as _Consulting Agreement_, and fill in its date (month, day and year).

Then, choose one of the sub-alternatives that come next and delete the one you are not using. Choose alternative 2a, "Raise," if you are giving the contractor a raise in return for signing the agreement. Nothing needs to be inserted here.

Choose alternative 2b, "Other Consideration," if you are giving the contractor something other than a raise in return for signing the agreement, such as stock options. In the blank, fill in a brief description of the additional benefit you will provide the contractor. (See Chapter 5, Section B for a discussion of the need to supply an additional benefit.)

b. Amendment

Under "Amendment," use Alternative #2, Adding Noncompetition, Nonsolicitation and/or Nondisclosure Clauses to Existing

Written Agreement, and delete Alternative #1.

Subsection a on the amendment form adds five sections to your original agreement: the nondisclosure, noncompetition and nonsolicitation clauses, as well as the clause giving you a right to an injunction and the survivability clause. You need to insert numbers in the blanks in front of these sections. Look at your original agreement and find a logical place where they could go and then assign section numbers to the sections accordingly.

For information on filling out the blanks in the nondisclosure of confidential information, noncompetition and nonsolicitation clauses, see Section C, above.

In the "Reasonable Restriction/Survivability" clause and the "Right to an Injunction" clause, fill in the section numbers you assigned to the nondisclosure, noncompetition and nonsolicitation sections. For instance, if you make the nondisclosure, noncompetition and nonsolicitation clauses Sections 13, 14 and 15, you should add these three numbers to the three blanks in the "Reasonable Restriction; Survivability" clause and the "Right to an Injunction" clause.

Next, in subsection b, you'll make an amendment to your original agreement to record the additional benefit that you're giving to the contractor in return for agreeing to the noncompete restrictions. You can make changes to the language in your original agreement, where you describe the contractor's compensation (if you are giving the contractor a raise); or you can add a new clause to your contract that describes the additional benefit the contractor will receive in exchange for agreeing to the noncompete restrictions. For instance, if the contractor's pay will remain the same but you have agreed to give the contractor equity in your company in exchange for the noncompete agreement, you'll need to add a new clause.

Use the first alternative to amend the compensation clause from your original contract. If you are changing the language from that original clause, insert the number of the clause from the original agreement in the first two blanks and insert the full text of the amended clause on the blank line.

Use the second alternative to add a new clause to your contract describing the additional benefit the contractor will receive. If you are adding a new clause, look at your original agreement and find a logical place where it could go and number it accordingly. Insert that number into the first two blanks and insert the full text of the new clause on the blank line.

H. Completing Your Agreement

Before you sign and date your agreement and make copies of it, read the general instructions below, which apply to all of the forms in this book.

1. Signing the Agreement

Legally, it's always important for the parties to a contract (in this case, the contractor and you, the client) to sign it correctly. First, of course, there's the obvious importance of getting each party's name right.

Second, you need to make sure each party's signature is "structured" correctly to make it clear who's signing the agreement, and in what capacity. This is particularly important if an entity (such as a partnership or a corporation), rather than a person, signs the agreement. In that case the "signature block" needs to state the title of the person signing the agreement (president or general partner, for example) to show that that person has the authority to sign the contract.

The following instructions apply to the independent contractor, too. Independent contractors sometimes operate their businesses as corporations or LLCs; or they may use a fictitious business name. That's fine—just follow the same rules in constructing the contractor's signature block as you would for your other business. The following subsections show you the signature blocks that you can choose from, depending on how your business (and that of your contractor) is organized.

a. Sole Proprietorships

If you run your business as a sole proprietorship (a one-person business that isn't registered with the state as a corporation or an LLC), you are fully liable for all business contracts and debts.

Simply sign your full name, which makes the agreement binding on you and your business. If you have a fictitious business name (also called a d/b/a) and you want to be more precise, you can add "doing business as" after your name, to make it clear that you are entering into the agreement on behalf of your business.

To create a sole proprietor signature block out of the lines we provide, delete the first two lines and sign your name on the third. Type or print your name on the fourth line. If you wish to include your business name, on the last line, delete the pre-printed "Its" and type in "d/b/a" and the name of the business, as in the clause shown below.

By: _Clark Kent_

d/b/a The Caped Crusader

b. Limited Liability Companies

Setting up the signature blocks correctly is particularly important for business structures that offer protection from personal liability for business debts (known as "limited liability"), such as corporations and limited liability companies (LLCs). Stating a person's title and the name of the company under the signature preserves the limited personal liability of the person signing the agreement and of the business's owners.

If you run your business as a limited liability company (LLC), you know that the owners of LLCs are called members and the contract that governs the members' relationship to each other is called the operating agreement. Your LLC is probably managed by the members, but it might be run by one or more properly authorized managers. If the LLC is large or has investors who don't participate in its management, it might even have officers who manage it, just like a corporation, including a president, vice president and secretary. The signature block will vary depending on who runs the LLC—members, managers or officers.

i. How Many Signatures?

Before you choose the signature block for your LLC, understand that an LLC operating agreement may provide that two or more members' or managers' signatures are required to bind the LLC to certain types of contracts. Check your LLC operating agreement to make sure that the manager, member or officer signing the agreement on behalf of the LLC has the power to bind the LLC to contracts by him or herself. If your LLC has officers, the president or other high-ranking officer can probably sign the agreement, but again, it's worth consulting your company's operating agreement to be sure this officer has the authority to do this.

ii. Member-Managed LLCs

If your LLC is member-managed, any one member can normally sign an agreement and bind the LLC. On the first line of the signature block, the member should insert the name of the company (including the abbreviation LLC or L.L.C.), and on the second line, the state in which the company was formed and the words "limited liability company." On the next three lines, the member should sign his name, type or print his name and add the word "Member."

Kryptonite Busters, LLC,
a Delaware limited liability company
By: _____*Lex Luthor*_____
Its: _____*Member*_____

---

iii. Manager-Managed LLCs

If your LLC is manager-managed, the agreement should probably be signed by a manager and should look like the signature block that follows. If it turns out that a member or an officer has the right to bind the LLC, then insert the appropriate title, such as "member" or "president."

Kryptonite Busters, LLC,
a Delaware limited liability company
By: _____*Otis White*_____
Its: _____*Member*_____

If you are entering into a noncompete agreement with a key executive as part of a formal employment contract, consider having all members of your LLC sign a resolution ratifying the agreement, even if your LLC member or manager has legal authority to sign contracts. *This can head off any disagreements or confusion between the members or managers later. For more information on LLC resolutions and recordkeeping, see* Your Limited Liability Company: An Operating Manual, *by Anthony Mancuso (Nolo).*

c. Corporations

If your business is set up as a corporation, you know that the owners of a corporation are called shareholders, the people who direct the policy of the corporation are the directors, and the executive employees who run the corporation on a daily basis are the officers, usually consisting of a president, a vice president, a secretary and a treasurer. In small corporations, the shareholders wear many hats and are usually directors as well as officers. Corporate shareholders, officers and directors are not personally liable for business debts, which means they usually can't be held personally liable to pay these amounts except in extreme circumstances.

If you are in doubt as to which corporate officers have power to sign contracts, check your company's bylaws. Usually, the president or chief executive officer (CEO)

of a corporation will have the authority to sign contracts on behalf of the corporation, but sometimes the corporation's bylaws or even a state law will require two officers to sign a contract entered into on the corporation's behalf. Directors don't normally sign agreements, but they can—check your bylaws to see if they are authorized to do so.

Corporate officers and directors need to make sure they sign all agreements in their correct capacity in order to make sure they protect their limited personal exposure for business debts. The officer or director who signs the agreement on behalf of the company needs to make it clear that she is signing the agreement in her corporate, not her individual, capacity. The name of the corporation (including the abbreviation "Inc." or" Corp.") goes on the first line of the signature block. The state in which the company was incorporated and the word "corporation" should be inserted on the second line. On the next three lines, the officer or director should sign his name, type or print his name and add her title.

> *Jailbreak Specialists, Inc.,*
> *a Delaware corporation*
> By: *Harry Houdini*
> Its: *President and Chief Executive Officer*

If you're a small or family corporation entering into a noncompete agreement with a high-level employee as part of a formal em-

ployment contract, consider getting shareholder approval for the agreement, even if your bylaws don't require it. *This can prevent non-director or officer shareholders from feeling unfairly excluded from the corporate decision-making process, and can head off disagreements later. For more information about corporate resolutions and recordkeeping, see* The Corporate Minutes Book: The Legal Guide to Taking Care of Corporate Business, *by Anthony Mancuso (Nolo).*

d. General Partnerships

If you are a partner in a general partnership, you know that you are personally liable for all business contracts and debts. It's still important, however, to structure the signatures on a contract correctly to make it clear that the partnership is the party to the contract, not the individual partner signing the contract. This is important because even though general partners are liable for the partnership's debts, they do have the right to ask the other partners to pay their share of any business debt they pay. If a partner signs individually, he may forfeit this right.

A general partner of a partnership can sign all agreements on behalf of the partnership. Consult your partnership agreement to make sure that one general partner's signature is enough to bind the company. If you're not sure, all of the general partners should sign the agreement.

The name of the partnership goes on the first line of the signature block, and the state in which the company was formed and the word "partnership" should be inserted on the second line. On the next three lines, the partner should sign her name, type or print her name and add her title.

Oblivious Reporters,
a Delaware partnership
By: *Lois Lane*
Its: *General Partner*

 For more information about creating, running and operating partnerships, see The Partnership Book, *by Denis Clifford and Ralph Warner (Nolo).*

e. Limited Partnerships

Limited partnerships have general partners, who run the business and are personally liable for business debts, but they also have limited partners, who don't manage the business and are liable for business debts only up to the amount of their investment.

Limited partners can't sign agreements on behalf of the partnership because they don't have the authority to bind the partnership The general partner(s) of a partnership must sign all agreements. Consult your partnership agreement to determine if more than one general partner's signature is necessary to bind the partnership to an agreement.

The name of the partnership goes on the first line of the signature block, and the state in which the company was organized and the word "partnership" should be inserted on the second line. On the next three lines, the partner should sign her name, type or print her name and add her title.

Oblivious Reporters, L.P.,
a Delaware limited partnership
By: *Lois Lane*
Its: *General Partner*

---

f.   Multi-Tiered Companies

Generally, the law does not require all of the members of a limited liability company, or all of the partners in a general partnership, to be natural persons. For various reasons (usually for tax reasons, to protect an owner's privacy or to shield an owner even more from personal liability) another company may be the manager of an LLC or the general partner of a partnership. In that case, you should list both company names.

The name of the primary company—the company that is a party to the contract—goes on the first line of the signature block, and the state in which the company was organized and its type of legal structure, such as "limited liability company" or "limited partnership," should be inserted on the second line. Then insert the name of the company that's the general partner or manager of the main company, and fi-

nally the name of the person signing the document and his title.

Bumbling Assistants, L.P.,
a Delaware limited partnership
By: *Fresh off the Farm, LLC, a Delaware limited liability company*
Its: *General Partner*
By: *Jimmy Olsen*
Its: *Manager*

---

2. Altering the Agreement Before It's Signed

You can keep your noncompete agreement on your computer and easily alter it up to the day you sign the agreement.

If for some reason you must change the agreement before it has been signed but after it has been printed (for example, you've printed out a hard copy and your computer isn't available), you can simply write the changes in by hand and cross out anything you want to remove. But it's important that both parties initial each of these changes before they sign the agreement to make sure it's clear that both parties have agreed to them. Although this is a perfectly legal way to alter an agreement, it's almost always a better idea to make the changes on your computer if you can. This reduces the chance of confusion later.

If you need to change the agreement *after* it's been signed, use Form IC-9, the amendment form.

3. Making Copies of the Agreement

Both you and the contractor should have a signed original of the agreement for your files. To accomplish this, when you're ready to sign the agreement, prepare two copies of the agreement. Sign both of them, and then have the worker do the same. If you or your worker received the advice of an attorney before signing the noncompete agreement, you might want to provide the attorney with a signed original as well.

Don't sign in black ink. *It's helpful to sign contracts in blue ink so that you'll know which documents are copies and which are originals. (Marking originals "Original" and copies "Copy" is also useful.)*

Keep the original in a safe place—the contractor's personnel file is a good place. While a copy is usually enough to prove the legitimacy of a signature if someone disputes its authenticity, it's always better to have an agreement with the original signature.

4. To Fax or Not to Fax

Often, parties signing an agreement aren't in the same place at the same time. It's perfectly legal to have an independent contractor sign the agreement and fax it back to you. But if you do this, it's best to ask the worker to also sign two duplicate originals and mail one back to you, so that you'll have an original for your files.

5. Changing the Agreement After It's Signed

You may want to make changes to the agreement after it's signed. This is easy to do, but it's important to make sure that any changes to your agreement are in writing. The agreements in this book require all amendments to be in writing and signed by both parties. An amendment form, IC-9, is included on the CD-ROM. The instructions for the amendment form are in Section G, above.

6. Naming Your Agreement

Although we provide job descriptions in our independent contractor agreement titles to make it easier for you to find them, we suggest that you delete this job description from the title. The final title of your agreement should be "Independent Contractor Agreement."

The Termination Agreement for Independent Contractors should be titled "Termination Agreement."

If you are creating an amendment to an agreement, it should be titled "Amendment to Independent Contractor Agreement."

Form IC-7: Independent Contractor Agreement (General Agreement)

1.   Introduction

This agreement ("Agreement") is made and entered into as of _____, _____ ,

between_____ ("Contractor") and _____, a
_____ ("Company").

2.   Purpose

Company is in the business of _____.

[]   Alternative # 1: New Contractor

Company would like to retain Contractor as a _____. In exchange for
Company's retaining Contractor's services, and for other good and valuable consideration,
the receipt and sufficiency of which is hereby acknowledged, Company and Contractor
agree as follows:

[]   Alternative # 2: Existing Contractor With Prior Oral Agreement

Contractor was previously retained by Company as a _____ pursuant to an
oral independent contractor agreement dated which began on _____, _____ .

Company shall continue to retain Contractor's services as a _____, but on the
terms and conditions set forth in this Agreement.

As _____, Contractor has access to Company's Confidential Information, as
defined in this Agreement. In exchange for Company's retaining Contractor's services as a
_____, and for other good and valuable consideration, the receipt and
sufficiency of which is hereby acknowledged, Company and Contractor agree as follows:

3.   Duties

Contractor's duties will include:

_____

_____

_____

Contractor acknowledges that because Contractor is an independent contractor, Company will control only the results of the services Contractor provides to Company and not the means by which Contractor provides services.

4.   Compensation

In exchange for the services to be rendered by Contractor under this Agreement,

[ ]   Alternative # 1: Flat Fee

Company shall pay Contractor the sum of _____ Dollars ($_____), payable as follows: _____.

[ ]   Alternative # 2: Weekly or Monthly Fee

Company shall pay Contractor the sum of _____ Dollars ($_____) per [week/month], beginning on the ___ day after the date of this Agreement and continuing on the same day of each [week/month].

[ ]   Alternative # 3: Hourly Fee With Invoice

Company shall pay Contractor the sum of _____ Dollars ($_____) per hour. Contractor shall submit invoices to Company each [month/week] detailing the hours worked and services performed and the total fee due. Company shall pay Contractor the invoiced amount within _____ (___) days of receiving an invoice.

5.   Term of Services

[ ]   Alternative # 1: Fixed Term

This Agreement will begin on the date set forth in Section 1 and will continue for _____ (___) [weeks/months/years], ending on _____, _____.

[ ]   Alternative # 2: Project-Based Term

This Agreement will begin on the date set forth in Section 1 and will continue until _____ but shall not end later than _____.

6.   No Withholding or State Insurance

Because Company is retaining Contractor as an independent contractor and not as an employee, Company will not withhold from Contractor's compensation any state or federal income taxes, and Company will not withhold or pay any Social Security, Medicare, federal unemployment insurance (FUTA), workers' compensation insurance, state unemployment or disability insurance payments on Contractor's behalf. Contractor agrees and covenants to report all income received from Company and make all required income tax and other tax payments in connection with Contractor's compensation. Company will provide Contractor with a Form 1099 summarizing Contractor's compensation for each tax year.

7.   No Partnership

This Agreement does not create any partnership or joint venture between Company and Contractor or any relationship other than client and independent contractor. Except as described in Section 3, or unless Contractor obtains Company's written consent, Contractor shall not have the authority to and shall not bind the Company to any contract or agreement.

8.   No Other Benefits

Except as specifically set forth in this Agreement, Company is not responsible for providing and will not provide Contractor with any benefits, including but not limited to health insurance, pension benefits or any other benefits Company provides to its employees.

9.   Termination of Services

If either Contractor or Company violates, breaches or fails to perform any provision of this Agreement, either party shall have the right, with written notice, to immediately terminate services under this Agreement.

10.   Additional Agreements

Company and Contractor additionally agree that:_____

_____

_____

11.   Nondisclosure of Confidential Information

a.   Company may need to disclose to Contractor or give Contractor access to Confidential Information so that Contractor may properly fulfill his or her duties to Company. "Confidential Information" means Company's trade secrets, including, but not limited to, customer lists (including names, addresses, attributes, requirements, special needs and other data); names, locations of and agreements with vendors, suppliers and strategic business alliance partners; contemplated new products or services; _____; or any other information that is not generally known and from which the Company derives an economic benefit. The Confidential Information may be written, such as computer source code, programs, hardware and software, tapes, disks, documents, drawings, data or product specifications, or unwritten, such as unwritten knowledge, ideas, processes, practices or know-how. Confidential Information does not include information that is in the public domain, information that is generally known in Company's industry or information that Contractor acquired completely independently of his or her services for Company.

b.   For as long as the Confidential Information is not generally known and Company derives an economic benefit from the Confidential Information, Contractor shall not use or disclose to any other person or entity any Confidential Information or any copy or summary of any Confidential Information unless Contractor is required to do so to perform Contractor's duties to Company or as required by law.

c.   While Contractor is performing services for Company and afterward, Contractor shall not remove or copy any Confidential Information or participate in any way in the removal or copying of any Confidential Information without Company's written consent. Contractor shall immediately return to Company all Confidential Information when Contractor ceases performing services for Company, or any time Company requires such Confidential Information to be returned.

d.   Contractor will not obtain or attempt to obtain any Confidential Information for any purpose whatsoever except as required by Company to enable Contractor to perform his or her duties.

e.   Contractor will not disclose to Company or misuse any third party's trade secrets, including any trade secret information of Contractor's former employer or client, _____. Contractor represents and warrants that the execution of this Agreement by Contractor will not violate or conflict with the terms of any other agreement to which Contractor is a party.

12. Noncompetition

Contractor agrees that in order to protect the Confidential Information described above, while Contractor is performing services for Company, and for a period of _____ [years/months] thereafter (collectively, the "Term"), Contractor shall not:

a.   plan for, acquire any financial interest in or perform services for (as an employee, consultant, officer, director, independent contractor, principal, agent or otherwise) any business that would require Contractor to use or disclose any Confidential Information, or

b.   perform services (as an employee, consultant, officer, director, independent contractor, principal, agent or otherwise) that are similar to Contractor's current duties or responsibilities for any person or entity that, during the Term, engages in any business activity in which Company is then engaged or proposes to be engaged and that conducts its business in the Territory.

c.   "Territory" means

[ ]   Alternative # 1: General Territory

any geographic area in which Company conducts its business during the Term.

[ ]   Alternative # 2: Specific Territory

_____.

13. Nonsolicitation

While Contractor is performing services for Company, and for a period of _____ [years/months] thereafter, Contractor shall not:

a.   employ, attempt to employ or solicit for employment by any other person or entity, any Company employees;

b.   encourage any consultant, independent contractor or any other person or entity to end their relationship or stop doing business with Company, or help any person or entity to do so or attempt to do so; or

c.   solicit or attempt to solicit or obtain business or trade from any of Company's current customers or clients with whom Contractor had contact or about whom Contractor acquired knowledge while performing services for Company, or help any person or entity do so or attempt to do so.

14. Right to an Injunction

Contractor acknowledges that his or her services to Company are special and unique and that, while performing these services, Contractor will have access to and Company may disclose to Contractor the Confidential Information described above. Contractor also acknowledges that performing services for Company will place him or her in a position of confidence and trust with Company and its employees, clients and customers.

If Contractor breaches or threatens to breach any of the provisions of Sections 11, 12 or 13 of this Agreement, Company will sustain irreparable harm. Company shall be entitled to an injunction to stop any breach or threatened breach of this Agreement, including the provisions of Sections 11, 12 or 13. Contractor acknowledges and agrees that monetary damages would not adequately compensate Company for any breach or threatened breach of these sections and that if Company seeks injunctive relief to put an immediate halt to the offending conduct, Contractor shall not claim that monetary damages would be an adequate remedy.

15. Reasonable Restrictions; Survivability

Contractor acknowledges that the restrictions set forth in Sections 11, 12, 13 and 14 of this Agreement are reasonable and necessary for the protection of Company, its business and its Confidential Information. The provisions of Sections 11, 12, 13 and 14 of this Agreement shall survive the termination, for any reason, of Contractor's employment with Company.

16. Severability

If a court determines that any provision of this Agreement is invalid or unenforceable, any invalidity or unenforceability will affect only that provision and shall not make any other provision of this Agreement invalid or unenforceable. Instead, such provision shall be modified, amended or limited to the extent necessary to render it valid and enforceable.

17. Applicable Law

This Agreement shall be governed by and construed in accordance with the laws of the State of _____.

18. Jurisdiction

Contractor and Company consent to the exclusive jurisdiction and venue of the federal and state courts located in _____, _____, in any action arising out of or relating to this Agreement. Contractor and Company waive any other venue to which either party might be entitled by domicile or otherwise.

19. Entire Agreement; No Other Change

This is the entire agreement between the parties. It supersedes and replaces any and all prior oral or written agreements between Company and Contractor that relate to the matters covered by this Agreement.

20. Assignment; Binding Effect

This Agreement shall bind the Company's successors and assigns, and Company may assign this Agreement to any party at any time, in its sole discretion, without Contractor's consent. This Agreement shall bind Contractor's heirs, successors and assignees. Contractor shall not assign any of Contractor's rights or obligations under this Agreement without Company's prior written consent.

21. Waiver

If Company waives any term or provision of this Agreement, that waiver shall be effective only in the specific instance and for the specific purpose for which Company gave the waiver. If Company fails to exercise or delays exercising any of its rights or remedies under this Agreement, Company retains the right to enforce that term or provision at a later time.

22. Amendment

This Agreement may be modified, changed or amended only in writing, and such writing must signed by both parties.

23. Counterparts

The parties may execute this Agreement in counterparts, each of which shall be considered an original, and all of which shall constitute the same document.

IN WITNESS WHEREOF, the parties have executed this Agreement as of the day and year first written above in Section 1.

"Company"

_____, a _____

By: _____

_____

[type or print name]

Its: _____

"Contractor"

_____

_____

[type or print name]

7

When Workers Depart: Revisiting Your Agreement

Your noncompete agreement will protect you only so long as your ex-worker honors it. In this chapter, we give you suggestions for maximizing the chances that the worker will do so. Making sure that the worker understands the practical consequences of the agreement is key.

If a worker has violated (or plans to violate) your noncompete agreement, following our procedures will give you a better chance of finding out (and stopping the violations) before too much actual damage has occurred. This chapter also covers what steps to take if the worker disregards your agreement, which range from gentle reminders to written notices and, if necessary, a trip to court.

Our recommendations apply whether the worker is departing voluntarily, is laid off or is fired. They also pertain to all types of restrictive agreements—full-blown noncompete agreements (with noncompetition, nondisclosure and nonsolicitation clauses) or scaled-down versions, such as those without the noncompetition component.

A. Understand Your Rights

Before we discuss the steps you should take when someone departs, we'll quickly go over your rights and options in the event that the worker doesn't honor the agreement. In addition to suing anyone who violates a noncompete or nondisclosure agreement in civil court, state and federal laws create criminal sanctions for stealing trade secrets.

1. Suing in Civil Court

You can sue a former worker for using or disclosing your trade secrets, soliciting your customers or employees or competing against you in violation of your agreement.

a. Misappropriation of Trade Secrets

Under the Uniform Trade Secrets Act (UTSA), and the laws of non-UTSA states, trade secret owners have the right to obtain certain civil legal remedies against someone who misappropriates trade secrets. (Civil remedies include court orders and/or money damages that you can obtain by going to court.) In addition, trade secret owners have remedies under the UTSA against a former worker's new employer if the new employer knows or even suspects that the worker has revealed or plans to use a former employer's trade secrets.

To win a dispute based on state trade secret law, you must be able to show that the information is a trade secret (that is, it provides an economic advantage to your business and your business has taken reasonable efforts to keep it secret) and that the person accused of misappropriation improperly acquired the information or improperly disclosed it.

Don't be misled by the legalese—misappropriation doesn't necessarily mean that an employee steals into your offices in the dead of night and loads your confidential files onto the back of a truck. And misappropriation doesn't necessarily mean the worker uses or discloses the information; just the act of taking it, when the worker knows the information is a secret, can constitute misappropriation.

Here are some examples of the ways workers can misappropriate your trade secrets:

- photocopying documents containing sensitive information
- copying files or programs onto a computer disk
- printing out copies of databases and files
- emailing files to themselves at a private email account
- accessing your computer network remotely and downloading files or programs onto a home computer
- keeping or taking a Rolodex full of customer or client information, or even a collection of business cards
- downloading or copying information stored in an electronic organizer, PDA (personal digital assistant) or cell phone. Many of these devices now "hot sync" with personal computers, meaning that the worker can simply plug the device into her home computer and download the information onto her hard drive, or

- memorizing the information. Some people can remember scores of names, phone numbers and other important information and wouldn't need to photocopy things like customer lists or product formulas in order to use them.

This list is not exhaustive—a worker who wants your trade secrets will think of a creative away to take them. As you can see, the ease with which a worker can make off with your trade secrets (purposely or inadvertently) makes it even more critical to put a trade secret protection program in place at your business. (See Chapter 1, Section D, for more information.)

b. Violations of the Noncompetition or Nonsolicitation Clauses

Suppose your main competitor lures away one of your key employees with offers of more money and vacation time. Or your salesperson, an independent contractor, starts a new business and starts contacting all of your clients, urging them to bring their business to her instead. As you'll see below, your first step should be to contact the former worker, remind her of her obligations under your agreement and ask her to cease the activity that violates the agreement. If the ex-worker refuses to stop, even after your lawyer has sent her a letter, your next step is to ask a court to stop the former worker from competing against your company or soliciting your clients.

A judge will look at your agreement to see if it meets the rules we discussed in Chapter 1, Section B (for most states), or the specific state rules we discussed in Chapter 2, Section B. If the judge determines that your agreement meets your state's standards for noncompete agreements, the agreement will be enforceable. The judge will then decide whether the former worker has violated the agreement and whether the former worker's behavior (for example, working for a competitor) should be stopped right away. If you're lucky, the judge will put a stop to the behavior with a temporary order (an injunction); which will be re-examined later at trial.

If you and the worker don't settle the case, it may go to trial. A judge or jury will decide if the former worker violated the agreement and, if so, whether you're entitled to money damages for the financial harm suffered by your business.

c. Getting an Injunction

If a trade secret owner can establish that a trade secret was in fact improperly used, disclosed or acquired, a court can stop any further use or disclosure of the information by granting an injunction (a preliminary court order that could prohibit a former worker from going to work for a competitor or from disclosing your trade secrets).

Judges have this power to stop the misuse or disclosure of trade secrets before a trial because lawsuits tend to drag on for years. It would defeat the purpose of the lawsuit if the trade secret thief (called an "infringer") could keep using this information during months or years of litigation—by then, any money damages the trade secret owner would get at the end of the lawsuit wouldn't bring back lost business.

Similarly, if a business owner can prove that a former worker has violated an agreement containing nonsolicitation and noncompetition clauses, a court may grant an injunction to stop the former worker from soliciting your customers and employees and competing against you. This will decrease the chance that you will lose trade secrets, customers and employees while awaiting a trial.

The success of your case can turn on whether you have obtained an injunction at the outset. Lawyers often consider the judge's decision a preview of how the case will finally turn out. Consequently, litigants who have shown no signs of settling their dispute often come to the bargaining table once they've seen which way the judge is leaning. The employer who is armed with an injunction has a good chance of stopping the infringing behavior before the case goes to trial.

Different Types of Court Orders

You may have heard lawyers throwing around legal terms such as "TROs" (temporary restraining orders), "preliminary injunctions" and "permanent injunctions," and wondered what these terms meant. Here's a brief primer:

A **temporary restraining order,** or **TRO,** is just that—a temporary order issued by a judge restraining someone from doing something for a short period of time. A TRO lasts until the judge has a full hearing on the matter and can make a more informed decision about whether to issue a **preliminary injunction.** Depending on the urgency of the matter, a judge can issue a temporary restraining order without hearing from both parties.

A **preliminary injunction** is an order issued by a judge that prevents a party from doing something (or, sometimes, requires a party to do something). Before issuing a preliminary injunction, a judge will conduct a hearing in which both sides have a chance to present their arguments as to why the judge should, or should not, issue the injunction. Gen-

erally, a preliminary injunction lasts until the judge can conduct a full trial and decide whether to issue a **permanent injunction.**

A **permanent injunction** is a longer-lasting court order that prevents a party from doing something. But despite its name, it doesn't necessarily last forever. For instance, suppose you sue a former employee who signed a noncompete agreement that provided the employee couldn't compete against your company for two years. A judge might issue a permanent injunction enjoining (stopping) her from competing against you for that period of time—but since the injunction will only last two years, it's obviously not "permanent" in the usual sense of the word.

You might have noticed that each court order discussed above is issued by a judge. Juries aren't involved in these types of orders because only a judge is considered to be sufficiently qualified to decide whether to grant one.

In addition to injunctive relief, a court may eventually award you money damages. These can consist of lost profits resulting from the theft of your trade secrets, profits the former worker or her new employer earned from a wrongfully acquired trade secret and, occasionally, punitive damages (special damages that are used to punish the former worker and possibly the new employer).

2. Criminal Penalties

In addition to being at the receiving end of a civil suit, someone who steals your trade secrets may also be subject to criminal prosecution. Criminal laws affecting trade secrets differ from state to state, but typically such laws apply to anybody who intentionally and without permission:

- physically takes records or articles reflecting the trade secret
- copies or photographs these records or articles
- assists in either of these acts, or
- discloses the trade secret to another after having received knowledge of the secret in the course of a confidential employment relationship.

However, criminal prosecutions are rare for several reasons. Many businesses prefer not to bring law enforcement officials into the fray and would rather settle the matter between the parties. In a lot of cases, law enforcement officials don't want to prosecute a matter because there may not be enough evidence to get a conviction. (The standard of proof in criminal cases is higher than civil lawsuits, so unless you can get ironclad proof, a prosecutor is unlikely to zealously pursue the case.) Finally, although it sounds cynical, most prosecutors are simply too busy with murders, robberies and other violent crimes to pay much attention to the nonviolent or "white collar" type of crime that trade secret theft falls into. (But see "Silicon Valley Prosecutor Takes on Trade Secret Theft," below, for information on trade secret thieves who found themselves on the wrong end of a criminal trade secret theft prosecution.)

Silicon Valley Prosecutor Takes on Trade Secret Theft

In a highly publicized case, a district attorney in Santa Clara County, California, pursued a criminal trade secrets case against former employees of a software maker who left to start their own company—and took their former employer's source code with them.

For four years, the determined prosecutor gathered evidence, subpoenaed witnesses and stuck with an unpopular criminal case the defense insisted was a civil, not a criminal, matter. In the end, his persistence paid off. Just hours before jury selection for the trial was to begin, the defendants agreed to plead "no contest" (a slightly lesser plea than a guilty plea) to the charges, pay hefty fines and even endure some jail time for their part in the trade secret theft.

Many companies, and the lawyers who represent them, hope the outcome of this case will convince other prosecutors across the country—both federal and state—to actively pursue trade secret thieves and enforce the laws on the books.

Stealing trade secrets is also a federal crime. Under the Economic Espionage Act, it is illegal to steal a trade secret or to receive or possess trade secret information knowing that it is stolen. One purpose of the act is to protect U.S. businesses from high-tech trade secret theft (for example, over the Internet). The fines and penalties, including imprisonment, can be severe. Individuals can be imprisoned up to ten years and fined up to $500,000. (A corporation or other organization can be fined up to $5,000,000.) And if the trade secret theft benefits a foreign government, foreign instrumentality (any institution, organization or business substantially owned or controlled by a foreign government), or foreign agent, an infringer can be imprisoned for up to 15 years and fined up to $500,000. (A corporation or other organization can be fined up to $10,000,000.)

As with state criminal trade secret statutes, the FBI and the U.S. attorney in your area may not be eager to follow up on a complaint that seems small-time to them or lacks enough evidence to get a conviction. Don't pin your hopes on either of these agencies to help you out unless one of your workers is involved in foreign espionage or you own a very large company.

3. Other Legal Rights of an Employer

Most states also prohibit former workers from engaging in certain types of unfair or unethical behavior. If, after reading the points that follow, you decide to sue a former worker, your attorney will no doubt combine the following theories with claims of trade secret misappropriation and breach of contract into one civil complaint against the former worker:

- **Unfair competition.** An ex-worker may not harm a former employer by disparaging the former employer's business with untrue statements or interfering with the former employer's business contracts.
- **Interference with a contract.** A former worker cannot induce a customer, client, supplier or employee to breach (break) a contract with your company.
- **Interference with economic or business relations.** An ex-worker cannot deliberately interfere with, steal business from or try to damage your company.

B. Steps to Take When a Worker Departs

If a worker who has signed a noncompete agreement announces she is leaving, or circumstances require you to fire an employee or terminate a contractor's services, you need to handle the departure properly in order to protect your rights. In most businesses, it's relatively rare for a worker to leave and attempt to steal or misuse trade secrets or otherwise violate a noncompete or nondisclosure agreement, so all of the following steps may not be necessary, but you should be prepared nonetheless.

When a worker who's signed a noncompete agreement departs, voluntarily or involuntarily, begin looking for warning signs that she's going to violate your agreement. The earlier you can detect and head off a potential violation of the agreement (whether in the noncompetition, nonsolicitation or nondisclosure portion), the better chance you have of protecting your business and heading off a lawsuit.

Following are several steps you should take to help ensure that your employees or independent contractors (or their future employees or clients) don't violate your agreement after leaving your company.

It's not too late—ask a departing worker who hasn't signed a noncompete agreement to sign a severance or termination agreement upon departure. *See Chapter 3, Section D (for employees), and Chapter 5, Section C (for independent contractors), for more details. Then, follow the suggestions below to make sure your rights are protected.*

Step 1. Conduct an Exit Interview

As soon as you learn that a key employee or independent contractor is leaving (or right after you terminate the employee or contractor), sit down and review your agreement together.

How you conduct the interview—and what you ask—will depend on whether the worker is leaving voluntarily or was terminated. If you are terminating the worker, be prepared to have this discussion during the termination discussion. It's possible that a fired or laid-off worker will be angry and refuse to have a discussion with you. If this happens, skip to Step 2, below, and prepare a letter to the worker in which you restate the worker's obligations under the agreement—and keep your eyes and ears open for any potential problems.

If a worker gives notice, schedule this interview as soon as possible. The earlier you review the obligations under the agreement, the sooner you can deter any potential bad behavior (such as downloading sensitive files) that might otherwise occur during the worker's last couple of weeks.

 For more information on safely handling an employee's termination, see Dealing With Problem Employees: A Legal Guide, *by Amy DelPo and Lisa Guerin (Nolo).*

Step 1a. Remind the Worker About the Agreement

In the exit interview, whether the worker gave notice or was fired, give the worker a copy of the agreement she signed (she may have forgotten she even signed one or may no longer have a copy). During the interview, remind her of her obligations under the agreement and that you fully expect her (and any future employer) to honor all the provisions of the agreement.

Emphasize that the agreement does not allow the worker to:

• work in a similar capacity for a competing business for a certain amount of time (unless your agreement contains only nondisclosure and non-solicitation clauses)

• take part in the ownership of a competing business for a certain amount of time (unless your agreement contains only nondisclosure and non-solicitation clauses)

• use or disclose any of your confidential information, as defined in your agreement

• encourage any of your customers or clients to take their business away from your company, or

• encourage any of your current employees to leave your company to join the worker's new company.

Whatever the reason for the worker's departure, try to get a clear verbal assurance that the worker will not accept a job that violates the agreement, use any of your trade secrets or confidential information in any new job or lure away any customers or employees. A worker who is willing to say this to your face is probably less likely to violate your agreement—and if you're good at "reading" people, you might be able to tell if the worker means it or not.

Step 1b.   Find Out Where the Worker's Going (Workers Who Give Notice Only)

If a worker has given notice, try to get as much information from the employee or contractor as you can. That way, you'll know where to look (and monitor) to make sure your agreement is being honored. The following are some questions you might want to ask the departing worker:

- What company he will work for next?
- What will his new title be?
- What services he will perform in his new position? What kinds of projects will he be in charge of? (To properly assess the potential for problems, you need to know if the worker's duties and responsibilities in the new job will be similar to what they were at your company.)
- How did he find the job? (This is helpful in assessing whether or not one of your competitors tried to lure the worker away, so that you can take action if you need to.)
- Has he discussed his impending departure with any of your employees or contractors?

- Does he know if any of these employees or contractors plan to leave with him?
- Has he informed any of your clients or customers that he is leaving? (This is especially important if the employee or contractor has had significant client or customer contact.)
- Why is he leaving? Is it more money? More responsibility? Lifestyle issues? A problem with your company that no one has addressed? If your workers harbor personal resentment against your company, it's more likely that this person will violate the agreement.

Keep it friendly. *Although you might be on tenterhooks during your discussion, do your best to maintain a fair, even tone with the worker. Don't take an antagonistic stance or assume the worker is out to hurt your company. Not only would that make the worker uncomfortable (and no doubt angry), if the person is on the defensive, you'll be less likely to get good information.*

If the worker is leaving to join a competitor, research the worker's future employer to determine:

- what kinds of products or services the competitor provides
- whether the company has a new product or service launch in the works in which your trade secrets might come in handy, or

• whether the company has a history of or reputation for hijacking key employees from competitors in order to pick their brains for information.

 If you smell trouble, contact an employment lawyer. *If your discussion with the worker alerts you that trouble is on the horizon (for instance, the worker disagrees with you that she's obligated under the agreement, is otherwise hostile or refuses to tell you about her future plans), consider contacting an employment attorney. The moment you suspect you may be a victim, the advice of an employment lawyer can help protect your rights. For tips on finding a lawyer, see Chapter 8.*

Step 2.   Follow Up With a Letter

After the meeting, send the employee or contractor a letter summarizing your conversation and the restrictions imposed by the agreement (see our sample, below). If you decide to base your letter on our sample, customize it to suit your particular situation. Be sure to repeat what you made clear in the interview—that you're prepared to take legal action if your legal rights under the contract are not respected, but without taking an antagonistic tone. The following is an example of a letter an employer might send to a former employee.

Sample Letter to Departing Employee

Jenny Stewart
345 Maple Street
Berkeley, CA 94710

October 1, 2001

Dear Jenny:
I was very sorry to receive your resignation as Acme's Manager of Information Systems last Wednesday. You have been a valued employee and Acme is sorry to lose you.

The purpose of this letter is to remind you of your obligations under the noncompete agreement you signed on September 1, 1999. Specifically, as we discussed last week and as you acknowledged, this agreement prohibits you from either using or disclosing Acme's trade secrets or confidential information to any third party and from taking a similar position with any of our competitors for a period of six months after you leave Acme.

Additionally, you must not solicit any of our employees to join any new venture of your own or on your new employer's behalf, or encourage any of our customers to terminate their relationship with Acme.

As you are aware, the purpose of our agreement is to protect Acme's business interests. Therefore, any violation of the agreement would require Acme to take legal action against you or a future employer to enforce its rights.

Please accept our sincerest wishes for satisfaction in your new career.

Sincerely,

Stephanie A. Johnson
President
Acme Internet Solutions

➡️ **Skip the following steps if you trust your ex-worker and know the details of the new job.** *On the other hand, if the worker has been difficult and didn't acknowledge your rights under the noncompete agreement, definitely go on to the next steps.*

Step 3. Cut Off the Worker's Access to Information

If your former worker was not forthcoming during the interview about the new job or responsibilities, or was otherwise hostile and uncooperative, cut off this person's access to proprietary or confidential information. Depending on the situation, you may want to:

- Ask the worker to return copies of confidential data and keys or passcards to the building, individual offices or file cabinets.
- Take away computer disks, laptop computers or personal data storage devices (such as a Palm Pilot, or cellular phone) that contain confidential data. (If any of these items belong to the worker, you can ask to see their contents and ask the worker to delete or return any of your information. You cannot forcibly take these items away.)
- Change computer passwords and network access, and check for any unauthorized means of getting into

your network. This is particularly important if the departing worker was an IT specialist and had the ability to create a "backdoor," or shortcut, to your system that only the worker knows about.

- Change alarm codes and locks.
- Ask the worker to leave immediately. Many companies reserve this tactic for workers who are terminated, but it's become increasingly common for employers in highly competitive industries, such as investment banking and marketing, to ask an employee who gives notice to leave that same day. This is perfectly acceptable and shouldn't pose a problem, as long as you consistently react this way for every employee who leaves.

💡 **Don't embarrass or speak badly of a departing worker.** *Unless it's regular company policy, it's best to not escort a departing worker from the building by a security guard or in any way that draws attention to the situation. Doing so could embarrass and slander the worker, since you would be giving other employees the impression that this person is dishonest and can no longer be trusted with company information. Similarly, don't speak poorly of a worker who left on bad terms or discuss the circumstances of the departure with anyone who doesn't need to know. This behavior increases the chance that a departing worker could file a lawsuit alleging slander.*

To learn more about the ins and outs of safely firing employees, check out Dealing With Problem Employees: A Legal Guide, *by Amy DelPo and Lisa Guerin (Nolo).*

If you suspect that the employee or contractor may have already taken sensitive information, try to do some investigating. Find out if paper or computer files have been checked out and copied; ask the front desk or security to learn whether the worker has been in and out of the building at odd hours. (One employer discovered that his employee had been photocopying confidential files when he noticed that the copy count on the copy machine was unusually high.) Be sure to document your findings. This information will help you build your case—it proves that the worker possesses confidential information—if you need to go to a judge to ask for an injunction restraining the worker from disclosing your trade secrets or otherwise violating your agreement.

Step 4. Contact the New Employer

If you find out that your former worker's new employer or client will be a competitor, taking this next step may help prevent disclosures.

If you smelled trouble at any point along the way and hired a lawyer to help prevent your former worker from violating the agreement, the lawyer may advise you to send a letter informing your worker's future employer or client of the existence of the noncompete agreement. (We don't recommend sending one of these letters without some legal advice; if you're wrong—the new employer is not a competitor, or your agreement is somehow unenforceable—you could end up on the receiving end of a lawsuit by the former employee for interfering with a business relationship.) In the letter, let the new company know that, if the worker violates any provision of the agreement, you will take legal action against it, including going to court to ask for an injunction to stop the worker from taking the job with the company or to prevent the worker from disclosing trade secrets while on the job. If the worker has taken a job in a state like California, where a traditional noncompetition clause will not be enforced, focus on informing the new company that you expect it will take steps to make sure your trade secrets are respected and that your employees and clients will not be solicited.

Sending such a letter places the future company on notice about the existence of agreement. This may be helpful in the event the new company helps your former worker violate the agreement, because it demonstrates the company's bad faith, a factor that can influence a court. Also, your letter may force the new company to be careful about assigning duties and responsibilities to your former worker (for example, not assigning a particular project for a year).

If you're lucky, the problem could end there. Chances are, the new company wants to avoid litigation almost as much or more than you do.

Step 5. File a Lawsuit Against the Employee or Independent Contractor

If you are convinced a former employee or independent contractor intends to violate your agreement—or if you know or have evidence that the former worker has already violated it—it's time to take harsher measures.

Although your natural instinct might be to rush off to court, if the threat to your business isn't too immediate (for instance, the former worker is considering a job offer with a competitor but hasn't started yet), consider using mediation or arbitration instead of filing a lawsuit. With mediation, rather than suing in court to ask a judge to decide who's right, the two sides sit down together with a neutral third party to try to reach a mutually acceptable resolution. With arbitration, the two sides agree to let a mutually selected, neutral third party decide the dispute for them. Since the agreements in this book don't require mediation or arbitration, you'll have to convince your former worker it's the right thing to do. However, since mediation and arbitration can save you both a lot of time, money and emotional energy, it might be worth it.

 Nolo's website (http://www.nolo.com) has lots of helpful information about mediation, including free encyclopedia articles about mediation such as "Why Consider Mediation?" "The Six Stages of Mediation" *and* "Getting the Other Side to the Mediation Table," *as well as* How to Mediate Your Dispute, *by Peter Lovenheim (Nolo), a comprehensive resource for guiding your dispute through mediation.*

If your ex-worker refuses to mediate or arbitrate your dispute, or the threat to your business is so dire you don't have time to convince your former worker to agree to mediation or arbitration and then select a mediator or an arbitrator, you and your attorney may decide to go ahead and file a lawsuit. This lawsuit will probably ask the judge for a temporary restraining order (TRO) or a preliminary injunction (see "Different Types of Court Orders," in Section A1, above) to stop your former worker from violating the agreement. Your lawyer will advise you during this process, and may try to inform the employee or independent contractor that you are about to file a lawsuit—to see if the threat of litigation convinces the worker to stop the offending behavior.

If you go to court, the judge will decide whether to grant a TRO or injunction or require you to go to trial to prove that you have suffered actual damages because of the competitor's conduct. A TRO or preliminary injunction may be granted in a matter of days or weeks, and can:

- prevent your former worker from beginning work with a new company until the case has been resolved, and/or
- prevent your former worker from disclosing any confidential information or trade secrets to a future employer and from soliciting any of your customers, clients or employees, pending the outcome of the case.

The court's decision to issue a TRO or preliminary injunction often determines the outcome of the entire case. That's because judges grant injunctions only if there is a likelihood that the party asking for the injunction will win the lawsuit. As a result, after a judge grants or denies the TRO or preliminary injunction, the parties often decide to settle. If the judge grants an injunction, the worker will probably be barred from starting work for the new employer or client and from engaging in the prohibited behavior until the case is settled or decided at a trial.

If the judge *denies* the injunction, you can still pursue your case against the worker and hope to get money damages, but the worker will be free to start a new job or engage in the behavior you sought to stop. In this case, you might be the one who's more interested in settling for something less than the full enforcement of your agreement (for instance, you might agree to not try to enforce the noncompetition clause if the employee agrees to abide by the nonsolicitation clause), because now you're facing a long and fairly expensive trial process if you press forward. If you requested a TRO or preliminary injunction and didn't get one, you know that it's unlikely you'll succeed at trial.

How Injunctions Are Granted

The cases described below will help you understand some of the factors that go into a judge's decision whether to grant an injunction.

The employer in *The Hunter Group, Inc. v. Smith*, 1998 Westlaw 682154 (4th Cir.), was not successful in convincing a judge to put a fast halt to a former worker's behavior. The Hunter Group terminated the employee, Smith, who used to instruct Hunter's Education Services Group consultants on using PeopleSoft software. Shortly after being fired, Smith took a similar position at Deloitte, a direct competitor of Hunter's, in a similar capacity. Four other Hunter employees joined Deloitte's consulting group, taking jobs that were nearly identical to their jobs at Hunter. All five employees had signed noncompete agreements with Hunter.

Hunter sued, alleging violation of the noncompete agreements and other legal theories. The court granted Hunter's motion for a temporary restraining order but reversed itself later. Hunter appealed and lost.

The appellate court acknowledged that Hunter had been harmed when it lost the five employees, almost half of Hunter's 12-member Education Services Group. But the court decided that the source of the harm was not the departure of the employees, but the fact that Hunter hadn't trained enough consultants with the necessary expertise in PeopleSoft. Enjoining the individual defendants from performing consulting services at Deloitte would not remedy the scarcity of consultants at Hunter.

By contrast, here's a case where the judge granted an injunction. In *New England Circuit Sales Inc. v. Randall*, 1996 Westlaw 1171929 (D. Ma.), a judge prevented an executive who had worked for an e-commerce company from working for a competing Internet sales firm. Randall, the executive, began working for the company in June 1994, first as director of new business development and later as general manager of its direct sales. Randall twice signed employment agreements containing noncompetition and nondisclosure provisions, including a prohibition on working for a competitor for one year after leaving.

Randall resigned in February 1996, and the following month he accepted an employment offer from Internet Shopping Network (ISN), a direct competitor. His old company filed suit to enforce its noncompete agreements.

Citing the contents of an ISN press release, the judge found that Randall intended to use the confidential information he acquired from his old company in his new employment. The press release detailed upcoming changes and improvements to ISN's website, which were substantially similar to the content management techniques in place at NECX, which gave NECX an edge in the industry and which Randall had been privy to during his employment by NECX.

Without an injunction, the judge said, NECX would suffer irreparable injury because it would be extremely difficult to assess the amount of the damage NECX would incur after the fact. Further, without an injunction, the noncompete would be useless because its duration was only one year after Randall left NECX, and a trial would take place after the one-year period expired. The judge noted that the noncompete agreement was reasonable because it only prevented Randall from working for a business "substantially" similar to NECX's and only prevented Randall from working for a year.

The judge decided that Randall's noncompete agreement was enforceable because it protected a legitimate business interest and was reasonable in scope (legal requirements for enforceability in Massachusetts). The court also decided that because Randall had been exposed to highly confidential information in a "fast-emerging, even revolutionary, industry," the noncompetition and nondisclosure clauses were necessary to protect the plaintiff's legitimate business interests.

Step 6. File a Lawsuit Against the New Employer or Hiring Firm

If your company has a lot at stake, you and your lawyer might decide to sue the worker's new employer or client. You're most likely to consider this route if the new company is a dreaded competitor that hired your worker away, hoping to learn your secrets or steal your clients and customers.

Of course, the new employer or client was not a party to the noncompete agreement between you and the worker. Still, there are other separate legal actions, including misappropriation of trade secrets, unfair competition and interference with a contract, which you can bring against the new employer if necessary (these are some of the same legal rights you have against the worker, which we discussed in Section A, above).

In all likelihood, if you bring a lawsuit against the worker, your lawyer will advise you to bring suit against the new employer or client at the same time. The judge hearing the matters will probably combine the two lawsuits.

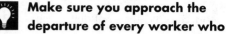 **Make sure you approach the departure of every worker who has signed a noncompete agreement the same way.** *If your enforcement of noncompete agreements against former workers is inconsistent, it will be more difficult for you to prove to a judge that you've been responsible about protecting your secrets, and as a result, the judge will be less inclined to rule in your favor.* ■

8

Help Beyond This Book

Throughout this book, we've flagged several situations in which it might be in your best interests to talk to an employment lawyer. That doesn't mean you can't use one of the forms in this book to prepare a comprehensive, solidly drafted noncompete agreement on your own. What it does mean is that you may encounter a few issues you'll need to talk to a lawyer about, particularly those that have to do with your state's specific laws. For example, as we just discussed in Chapter 7, if a departing worker shows every sign of disregarding your noncompete agreement, it can be wise to speak to a lawyer.

Fortunately, getting quality, inexpensive legal help is getting easier, but you still have to do some research to find the right lawyer. In this chapter, we provide you with a few tips and pointers on how to find a good lawyer—an employment law expert who thoroughly understands noncompete agreements—who will review your agreement or help you sue a former worker, without draining your bank account.

A. The "Legal Coach" Arrangement

Rather than hiring a lawyer to draft your noncompete agreement from scratch—leaving you with a document full of legalese that you can't read and can't afford—we suggest that you hire a lawyer who's willing to be your "legal coach." A legal coach is a lawyer who's willing to let you do most of the legwork in creating your agreement, but will be available to review your agreement and answer questions when you reach an impasse or encounter a complicated area of law.

The amount of work you hand over to a legal coach is up to you. Many small business owners find that it makes sense to teach themselves a good working knowledge of the legal basics surrounding employment issues (which seem to come up daily) and to talk to their lawyer only when they have a question that needs answering or a document that needs reviewing. Fortunately, legal information and resources are becoming easy to find on the Internet (see Section B, below). Many small business publications and trade associations also regularly publish helpful materials.

1. When to Use a Legal Coach

Throughout this book, we noted issues about which you should consult a lawyer. As a review, you might want to talk to an attorney if you:

- aren't sure what business information qualifies as a trade secret
- don't know which employees or contractors should be asked to sign noncompete agreements
- have a business in one of the states we discussed in Chapter 2, Section B1 (employees), and Chapter 2, Sec-

tion B2 (independent contractors), which have strict laws regarding noncompete agreements

- want to create an employment agreement for a fixed term
- want to add a work-for-hire clause or arbitration clause to an employee or contractor's noncompete agreement (see Chapter 6, Section F), or
- think an employee or contractor has violated, or is about to violate, your agreement.

2. How to Hire a Lawyer Who's Willing to Be Your Legal Coach

Many lawyers are not comfortable with the "legal coach" model, which has become acceptable only in the last decade. For example, some lawyers won't review documents you've created using self-help materials, since there is not enough profit in it to justify their trouble and malpractice risk.

To save yourself time and money, when you call a lawyer, make it clear that you are looking for someone who will help you help yourself. (See Section B, below, for tips on getting referrals to lawyers.) If the lawyer has a problem with this kind of relationship, keep shopping—plenty of good, local lawyers are anxious to find more business clients.

When you find a lawyer who seems agreeable to the arrangement you've proposed, ask if you can meet with the lawyer for a half-hour or so. During the in-person interview, discuss important issues such as the lawyer's experience and customary charges for services, as explained in Section C, below. Pay particular attention to the rapport between you and the lawyer— if you don't get along or you find the lawyer's personality or style objectionable, it will continue to drive you crazy. Unless you're dealing with an expert whom no one can replace, you might want to move on.

Remember, you are looking for a legal advisor who will work *with* you. Trust your instincts and seek a lawyer whose personality and business sense are compatible with your own. For instance, don't hire a lawyer who keeps you waiting for a long time, doesn't return your phone call within a day or so or is otherwise distracted or less than polite during your initial meeting.

If you already have a lawyer whom you turn to for help with routine small business matters, ask her if she's experienced with employment law matters and would be willing to review a document that you put together using self-help materials.

 A small business lawyer is not always an employment law expert. *Unless your small business lawyer spends a significant amount of time on employment law issues, and specifically on noncompete agreements (or nondisclosure/nonsolicitation agreements), ask for a referral to an employment law expert. Don't*

let your lawyer convince you that she can handle it even though she doesn't have much employment law experience. And don't be put off by the expense of hiring an "expert"—although an employment law expert might charge a slightly higher hourly rate than a general small business lawyer, you'll pay for less of the expert's time since you won't have to pay for your lawyer to learn an unfamiliar area of law.

B. Finding a Lawyer

When looking for an employment law expert, the best approach is to ask your own small business lawyer (if you have one). Your lawyer may routinely refer employment law issues to a friend or business acquaintance. And, since your lawyer will want to keep your business, you're likely to be steered towards someone who meets your criteria (knowledgeable, helpful and reasonable).

If you don't already have a small business lawyer or the one you have can't make a recommendation, ask people who own or operate efficiently run businesses of comparable size and scope to yours. You'll be banking on the assumption that a successful businessperson knows how to pick a good lawyer, too. If the businessperson you talk to has successfully used an employment lawyer to draft employment or noncompete agreements, so much the better.

If you talk to several businesspeople, chances are you'll come away with some good leads. And, of course, other knowledgeable people in your network, such as your banker, accountant, insurance agent or real estate broker may be able to provide the names of lawyers whom they trust to help them with employment matters.

How shouldn't you search for a lawyer? Don't just pick a name out of a phone book, legal directory or advertisement—you really have no way of knowing what you will be getting. Lawyer referral services operated by bar associations are usually equally unhelpful. Often, these services simply supply the names of lawyers who have signed on to the service for a fee and accept the lawyer's word for what types of skills she has. Additionally, many good, successful lawyers who already have enough business don't sign up for these services.

What about looking for a lawyer online? Many lawyers have their own websites, and there are a number of online lawyer directories. Although none of these can replace the knowledgeable recommendation of a savvy businessperson, some of the better websites have the potential to become useful places to convey information about lawyers. While we can't specifically recommend any of the online directories (none of them do a great job of providing practical information about lawyers yet), keep an eye out for sites that:

- provide in-depth biographical information about each lawyer. You want to know where the lawyers went to school, how long they have been in practice, what their specialties are and whether they have advanced training in employment law, have published articles or books on the subject or are a member of relevant trade organizations, and

- give you helpful information about how the listed lawyers like to practice. For example, if a lawyer's bio or statement emphasizes helping small businesspeople understand the legal information they need to actively participate in solving their own legal problems, you may wish to set up an appointment.

 Verify information using your state bar association's website.
In many states, you can confirm an attorney's background information (bar admission date and schools attended) on the state bar association's website. Most of these sites will also tell you if the lawyer has a record of bar discipline. If the lawyer you're interested in isn't a member of the bar in your state or has a record of discipline, keep looking.

C. Paying for a Lawyer

Few small business people can afford to buy all of the legal information they need at upwards of $200 per hour. The fact that you are reading this book is good evidence that you understand the need to obtain as much legal information on your own as possible and use a lawyer only when you require added negotiating, drafting or litigating skills. For most day-to-day legal concerns, you need only a legal coach or mentor adept at helping you help yourself, not someone who wants to mail you a bill every Friday.

1. How Much Should It Cost?

For each job you ask a lawyer to do, such as reviewing your noncompete agreement, ask how much it will cost. If the lawyer hems and haws and won't give you at least a ballpark estimate, keep looking. It means that lawyer doesn't know what he's doing or is unwilling to acknowledge that you're on a budget.

If the lawyer gives you a price that you feel is too high, say so. With this book, you should be able to learn about most of the legal issues and do most of the routine work of creating a noncompete agreement yourself, which should reduce the lawyer's fee.

Find out who will be working on your project or case—lawyers often offload work to legal assistants, paralegals or less experienced associates. If you're going to pay the attorney's hourly rate, make sure you are actually getting the attorney's time. If others will work on your matter and you're trying to negotiate a flat rate for your project, make sure it's based on the hourly rates of the people who will actually be working on the project and the estimated time each will spend working on it.

2. Billing Increments

When you approach a lawyer, it's important to be up-front about money and to get a clear understanding about how and when you'll be charged. For example, if you call a lawyer from time to time for general advice or to be steered to a good information source, how will you be billed? Some lawyers bill a flat amount for a call or a meeting; others bill to the nearest six-, ten- or 20-minute interval. (This means that if you talk to a lawyer for two minutes on the phone, you may billed for six, ten or 20 minutes.)

Whatever the lawyer's billing system, you need to understand it. If you're uncomfortable with the system, ask to be billed in shorter time increments or to pay a flat fee for the project. Many lawyers are willing to negotiate, but you'll never know if you don't ask. Frankly, at $200 or so per hour, we think it's silly to pay for 20 min-

utes of a lawyer's time if you need only six or 12 minutes.

Although it might seem counterintuitive, don't call your lawyer every time you have a question. Unless your question is urgent, schedule a time each week or month to speak to your lawyer. As issues and questions occur to you, jot them down. Save your list of questions to ask when you and your attorney speak.

To show you how this can save you some money, let's assume you have three minor questions you want to ask your attorney. Suppose she bills in ten-minute increments and charges $240 an hour (that's $40 for every ten minutes!). If you call your lawyer to ask each question separately, and you spend six minutes on the first call, three minutes on the second, and eight minutes on the third, you'll get charged $40 each time, or $120 for all three calls. But if you save all three questions for one 17-minute phone call, you'll only pay $80 (the charge for a 20-minute phone call). Over time, the savings will add up. And, believe it or not, your attorney—whose phone rings off the hook all day—will be happy to use time with you more efficiently.

3. Written Fee Agreements

Especially if you're hiring a lawyer to help with a significant legal problem (for example, bringing a lawsuit against a former employee), it's a good idea to get your fee arrangement in writing. In several states, fee agreements between lawyers and clients must be in writing only if the expected fee is $1,000 or more (or if the fee is contingent on the outcome of the lawsuit). But required or not, it's a good idea to get put your fee arrangement in writing.

Make sure your written fee agreement records the hourly rates of the attorney, plus those of any other people who might work on your matter. If you don't want the attorney to hand off the work to others with less experience, speak up before you sign the agreement—once you've signed the agreement, it will be difficult, if not impossible, to change it.

When you get a fee agreement from an attorney, read the fine print. While you and your lawyer may settle on an agreeable hourly fee, you may be shocked to find out how much you're charged for seemingly mundane things like photocopying, faxing, overnight delivery and courier services, as well as long-distance calls. Many lawyers mark up their costs for performing all of these services—they call this "overhead." (Lawyers *love* faxing—they often charge $1.00 a page!—as well as using expensive couriers and overnight delivery services.) This markup is especially true of large law firms who are often able to negotiate volume discounts on long-distance and overnight delivery service rates, but rarely pass this discount along to their clients. If a listed cost seems excessively high, say so—you may get the attorney to lower it or waive it altogether.

Make sure that any charges for such items will be put in written statements or invoices, and don't hesitate to make it clear that unless it's life-threatening or urgent, you'd like documents sent to you by regular old U.S. mail or, if you're tech-savvy, by email.

4. Agreeing to Arbitration

Like many people, including doctors, dentists and contractors, attorneys are choosing alternatives to court, such as arbitration or mediation, to resolve disputes with their clients. It's very possible that your attorney's fee agreement will contain an arbitration clause, which will require you to waive your right to sue in court. You'll have to submit any disputes, including malpractice claims, to an out-of-court arbitrator.

Arbitration and mediation can save you thousands of dollars in legal fees and can help you solve a problem much faster than if you went to court. But before you agree to arbitrate all disputes with your attorney, make sure you read any arbitration clause carefully to make sure it doesn't contain any nasty surprises. For instance, the arbitration clause may require you to pay for all of the legal bills—including those of the lawyer—if you lose the dispute. If it does, negotiate to have the arbitrator decide who pays legal fees.

5. Deposits

Many lawyers will ask you for money up front before they start working. This is sometimes called a "retainer" or a deposit. These up-front fees often range from $1,000 to $5,000, but can be any amount. Some firms require the same amount for all clients, some tailor the amount of the deposit to the complexity of the matter and some ask for deposits depending on how the attorney feels about the client or the case. (If an attorney is uncomfortable taking a client's case, it's not unusual to ask for a very large, unreasonable fee, which makes it possible to turn the client away without actually having to say "no.")

The attorney uses this money to pay the hourly fees plus the costs incurred representing you. Ethical rules require attorneys to place your money in a separate "trust account" and to provide you, the client, with detailed information about it, including regular statements detailing how the money is being spent and how much money is left.

We don't recommend paying large deposits if you can help it. Why? Because once you fork over the money and the attorney starts working, if you are not satisfied with the lawyer's work, you'll have a tough time getting even a partial refund. Far better to pay for a few hours of the lawyer's time and go from there.

⚠ Never send a large deposit to a lawyer whom you've met only over the phone. *With the increase in Internet and Yellow Pages advertising, it's easier than ever for people to find lawyers, but it's also easier to get burned. Don't write a check until you've met a lawyer face to face and have reached an agreement on fees. Sadly, lots of people have shelled out large amounts of money to attorneys they've never met, who don't show up for a critical meeting or vanish altogether—with the money, of course.*

6. The Attorney/Client Relationship

Some attorneys and clients hit it off and become very friendly over the course of their relationship. While this may sound attractive, it will probably not happen for you. If you hire a lawyer, you two will probably be on a purely professional footing—and that's it. But, while your lawyer is not your best friend, he does owe you a few duties, which you should understand before you delve into the details of your business and legal problem.

a. Confidentiality and Attorney/Client Privilege

If you've watched even one legal television show, you probably know about the attorney's duty of confidentiality and the attorney/client privilege. The duty of confidentiality is the ethical rule that requires your attorney to keep everything you say confidential. The attorney/client privilege means that your attorney cannot reveal anything you've told your attorney in a court of law, even if the lawyer's been subpoenaed (ordered to come to court and testify). Lawyers can be disbarred (lose their license to practice law) if they violate either rule.

The privilege and confidentiality requirements extend to other people who work in your attorney's firm. These protections do not, however, cover information that is public knowledge. Nor will they protect you if you yourself reveal the information to someone other than your lawyer (or in some states, your spouse). Losing the protections this way is known as "waiving" them.

Most lawyers are very concerned about client confidentiality and go to great lengths to protect it. You can usually rest easy when you disclose confidential business information to your lawyer, because most lawyers are not about to disclose it to the rest of the world.

 Listen to what your lawyer says about *other* clients. *While it's unusual, it's not unheard of for a lawyer to get lazy about protecting clients' information, particularly if it makes a good story. Don't let your woes become the next tale—look elsewhere for a lawyer.*

b. Conflict of Interest and Business Clients

When an individual hires a lawyer for a personal matter, such as a divorce or for representation in a criminal case, the attorney represents that person alone—which means that the attorney's advice must be geared towards that person's best interests and no one else's. And if you're a sole proprietor, you and your business are indistinguishable, as far as the lawyer is concerned. But when a partnership or company, such as a corporation or limited liability company, hires a lawyer, whom does the lawyer represent then?

When you hire a lawyer to represent your business, it's important to understand that in most states, by law, your attorney owes a duty of loyalty to the entity—the business—not the person who works for or even founded the company. This doesn't matter so much if you run your business by yourself (whether as a sole proprietorship or a limited liability company), because generally your personal interests and your company's interests are the same.

However, if you operate your business with other people—whether as a partnership, corporation or a limited liability company—there's a chance that what's good for the company isn't good for one of the owners, individually. For instance, if you operate your business as a partnership with another person and you hire an attorney to negotiate a commercial lease, the attorney is obligated to do what's best for the partnership. If one partner's best friend owns the building and that partner wants the friend to receive high rent, the lawyer is still obligated to negotiate a lower price, because that's what's best for the partnership.

This also means that if you and your partner disagree about a particular course of action for your business, your attorney will do only what both of you agree should be done, not what one of you tells the lawyer to do. Don't expect your attorney to take sides in a dispute between the two of you, because she can't. You might be able to air your differences, but in the end the lawyer may recommend that each of you get your own personal lawyers to work out the problem.

Sometimes you will want the lawyer to represent your business *and* its owners, individually. If you request this, your lawyer will probably ask you to sign something called a "conflict waiver." This waiver is necessary because ethical rules normally prevent lawyers from representing a client whose interests are or might be different from another client's.

There's another rule concerning your lawyer's duties that you should be aware of. A lawyer who represents a business entity usually has no duty to keep information among business owners or employees confidential. That means that legally and ethically, your attorney is not required to keep the information you've

shared a secret from your business partner, and may even be required to inform your business partner if not doing so would harm the organization. Similarly, if you and your partner get into a dispute that leads to a court battle, your lawyer can probably reveal anything you told the lawyer. So think twice before you start spouting off to your lawyer about how you're going to clean out the corporate bank account and move to Rio.

D. Doing Self-Help Research

Law is information, not magic. If you can look up necessary information yourself, you need not purchase it from a lawyer. Finding basic employment law information is not difficult. Much of the research necessary to understand your state's laws on noncompete agreements can be done by using the Internet.

Of course, interpreting typically obtuse legal language can be difficult, so if important issues are involved, it can make sense to check your conclusions with a lawyer. If you have energy and time, you can read one of the professional practice manuals or treatises lawyers often rely on.

Almost every county has a law library that's open to the public, as do many public or state universities with law schools. Ask a law librarian for help finding these manuals and treatises. Two of the major legal publishers are Reed-Elsevier and West

Publishing. In California, CEB (Continuing Education of the Bar) publishes a number of useful treatises on California law. Your law librarian can point you to the clearest, best-written summaries of the law.

In doing legal research for your business, there are a number of sources for legal rules, procedures and issues you may wish to examine. Here are a few:

- **State laws on noncompete agreements.** These state laws should be your primary focus for finding the rules a state has adopted regarding noncompete agreements. (But note that many states do not have any written laws on noncompete agreements.) We've summarized all of the noncompete laws that do exist in Chapter 2, Section B1, and Chapter 4, Section C2, and provide the full text of each one in Appendix 2. You can also go to Nolo's Legal Research Center to find them, at http://www.nolo.com/research/index.html.

- **Other state laws, such as trade secrets laws and business and labor laws.** These laws govern the rights and duties of employers and employees. You can go to Nolo's Legal Research Center to find the website for your state's laws, then search for the particular law you need.

- **Federal laws.** The Economic Espionage Act of 1996 created federal criminal and civil penalties for stealing or misusing trade secrets. You can find this law by going to the federal laws page in Nolo's Legal Research Center and using the U.S. Code search box or the Code of Federal Regulations search box.

- **Secondary sources.** Also important in researching business law are sources that provide background information on particular areas of law. One example is this book. Others are commonly found in the business, legal or reference section of your local library or bookstore (for example, see the Nolo small business and employment titles in the next section).

E. Nolo Employment and Small Business Resources

A good place to start when you have a legal question is always Nolo's Online Legal Encyclopedia (http://www.nolo.com/encyclopedia/index.html). It contains a lot of free, helpful information on all sorts of business and employment topics. Also on Nolo's website you can check our answers to Frequently Asked Questions (FAQs)—a collection of answers to over one thousand of the questions our customers ask most often.

For further learning, below are several titles published by Nolo that offer valuable employment law information to small business owners:

- *The Employer's Legal Handbook*, by Fred S. Steingold. The most complete guide to your legal rights and responsibilities, this book shows you how to comply with the most recent workplace laws and regulations, run a safe and fair workplace and avoid employee lawsuits.
- *Hiring Independent Contractors: An Employer's Legal Guide*, by Stephen Fishman. This book shows you how to safely hire independent contractors based on the most recent IRS rules, assess who qualifies as an independent contractor, hire ICs without risking a tax audit, retain ownership of intellectual property when using contractors, handle an IRS audit and take advantage of the IRS's "Safe Harbor" law.
- *Dealing With Problem Employees: A Legal Guide*, by Amy DelPo and Lisa Guerin. This book helps employers investigate employee problems, apply progressive discipline to employees and fire employees safely, if necessary.
- *Firing Without Fear*, by Barbara Kate Repa. This book helps make the event of "dropping the ax" as even-handed and fair-minded as possible by explaining the laws, the myths and the realities of firing. Its commonsense advice and pragmatic tips help bring civility to the process, and its clear explanations of

the laws help define the legal dos and don'ts involved.

In addition, Nolo offers a whole host of small business titles that help you accomplish everyday business tasks without the help of a lawyer, from protecting your intellectual property to preparing minutes for your corporation. They include:

- *Quicken Lawyer Business*. This software provides the legal information and forms you need on your desktop. Features the text of seven best-selling Nolo books:
  - *Legal Guide for Starting & Running a Small Business*
  - *Legal Forms for Starting & Running a Small Business*
  - *The Employer's Legal Handbook*
  - *Domain Names*
  - *Tax Savvy for Small Business*
  - *How to Write a Business Plan*
  - *Marketing Without Advertising*.
- *Nondisclosure Agreements: Protect Your Trade Secrets & More*, by Stephen Fishman and Richard Stim. This book provides several nondisclosure agreements you can use to protect your trade secrets, whether you're dealing with potential business partners, lenders, employees or licensees.
- *Trademark: Legal Care for Your Business & Product Name*, by Stephen Elias. In this book, you'll learn how to choose distinctive trademarks that competitors can't

copy, search for other trademarks that might conflict with your own, register your name or other trademark with the U.S. Patent & Trademark Office, protect your marks from use by others and apply trademark law to domain names and Web pages.

- *Legal Guide to Starting & Running a Small Business*, by Fred S. Steingold. This book is an essential resource for every small business owner, whether just starting out or already established. Find out the basics about forming a business, negotiating a favorable lease, hiring and firing employees, writing contracts and resolving business disputes.

- *Legal Forms for Starting & Running a Small Business*, by Fred S. Steingold. A companion to *Legal Guide to Starting & Running a Small Business*, this book contains all the forms you need to accomplish a variety of daily legal tasks, from leasing commercial space to renting equipment. All forms are provided as tear-outs and on CD-ROM.

- *Leasing Space for Your Small Business*, by Janet Portman and Fred S. Steingold. An in-depth explanation of how to asses your needs for commercial space, evaluate potential rentals, choose and work with brokers and lawyers, understand complex leasing clauses and terms and negotiate for the best deal.

- *Your Limited Liability Company: An Operating Manual*, by Anthony Mancuso. Provides ready-to-use forms for holding formal LLC meetings and recording minutes; and contains forms and information for formally approving legal, tax and other important business decisions that arise in the course of operating an LLC. All forms are provided as tear-outs and on CD-ROM.

- *LLC Maker*, by Anthony Mancuso. Windows 95/98 software that assembles LLC articles of organization (or certificates of formation or organization) according to each state's legal requirements, plus an LLC operating agreement and other LLC formation paperwork. Includes extensive legal and program help, plus state-by-state information screens— also automatically launches your Web browser to go straight to your state's LLC filing office website.

- *Incorporate Your Business*, by Anthony Mancuso. This book takes you through the process of forming a corporation in every state, including filing articles of incorporation, creating corporate bylaws, appointing directors to the board, holding and keeping minutes of the first organizational meeting of the board of directors and complying with securities laws.

- *The Corporate Minutes Book: The Legal Guide to Taking Care of Corporate Business*, by Anthony Mancuso. Because meeting minutes are the primary paper trail of a corporation's legal life, it's important to know when and how to prepare corporate minutes. This book provides all the answers, instructions and forms you need to get the job done. All forms provided as tear-outs and on CD-ROM.
- *Tax Savvy for Small Business*, by Frederick W. Daily. This book gives business owners information about federal taxes and explains how to make the best tax decisions for business, maximize profits and stay out of trouble with the IRS.

- *How to Create a Buy-Sell Agreement & Control the Destiny of Your Small Business*, by Anthony Mancuso and Bethany K. Laurence. This book shows you how to adopt comprehensive buy-sell provisions to handle the purchase and sale of ownership interests in an LLC, partnership or corporation when an owner withdraws, dies, becomes disabled or wishes to sell an interest to an outsider. It comes with an easy-to-use agreement—simply check the appropriate options, then fill in the blanks. The buy-sell agreement is included as a tear-out and on CD-ROM. ■

Appendix 1

How to Use the CD-ROM

The tear-out forms in Appendix 3, as well as other forms discussed in this book, are included on a CD-ROM in the back of the book. This CD-ROM, which can be used with Windows computers, installs files that can be opened, printed and edited using a word processor or other software. It is *not* a stand-alone software program. Please read this Appendix and the README.TXT file included on the CD-ROM for instructions on using the Forms CD.

Note to Mac users: This CD-ROM and its files should also work on Macintosh computers. Please note, however, that Nolo cannot provide technical support for non-Windows users.

How to View the README File

If you do not know how to view the file README.TXT, insert the Forms CD-ROM into your computer's CD-ROM drive and follow these instructions:

- Windows 9x, 2000 and ME: (1) On your PC's desktop, double-click the My Computer icon; (2) double-click the icon for the CD-ROM drive into which the Forms CD-ROM was inserted; (3) double-click the file README.TXT.

- Macintosh: (1) On your Mac desktop, double-click the icon for the CD-ROM that you inserted; (2) double-click on the file README.TXT.

While the README file is open, print it out by using the Print command in the File menu.

A. Installing the Form Files Onto Your Computer

Word processing forms that you can open, complete, print and save with your word processing program (see Section B, below) are contained on the CD-ROM. Before you can do anything with the files on the CD-ROM, you need to install them onto your hard disk. In accordance with U.S. copyright laws, remember that copies of the CD-ROM and its files are for your personal use only.

Insert the Forms CD and do the following:

1. Windows 9x, 2000 and ME Users

Follow the instructions that appear on the screen. (If nothing happens when you insert the Forms CD-ROM, then (1) double-click the My Computer icon; (2) double-click the icon for the CD-ROM drive into which the Forms CD-ROM was inserted; and (3) double-click the file WELCOME.EXE.)

By default, all the files are installed to the \Noncompete Forms folder in the \Program Files folder of your computer. A folder called "Noncompete Forms" is added to the "Programs" folder of the Start menu.

2. Macintosh Users

Step 1: If the "Noncompete Forms CD" window is not open, open it by double-clicking the "Noncompete Forms CD" icon.

Step 2: Select the "Noncompete Forms" folder icon.

Step 3: Drag and drop the folder icon onto the icon of your hard disk.

B. Using the Word Processing Files to Create Documents

This section concerns the files for forms that can be opened and edited with your word processing program.

All word processing forms come in rich text format. These files have the extension ".RTF." For example, the form for the General Employee Agreement discussed in Chapter 4 is on the file General.rtf. All forms and their filenames are listed at the beginning of Appendix 3.

RTF files can be read by most recent word processing programs including all versions of MS Word for Windows and Macintosh, WordPad for Windows, and recent versions of WordPerfect for Windows and Macintosh.

To use a form from the CD to create your documents you must: (1) open a file in your word processor or text editor; (2) edit the form by filling in the required information; (3) print it out; (4) rename and save your revised file.

The following are general instructions on how to do this. However, each word processor uses different commands to open, format, save and print documents. Please read your word processor's manual for specific instructions on performing these tasks.

Do not call Nolo's technical support if you have questions on how to use your word processor.

Step 1: Opening a File

There are three ways to open the word processing files included on the CD-ROM after you have installed them onto your computer.

- Windows users can open a file by selecting its "shortcut" as follows: (1) Click the Windows "Start" button; (2) open the "Programs" folder; (3) open the "Noncompete Forms" subfolder; (4) open the appropriate subfolder; and (5) click on the shortcut to the form you want to work with.
- Both Windows and Macintosh users can open a file directly by double-clicking on it. Use My Computer or Windows Explorer (Windows 9x, 2000 or ME) or the Finder (Macintosh) to go to the folder you

installed or copied the CD-ROM's files to. Then, double-click on the specific file you want to open.

- You can also open a file from within your word processor. To do this, you must first start your word processor. Then, go to the File menu and choose the Open command. This opens a dialog box where you will tell the program (1) the type of file you want to open (*.RTF); and (2) the location and name of the file (you will need to navigate through the directory tree to get to the folder on your hard disk where the CD's files have been installed). If these directions are unclear you will need to look through the manual for your word processing program—Nolo's technical support department will *not* be able to help you with the use of your word processing program.

Where Are the Files Installed?

Windows Users

- RTF files are installed by default to a folder named \Noncompete Forms in the \Program Files folder of your computer.

Macintosh Users

- RTF files are located in the "Noncompete Forms" folder.

Step 2: Editing Your Document

Fill in the appropriate information according to the instructions and sample agreements in the book. Underlines are used to indicate where you need to enter your information, frequently followed by instructions in brackets. *Be sure to delete the underlines and instructions from your edited document.* If you do not know how to use your word processor to edit a document, you will need to look through the manual for your word processing program—Nolo's technical support department will *not* be able to help you with the use of your word processing program.

Some of the forms have check boxes before text. The check boxes indicate:

- Optional text, where you choose whether to include or exclude the given text.

- Alternative text, where you select one alternative to include and exclude the other alternatives.

If you are using the tear-out forms in Appendix 3, you simply mark the appropriate box to make your choice.

If you are using the Forms CD, however, we recommend that instead of marking the check boxes, you do the following:

Optional text

If you don't want to include optional text, just delete it from your document.

If you do want to include optional text, just leave it in your document.

In either case, delete the check box itself as well as the italicized instructions that the text is optional.

Alternative text

First delete all the alternatives that you do not want to include.

Then delete the remaining check boxes, as well as the italicized instructions that you need to select one of the alternatives provided.

Step 3: Printing Out the Document

Use your word processor's or text editor's "Print" command to print out your document. If you do not know how to use your word processor to print a document, you will need to look through the manual for your word processing program—Nolo's technical support department will *not* be able to help you with the use of your word processing program.

Step 4: Saving Your Document

After filling in the form, use the "Save As" command to save and rename the file. Because all the files are "read-only" and you will not be able to use the "Save" command. This is for your protection. *If you save the file without renaming it, the underlines that indicate where you need to enter your information will be lost and you will not be able to create a new document with this file without recopying the original file from the CD-ROM.*

If you do not know how to use your word processor to save a document, you will need to look through the manual for your word processing program—Nolo's technical support department will *not* be able to help you with the use of your word processing program. ■

Appendix 2

Noncompete Statutes

The following is the full text of the state noncompete statutes we discuss throughout this book.

Alabama

Code of Alabama § 8-1-1. Contracts restraining business void; exceptions

(a) Every contract by which anyone is restrained from exercising a lawful profession, trade, or business of any kind otherwise than is provided by this section is to that extent void.

(b) One who sells the good will of a business may agree with the buyer and one who is employed as an agent, servant or employee may agree with his employer to refrain from carrying on or engaging in a similar business and from soliciting old customers of such employer within a specified county, city, or part thereof so long as the buyer, or any person deriving title to the good will from him, or employer carries on a like business therein.

(c) Upon or in anticipation of a dissolution of the partnership, partners may agree that none of them will carry on a similar business within the same county, city or town, or within a specified part thereof, where the partnership business has been transacted.

California

California Business and Professions Code § 16600. Void Contracts (Chapter 1 of the Business and Professions Code)

Except as provided in this chapter, every contract by which anyone is restrained from engaging in a lawful profession, trade, or business of any kind is to that extent void.

Colorado

Colorado Revisied Statutes § 8-2-113. Unlawful to intimidate workman— agreement not to compete

(1) It shall be unlawful to use force, threats, or other means of intimidation to prevent any person from engaging in any lawful occupation at any place he sees fit.

(2) Any covenant not to compete which restricts the right of any person to receive compensation for performance of skilled or unskilled labor for any employer shall be void, but this subsection (2) shall not apply to:

(a) Any contract for the purchase and sale of a business or the assets of a business;

(b) Any contract for the protection of trade secrets;

(c) Any contractual provision providing for recovery of the expense of educating and training an employee who has served an employer for a period of less than two years;

(d) Executive and management personnel and officers and employees who constitute professional staff to executive and management personnel.

(3) Any covenant not to compete provision of an employment, partnership, or corporate agreement between physicians which restricts the right of a physician to practice medicine, as defined in section 12-36-106, C.R.S., upon termination of such agreement, shall be void; except that

all other provisions of such an agreement enforceable at law, including provisions which require the payment of damages in an amount that is reasonably related to the injury suffered by reason of termination of the agreement, shall be enforceable. Provisions which require the payment of damages upon termination of the agreement may include, but not be limited to, damages related to competition.

Florida

Florida Statutes § 542.335 Valid restraints of trade or commerce.

(1) Notwithstanding § 542.18 and subsection (2), enforcement of contracts that restrict or prohibit competition during or after the term of restrictive covenants, so long as such contracts are reasonable in time, area, and line of business, is not prohibited. In any action concerning enforcement of a restrictive covenant:

(a) A court shall not enforce a restrictive covenant unless it is set forth in a writing signed by the person against whom enforcement is sought.

(b) The person seeking enforcement of a restrictive covenant shall plead and prove the existence of one or more legitimate business interests justifying the restrictive covenant. The term "legitimate business interest" includes, but is not limited to:

1. Trade secrets, as defined in § 688.002(4).

2. Valuable confidential business or professional information that otherwise does not qualify as trade secrets.

3. Substantial relationships with specific prospective or existing customers, patients, or clients.

4. Customer, patient, or client goodwill associated with:

    a. An ongoing business or professional practice, by way of trade name, trademark, service mark, or "trade dress";

    b. A specific geographic location; or

    c. A specific marketing or trade area.

5. Extraordinary or specialized training.

Any restrictive covenant not supported by a legitimate business interest is unlawful and is void and unenforceable.

(c) A person seeking enforcement of a restrictive covenant also shall plead and prove that the contractually specified restraint is reasonably necessary to protect the legitimate business interest or interests justifying the restriction. If a person seeking enforcement of the restrictive covenant establishes prima facie that the restraint is reasonably necessary, the person opposing enforcement has the burden of establishing that the contractually specified restraint is overbroad, overlong, or otherwise not reasonably necessary to protect the established legitimate business interest or interests. If a contractually specified restraint is overbroad, overlong, or otherwise not reasonably necessary to protect the legitimate business interest or interests, a court shall modify the restraint and grant only the relief reasonably necessary to protect such interest or interests.

(d) In determining the reasonableness in time of a postterm restrictive covenant not predicated upon the protection of trade secrets, a court shall apply the following rebuttable presumptions:

1. In the case of a restrictive covenant sought to be enforced against a former employee, agent, or independent contractor, and not associated with the sale of all or a part of:

    a. The assets of a business or professional practice, or

    b. The shares of a corporation, or

    c. A partnership interest, or

    d. A limited liability company membership, or

    e. An equity interest, of any other type, in a business or professional practice,

a court shall presume reasonable in time any restraint 6 months or less in duration and shall presume unreasonable in time any restraint more than 2 years in duration.

2. In the case of a restrictive covenant sought to be enforced against a former distributor, dealer, franchisee, or licensee of a trademark or service mark and not associated with the sale of all or a part of:

    a. The assets of a business or professional practice, or

    b. The shares of a corporation, or

    c. A partnership interest, or

    d. A limited liability company membership, or

    e. An equity interest, of any other type, in a business or professional practice,

    a court shall presume reasonable in time any restraint 1 year or less in duration and shall presume unreasonable in time any restraint more than 3 years in duration.

3. In the case of a restrictive covenant sought to be enforced against the seller of all or a part of:

    a. The assets of a business or professional practice, or

    b. The shares of a corporation, or

    c. A partnership interest, or

    d. A limited liability company membership, or

    e. An equity interest, of any other type, in a business or professional practice,

    a court shall presume reasonable in time any restraint 3 years or less in duration and shall presume unreasonable in time any restraint more than 7 years in duration.

(e) In determining the reasonableness in time of a postterm restrictive covenant predicated upon the protection of trade secrets, a court shall presume reasonable in time any restraint of 5 years or less and shall presume unreasonable in time any restraint of more than 10 years. All such presumptions shall be rebuttable presumptions.

(f) The court shall not refuse enforcement of a restrictive covenant on the ground that the person seeking enforcement is a third-party beneficiary of such contract or is an assignee or successor to a party to such contract, provided:

    1. In the case of a third-party beneficiary, the restrictive covenant expressly identified the person as a third-party beneficiary of the contract and expressly stated that the restrictive covenant was intended for the benefit of such person.

    2. In the case of an assignee or successor, the restrictive covenant expressly authorized enforcement by a party's assignee or successor.

(g) In determining the enforceability of a restrictive covenant, a court:

1. Shall not consider any individualized economic or other hardship that might be caused to the person against whom enforcement is sought.

2. May consider as a defense the fact that the person seeking enforcement no longer continues in business in the area or line of business that is the subject of the action to enforce the restrictive covenant only if such discontinuance of business is not the result of a violation of the restriction.

3. Shall consider all other pertinent legal and equitable defenses.

4. Shall consider the effect of enforcement upon the public health, safety, and welfare.

(h) A court shall construe a restrictive covenant in favor of providing reasonable protection to all legitimate business interests established by the person seeking enforcement. A court shall not employ any rule of contract construction that requires the court to construe a restrictive covenant narrowly, against the restraint, or against the drafter of the contract.

(i) No court may refuse enforcement of an otherwise enforceable restrictive covenant on the ground that the contract violates public policy unless such public policy is articulated specifically by the court and the court finds that the specified public policy requirements substantially outweigh the need to protect the legitimate business interest or interests established by the person seeking enforcement of the restraint.

(j) A court shall enforce a restrictive covenant by any appropriate and effective remedy, including, but not limited to, temporary and permanent injunctions. The violation of an enforceable restrictive covenant creates a presumption of irreparable injury to the person seeking enforcement of a restrictive covenant. No temporary injunction shall be entered unless the person seeking enforcement of a restrictive covenant gives a proper bond, and the court shall not enforce any contractual provision waiving the requirement of an injunction bond or limiting the amount of such bond.

(k) In the absence of a contractual provision authorizing an award of attorney's fees and costs to the prevailing party, a court may award attorney's fees and costs to the prevailing party in any action seeking enforcement of, or challenging the enforceability of, a restrictive covenant. A court shall not enforce any contractual provision limiting the court's authority under this section.

(2) Nothing in this section shall be construed or interpreted to legalize or make enforceable any restraint of trade or com-

merce otherwise illegal or unenforceable under the laws of the United States or of this state.

(3) This act shall apply prospectively, and it shall not apply in actions determining the enforceability of restrictive covenants entered into before July 1, 1996.

Louisiana

Louisiana Revised Statutes Title 23 § 921. Restraint of business prohibited; restraint on forum prohibited; competing business; contracts against engaging in; provisions for

A. (1) Every contract or agreement, or provision thereof, by which anyone is restrained from exercising a lawful profession, trade, or business of any kind, except as provided in this Section, shall be null and void.

(2) The provisions of every employment contract or agreement, or provisions thereof, by which any foreign or domestic employer or any other person or entity includes a choice of forum clause or choice of law clause in an employee's contract of employment or collective bargaining agreement, or attempts to enforce either a choice of forum clause or choice of law clause in any civil or administrative action involving an employee, shall be null and void except where the choice of forum clause or choice of law clause is expressly, knowingly, and voluntarily agreed to and

ratified by the employee after the occurrence of the incident which is the subject of the civil or administrative action.

B. Any person, including a corporation and the individual shareholders of such corporation, who sells the goodwill of a business may agree with the buyer that the seller will refrain from carrying on or engaging in a business similar to the business being sold or from soliciting customers of the business being sold within a specified parish or parishes, or municipality or municipalities, or parts thereof, so long as the buyer, or any person deriving title to the goodwill from him, carries on a like business therein, not to exceed a period of two years from the date of sale.

C. Any person, including a corporation and the individual shareholders of such corporation, who is employed as an agent, servant, or employee may agree with his employer to refrain from carrying on or engaging in a business similar to that of the employer and/or from soliciting customers of the employer within a specified parish or parishes, municipality or municipalities, or parts thereof, so long as the employer carries on a like business therein, not to exceed a period of two years from termination of employment. An independent contractor, whose work is performed pursuant to a written contract, may enter into an agreement to refrain from carrying on or engaging in a business similar to the business of the person with whom the independent contractor has contracted, on the same basis as if the independent contractor were an employee, for a period not to exceed two years from the date of the last work performed under the written contract.

D. Upon or in anticipation of a dissolution of the partnership, the partnership and the individual partners, including a corporation and the individual shareholders if the corporation is a partner, may agree that none of the partners will carry on a similar business within the same parish or parishes, or municipality or municipalities, or within specified parts thereof, where the partnership business has been transacted, not to exceed a period of two years from the date of dissolution.

E. (1) Parties to a franchise may agree that:

(a) The franchisor shall refrain from selling, distributing, or granting additional franchises to sell or distribute, within defined geographic territory, those products or services which are the subject of the franchise.

(b) The franchisee shall:

(i) During the term of the franchise, refrain from competing with the franchisor or other franchisees of the franchisor or engaging in any other business similar to that which is the subject of the franchise.

(ii) For a period not to exceed two years following severance of the franchise relationship, refrain from engaging in any other business similar to that which is the subject of the franchise and from competing with or soliciting the customers of the franchisor or other franchisees of the franchisor.

(2) As used in this Subsection:

(a) "Franchise" means any continuing commercial relationship created by any arrangement or arrangements as defined in 16 Code of Federal Regulations 436.2(a).

(b) "Franchisee" means any person who participates in a franchise relationship as a franchisee, partner, shareholder with at least a ten percent interest in the franchisee, executive officer of the franchisee, or a person to whom an interest in a franchise is sold, as defined in 16 Code of Federal Regulations 436.2(d), provided that no person shall be included in this definition unless he has signed an agreement expressly binding him to the provisions thereof.

(c) "Franchisor" means any person who participates in a franchise relationship as a franchisor as defined in 16 Code of Federal Regulations 436.2(c).

F. (1) An employee may at any time enter into an agreement with his employer that, for a period not to exceed two years from the date of the termination of employment, he will refrain from engaging in any work or activity to design, write, modify, or implement any computer program that directly competes with any confidential computer program owned, licensed, or marketed by the employer, and to which the employee had direct access during the term of his employment or services.

(2) As used in this Subsection, "confidential" means that which:

(a) Is not generally known to and not readily ascertainable by other persons.

(b) Is the subject of reasonable efforts under the circumstances to maintain its secrecy.

(3) As used in this Subsection, "computer program" means a plan, routine, or set of statements or instructions, including any subset, subroutine, or portion of instructions, regardless of format or medium, which are capable, when incorporated into a machine-readable medium, of causing a computer to perform a particular task or function or achieve a particular result.

(4) As used in this Subsection, "employee" shall mean any individual, corporation, partnership, or any other entity which contracts or agrees with an employer to perform, provide, or furnish any services to, for, or on behalf of such employer.

G. Any agreement covered by Subsections B, C, D, E, or F of this Section shall be considered an obligation not to do, and failure to perform may entitle the obligee to recover damages for the loss sustained and the profit of which he has been deprived. In addition, upon proof of the obligor's failure to perform, and without the necessity of proving irreparable injury, a court of competent jurisdiction shall order injunctive relief enforcing the terms of the agreement.

Montana

Montana code § 28-2-703. Contracts in restraint of trade generally void

Any contract by which anyone is restrained from exercising a lawful profession, trade, or business of any kind, otherwise than is provided for by 28-2-704 or 28-2-705, is to that extent void.

North Dakota

North Dakota Century Code § 9-08-06. In restraint of business void—Exceptions.

Every contract by which anyone is restrained from exercising a lawful profession, trade, or business of any kind is to that extent void, except:

1. One who sells the goodwill of a business may agree with the buyer to refrain from carrying on a similar business within a specified county, city, or a part of either, so long as the buyer or any person deriving title to the goodwill from him carries on a like business therein.

2. Partners, upon or in anticipation of a dissolution of the partnership, may agree that all or any number of them will not

carry on a similar business within the same city where the partnership business has been transacted, or within a specified part thereof.

Oklahoma

Oklahoma State Statutes Title 15, § 217

Every contract by which any one is restrained from exercising a lawful profession, trade or business of any kind, otherwise than as provided by Sections 218 and 219 of this title, or otherwise than as provided by Section 2 of this act, is to that extent void.

Title 15, § 219A

A. A person who makes an agreement with an employer, whether in writing or verbally, not to compete with the employer after the employment relationship has been terminated, shall be permitted to engage in the same business as that conducted by the former employer or in a similar business as that conducted by the former employer as long as the former employee does not directly solicit the sale of goods, services or a combination of goods and services from the established customers of the former employer.

B. Any provision in a contract between an employer and an employee in conflict with the provisions of this section shall be void and unenforceable.

Oregon

Oregon Revised Statutes § 653.295. When noncompetition and bonus restriction agreements enforceable; applicability of restrictions

(1) A noncompetition agreement entered into between an employer and employee is void and shall not be enforced by any court in this state unless the agreement is entered into upon the:

(a) Initial employment of the employee with the employer; or

(b) Subsequent bona fide advancement of the employee with the employer.

(2) Subsection (1) of this section applies only to noncompetition agreements made in the context of an employment relationship or contract and not otherwise.

(3) (a) Subsection (1)(a) of this section applies only to noncompetition agreements entered into after July 22, 1977.

(b) Subsection (1)(b), subsections (4) and (5) and subsection (6)(a) of this section apply to employment relationships and bonus restriction agreements in effect or entered into after October 15, 1983.

(4) Subsection (1) of this section does not apply to bonus restriction agreements, which are lawful agreements that may be enforced by the courts in this state.

(5) Nothing in this section restricts the right of any person to protect trade secrets or other proprietary information by injunction or any other lawful means under other applicable laws.

(6) As used in this section:

(a) "Bonus restriction agreement" means an agreement, written or oral, express or implied, between an employer and employee under which:

(A) Competition by the employee with the employer is limited or restrained after termination of employment, but the restraint is limited to a period of time, a geographic area and specified activities, all of which are reasonable in relation to the services described in subparagraph (B) of this paragraph;

(B) The services performed by the employee pursuant to the agreement include substantial involvement in management of the employer's business, personal contact with customers, knowledge of customer requirements related to the employer's business or knowledge of trade secrets or other proprietary information of the employer; and

(C) The penalty imposed on the employee for competition against the employer is limited to forfeiture of profit sharing or other bonus compensation that has not yet been paid to the employee.

(b) "Employee" and "employer" have the meaning provided for those terms in ORS 652.310; and

(c) "Noncompetition agreement" means an agreement, written or oral, express or implied, between an employer and employee under which the employee agrees that the employee, either alone or as an employee of another person, shall not compete with the employer in providing products, processes or services, that are similar to the employer's products, processes or services for a period of time or within a specified geographic area after termination of employment.

South Dakota

South Dakota Codified Laws § 53-9-11 Employment contract—Covenants not to compete.

An employee may agree with an employer at the time of employment or at any time during his employment not to engage directly or indirectly in the same business or profession as that of his employer for any period not exceeding two years from the date of termination of the agreement and not to solicit existing customers of the employer within a specified county, first or second class municipality or other specified area for any period not exceeding two years from the date of termination of the agreement, if the employer continues to carry on a like business therein.

Texas

Texas Business and Commerce Code § 15.50. Criteria for enforceability of covenants not to compete

(a) Notwithstanding Section 15.05 of this code, and subject to any applicable provision of Subsection (b), a covenant not to compete is enforceable if it is ancillary to or part of an otherwise enforceable agreement at the time the agreement is made to the extent that it contains limitations as to time, geographical area, and scope of activity to be restrained that are reasonable and do not impose a greater restraint than is necessary to protect the goodwill or other business interest of the promisee.

(b) A covenant not to compete is enforceable against a person licensed as a physician by the Texas State Board of Medical Examiners if such covenant complies with the following requirements:

(1) the covenant must:

(A) not deny the physician access to a list of his patients whom he had seen or treated within one year of termination of the contract or employment;

(B) provide access to medical records of the physician's patients upon authorization of the patient and any copies of the medical records for a reasonable fee as established by the Texas State Board of Medical Examiners under Section 159.008, Occupations Code 5.08(o), Medical Practice Act (Article 4495b, Vernon's Texas Civil Statutes); and

(C) provide that any access to a list of patients or to patients' medical records after termination of the contract or employment shall not require such list or records to be provided in a format different than that by which such records are maintained except by mutual consent of the parties to the contract;

(2) the covenant must provide for a buy out of the covenant by the physician at a reasonable price or, at the option of either party, as determined by a mutually agreed upon arbitrator or, in the case of an inability to agree, an arbitrator of the court whose decision shall be binding on the parties; and

(3) the covenant must provide that the physician will not be prohibited from providing continuing care and treatment to a specific patient or patients during the course of an acute illness even after the contract or employment has been terminated. ■

Appendix 3

Forms for Businesses With Employees

Form	CD-ROM title
Form EMPL-1: Noncompetition, Nondisclosure and Nonsolicitation Agreement for IT Professionals	ITPro.rtf
Form EMPL-2: Noncompetition, Nondisclosure and Nonsolicitation Agreement for High-Level Executives With Access to Proprietary Information	Executive.rtf
Form EMPL-3: Noncompetition, Nondisclosure and Nonsolicitation Agreement for Salespeople	Sales.rtf
Form EMPL-4: Noncompetition, Nondisclosure and Nonsolicitation Agreement for Business Development or Marketing Managers	Marketing.rtf
Form EMPL-5: Noncompetition, Nondisclosure and Nonsolicitation Agreement for Research and Development Employees	ResDev.rtf
Form EMPL-6: General Noncompetition, Nondisclosure and Nonsolicitation Agreement	General.rtf
Form EMPL-7: Severance Agreement for Employee	Severance.rtf
Form EMPL-8: Amendment of Employee Agreement	Amendment.rtf

CD-ROM only.

Forms to Use With Independent Contractors

Form	CD-ROM title
● Form IC-1: Independent Contractor Agreement for Web Engineers/Designers	Web.rtf
● Form IC-2: Independent Contractor Agreement for Software Engineers/Beta Testers	Betatest.rtf
● Form IC-3: Independent Contractor Agreement for Salespeople	Sales.rtf
● Form IC-4: Independent Contractor Agreement for Brokers/Agents	Broker.rtf
● Form IC-5: Independent Contractor Agreement for Marketing/Market Research Consultants	Marketing.rtf
● Form IC-6: Independent Contractor Agreement for Research and Development Consultants	ResDev.rtf
● Form IC-7: Independent Contractor Agreement (General Agreement)	General.rtf
Form IC-8: Termination Agreement for Independent Contractor	Termination.rtf
Form IC-9: Amendment of Independent Contractor Agreement	Amendment.rtf

● CD-ROM only.

Form EMPL-6: General Noncompetition, Nondisclosure and Nonsolicitation Agreement

1. Introduction

This Agreement ("Agreement"), is made and entered into as of _____, _____ ,

between_____ ("Employee") and _____, a
_____ ("Company").

2. Purpose

Company is in the business of _____.

[ ]   Alternative # 1: New Employee

Company would like to employ Employee as its _____. Employee's duties
shall include _____. In exchange for Company's employing Employee, and
for other good and valuable consideration, the receipt and sufficiency of which is hereby
acknowledged, Company and Employee agree as follows:

[ ]   Alternative # 2: Existing Employee

Employee was previously employed by Company as its _____. Company would
like to employ Employee as its _____. Employee's duties shall include
_____. Employee will have greater responsibility and will have access to
Company's Confidential Information (as defined in this Agreement). In exchange for
Company's employing Employee as its _____, and for other good and
valuable consideration, the receipt and sufficiency of which is hereby acknowledged,
Company and Employee agree as follows:

3. Acknowledgment of At-Will Employment

Employee acknowledges that his or her employment with Company is at will and that
Company may terminate Employee at any time for any reason.

4. Nondisclosure of Confidential Information

a.   Company may need to disclose to Employee or give Employee access to Confidential
Information so that Employee may properly fulfill his or her duties to Company. "Confidential
Information" means Company's trade secrets, including, but not limited to, customer lists
(including names, addresses, attributes, requirements, special needs and other data); names,
locations of and agreements with vendors, suppliers and strategic business alliance partners;

contemplated new products or services; _____; or other information that is not generally known and from which the Company derives an economic benefit. The Confidential Information may be written, such as computer source code, programs, hardware and software, tapes, disks, documents, drawings, data or product specifications, or unwritten, such as unwritten knowledge, ideas, processes, practices or know-how. Confidential Information does not include information that is in the public domain, information that is generally known in Company's industry or information that Employee acquired completely independently of his or her services for Company.

b.   For as long as the Confidential Information is not generally known and the Company derives an economic benefit from the information, Employee shall not use or disclose to any other person or entity any Confidential Information or any copy or summary of any Confidential Information unless Employee is required to do so to perform Employee's duties to Company or as required by law.

c.   While Employee is employed by Company and afterward, Employee shall not remove or copy any Confidential Information or participate in any way in the removal or copying of any Confidential Information without Company's written consent. Employee shall immediately return to Company all Confidential Information when Employee's employment with the Company terminates, or any time Company requires such Confidential Information to be returned.

d.   Employee will not obtain or attempt to obtain any Confidential Information for any purpose whatsoever except as required by Company to enable Employee to perform his or her job duties.

e.   Employee will not disclose to Company or misuse any third party's trade secrets, including any trade secret information of Employee's former employer, _____, nor will Employee solicit any former employees or consultants of _____ on Company's behalf. Employee represents and warrants that the execution of this Agreement by Employee will not violate or conflict with the terms of any other agreement to which Employee is a party.

5.   Noncompetition

Employee agrees that in order to protect the Confidential Information described above, while Employee is employed by Company, and for a period of _____ [years/months] thereafter (collectively, the "Term"), Employee shall not:

a.   plan for, acquire any financial interest in or perform services for (as an employee, consultant, officer, director, independent contractor, principal, agent or otherwise) any business that would require Employee to use or disclose any Confidential Information, or

b.   perform services (as an employee, consultant, officer, director, independent contractor, principal, agent or otherwise) that are similar to Employee's current duties or responsibilities for any person or entity that, during the Term, engages in any business activity in which Company is then engaged or proposes to be engaged and that conducts its business in the Territory.

c.   "Territory" means

[]   Alternative # 1: General Territory

any geographic area in which Company conducts its business during the Term.

[]   Alternative # 2: Specific Territory

_____.

6.   Nonsolicitation

While Employee is employed by Company, and for a period of _____ [years/months] thereafter, Employee shall not:

a.   employ, attempt to employ or solicit for employment by any other person or entity, any Company employees;

b.   encourage any consultant, independent contractor or any other person or entity to end their relationship or stop doing business with Company, or help any person or entity do so or attempt to do so; or

c.   solicit or attempt to solicit or obtain business or trade from any of Company's current customers or clients with whom Employee had contact or about whom Employee acquired knowledge while employed by Company, or help any person or entity do so or attempt to do so.

7.   Right to an Injunction

Employee acknowledges that his or her services to Company are special and unique and that, while performing these services, Employee will have access to and Company may disclose to Employee the Confidential Information described above. Employee also acknowledges that his or her position in Company will place him or her in a position of confidence and trust with Company and its employees, clients and customers.

If Employee breaches or threatens to breach any of the provisions of Sections 4, 5 or 6 of this Agreement, Company will sustain irreparable harm. Company shall be entitled to an injunction to stop any breach or threatened breach of this Agreement, including the provisions of Sections 4, 5 or 6. Employee acknowledges and agrees that monetary damages would not adequately compensate Company for any breach or threatened breach of these sections and that if Company seeks injunctive relief to put an immediate halt to the offending conduct, Employee shall not claim that monetary damages would be an adequate remedy.

8. Reasonable Restrictions; Survivability

Employee acknowledges that the restrictions set forth in Sections 4, 5, 6 and 7 of this Agreement are reasonable and necessary for the protection of Company, its business and its Confidential Information. The provisions of Sections 4, 5, 6 and 7 of this Agreement shall survive the termination, for any reason, of Employee's employment with Company.

9. Severability

If a court determines that any provision of this Agreement is invalid or unenforceable, any invalidity or unenforceability will affect only that provision and shall not make any other provision of this Agreement invalid or unenforceable. Instead, such provision shall be modified, amended or limited to the extent necessary to render it valid and enforceable.

10. Applicable Law

This Agreement shall be governed by and construed in accordance with the laws of the State of _____.

11. Jurisdiction

Employee and Company consent to the exclusive jurisdiction and venue of the federal and state courts located in _____, _____, in any action arising out of or relating to this Agreement. Employee and Company waive any other venue to which either party might be entitled by domicile or otherwise.

12. Entire Agreement

This is the entire agreement between the parties. It supersedes and replaces any and all prior oral or written agreements between Company and Employee that relate to the matters covered by this Agreement.

13. Assignment; Binding Effect

This Agreement shall bind the Company's successors and assigns, and Company may assign this Agreement to any party at any time, in its sole discretion, without Employee's consent.

This Agreement shall bind Employee's heirs, successors and assignees. Employee shall not assign any of Employee's rights or obligations under this Agreement without Company's prior written consent.

14. Waiver

If Company waives any term or provision of this Agreement, that waiver shall be effective only in the specific instance and for the specific purpose for which Company gave the waiver. If Company fails to exercise or delays exercising any of its rights or remedies under this Agreement, Company retains the right to enforce that term or provision at a later time.

15. Amendment

This Agreement may be modified, changed or amended only in writing, and such writing must be signed by both parties.

16. Counterparts

The parties may execute this Agreement in counterparts, each of which shall be considered an original, and all of which shall constitute the same document.

IN WITNESS WHEREOF, the parties have executed this Agreement as of the day and year first written above in Section 1.

"Company"

_____, a _____

By: _____

_____

[type or print name]

Its: _____

"Employee"

_____

_____

[type or print name]

Form EMPL-7: Severance Agreement for Employee

1. Introduction

This severance agreement ("Agreement"), dated as of _____, _____,

is entered into by and between _____ ("Employee") and
_____, a _____ ("Company").

2. Purpose

Company is in the business of _____.

[ ]   Alternative # 1: Contracted Employee

Pursuant to an employment agreement dated as of _____, _____ ("Employment
Agreement"), Employee is currently employed by Company as its _____. Company
and Employee desire to terminate the Employment Agreement and Employee's employment
under the Employment Agreement on the terms and conditions set forth in this Agreement.

In exchange for the mutual covenants and agreements contained in this Agreement, and for
other good and valuable consideration, the receipt and sufficiency of which is hereby
acknowledged, Company and Employee agree as follows:

[ ]   Alternative # 2: At-Will Employee

Employee is employed by Company as its _____. Company and Employee desire
to terminate Employee's employment with Company on the terms and conditions set forth in
this Agreement.

In exchange for the mutual covenants and agreements contained in this Agreement, and for
other good and valuable consideration, the receipt and sufficiency of which is hereby
acknowledged, Company and Employee agree as follows:

3. Nondisclosure of Confidential Information

a.   While Employee has been employed by Company, Company has disclosed to
Employee or given Employee access to Confidential Information so that Employee could
properly fulfill his or her duties to Company.

[ ]   Alternative # 1: IT Professionals and Research & Development Employees

"Confidential Information" means Company's trade secrets, including, but not limited to, technology; equipment research, design and development; product formulas, pricing information, research, design and development; engineering or manufacturing processes or methods; database, website or network specifications or data; licensing arrangements; any titles, themes, stories, treatments, ideas, art work or logos; computer hardware and software; _____; or other information that is not generally known and from which the Company derives an economic benefit.

[ ]   Alternative # 2: High-Level Executives and Business Development/Marketing Managers

"Confidential Information" means Company's trade secrets, including, but not limited to, customer lists (including names, addresses, attributes, requirements, special needs and other data); business plans or strategies; advertising, marketing or publicity campaigns; credit information; sales projections; market research and analyses (including focus group or survey results); personnel and hiring information (including salary, sales commission and bonus data); names, locations of and agreements with vendors, suppliers and strategic business alliance partners; accounting or financial data; licensing arrangements; product pricing information; contemplated new products or services; _____; or other information that is not generally known and from which the Company derives an economic benefit.

[ ]   Alternative # 3: Salespeople and Other Employees

"Confidential Information" means Company's trade secrets, including, but not limited to, customer lists (including names, addresses, attributes, requirements, special needs and other data); personnel and hiring information (including salary, sales commission and bonus data); sales projections; names, locations of and agreements with vendors, suppliers and strategic business alliance partners; product pricing information; contemplated new products or services; _____; or other information that is not generally known and from which the Company derives an economic benefit.

The Confidential Information may have been written, such as computer source code, programs, hardware and software, tapes, disks, documents, drawings, data or product specifications, or unwritten, such as unwritten knowledge, ideas, processes, practices or know-how. Confidential Information does not include information that is in the public domain, information that is generally known in Company's industry or information that Employee acquired completely independently of his or her services for Company.

b.   For as long as the Confidential Information is not generally known and the Company derives an economic benefit from the information, Employee shall not use or disclose to any other person or entity any Confidential Information or any copy or summary of any Confidential Information unless Employee is required to do so by law.

c.   Employee shall not remove or copy any Confidential Information or participate in any way in the removal or copying of any Confidential Information without Company's written consent. On or prior to the Termination Date, Employee shall immediately return to Company all Confidential Information.

4.   Noncompetition

Employee agrees that in order to protect the Confidential Information described above, during the Term (as defined in Section 9 of this Agreement), Employee shall not:

a.   plan for, acquire any financial interest in or perform services for (as an employee, consultant, officer, director, independent contractor, principal, agent or otherwise) any business that would require Employee to use or disclose any Confidential Information, or

b.   perform services (as an employee, consultant, officer, director, independent contractor, principal, agent or otherwise) that are similar to Employee's current duties or responsibilities for any person or entity that, during the Term, engages in any business activity in which Company is then engaged or proposes to be engaged and that conducts its business in the Territory.

c.   "Territory" means

[ ]   Alternative # 1: General Territory

any geographic area in which Company conducts its business during the Term.

[ ]   Alternative # 2: Specific Territory

5.   Nonsolicitation

During the Term, Employee shall not:

a.   employ, attempt to employ or solicit for employment by any other person or entity, any Company employees;

b.   encourage any consultant, independent contractor or any other person or entity to end their relationship or stop doing business with Company, or help any person or entity do so or attempt to do so; or

c.   solicit or attempt to solicit or obtain business or trade from any of Company's current customers or clients with whom Employee had contact or about whom Employee acquired knowledge while employed by Company, or help any person or entity do so or attempt to do so.

6.   Right to an Injunction

Employee acknowledges that his or her services to Company were special and unique and that, while performing these services, Employee had access to and Company may have disclosed to Employee the Confidential Information described above. Employee also acknowledges that his or her position in Company placed him or her in a position of confidence and trust with Company and its employees, clients and customers.

If Employee breaches or threatens to breach any of the provisions of Sections 3, 4 or 5 of this Agreement, Company will sustain irreparable harm. Company shall be entitled to an injunction to stop any breach or threatened breach of this Agreement, including the provisions of Sections 3, 4 or 5. Employee acknowledges and agrees that monetary damages would not adequately compensate Company for any breach or threatened breach of these sections and that if Company seeks injunctive relief to put an immediate halt to the offending conduct, Employee shall not claim that monetary damages would be an adequate remedy.

7.   Reasonable Restrictions; Survivability

Employee acknowledges that the restrictions set forth in Sections 3, 4, 5 and 6 of this Agreement are reasonable and necessary for the protection of Company, its business and its Confidential Information. The provisions of Sections 3, 4, 5 and 6 of this Agreement shall survive the termination of the severance payments to Employee pursuant to Section 10 of this Agreement.

8.   Termination of Employment

Employee's employment with Company shall terminate as of _____, _____ ("Termination Date"). On Termination Date, Employee shall cease to be either an employee or an agent of Company and Employee shall not make any representation to any third party that he or she is an employee or agent of Company or has the authority to bind Company to any agreement.

9. Severance Payments

In consideration of Employee's promises in this Agreement, Company shall pay Employee a severance allowance, payable monthly on the _____ day of each month, of _____ Dollars ($_____), beginning on _____, _____, and ending on _____, _____ (the "Term").

In Company's sole discretion, this severance allowance may be subject to Company's normal withholding and payroll practices, including but not limited to the withholding of state and federal income taxes.

10. Continuation of Benefits

During the Term, Employee shall continue to be eligible for and Company shall continue to provide the following benefits to Employee: _____
_____
_____. In addition, Company shall make available to Employee all benefits for which Employee is eligible under Consolidated Omnibus Budget Reconciliation Act ("COBRA").

11. Termination of Obligations

If Employee breaches any of Employee's obligations under Sections 4, 5 or 6 of this Agreement, Company's obligations under this Agreement will immediately terminate and Employee will immediately refund to Company the full amount of any severance payments made to Employee pursuant to Section 9.

12. Confidentiality

Employee shall not directly or indirectly disclose either the existence of this Agreement or any of the terms of this Agreement other than to Employee's attorney, except to the extent that disclosing such terms is required by law.

13. Notice

All notices, requests, demands and other communications hereunder must be in writing and shall be considered properly given if delivered by hand or mailed within the continental United States by first-class, registered mail, return receipt requested, postage and registry fees paid, to the applicable party and addressed as follows:

To Company:

_____

_____

_____

_____

with a copy to Company's attorney:

_____

_____

_____

_____

To Employee:

_____

_____

_____

_____

with a copy to Employee's attorney:

_____

_____

_____

_____

14. Severability

If a court determines that any provision of this Agreement is invalid or unenforceable, any invalidity or unenforceability will affect only that provision and shall not make any other provision of this Agreement invalid or unenforceable. Instead, such provision shall be modified, amended or limited to the extent necessary to render it valid and enforceable.

15. Applicable Law

This Agreement shall be governed by and construed in accordance with the laws of the State of _____.

16. Jurisdiction

Employee and Company consent to the exclusive jurisdiction and venue of the federal and state courts located in _____, _____, in any action arising out of or relating to this Agreement. Employee and Company waive any other venue to which either party might be entitled by domicile or otherwise.

17. Entire Agreement

This is the entire agreement between the parties. It supersedes and replaces any and all prior oral or written agreements between Company and Employee that relate to the matters covered by this Agreement.

18. Assignment; Binding Effect

This Agreement shall bind the Company's successors and assigns, and Company may assign this Agreement to any party at any time, in its sole discretion, without Employee's consent. This Agreement shall bind Employee's heirs, successors and assignees. Employee shall not assign any of Employee's rights or obligations under this Agreement without Company's prior written consent.

19. Waiver

If Company waives any term or provision of this Agreement, that waiver shall be effective only in the specific instance and for the specific purpose for which Company gave the waiver. If Company fails to exercise or delays exercising any of its rights or remedies under this Agreement, Company retains the right to enforce that term or provision at a later time.

20. Amendment

This Agreement may be modified, changed or amended only in writing, and such writing must be signed by both parties.

21. Counterparts

The parties may execute this Agreement in counterparts, each of which shall be considered an original, and all of which shall constitute the same document.

IN WITNESS WHEREOF, the parties have executed this Agreement as of the day and year first written above in Section 1.

"Company"

_____, a _____

By: _____

_____

[type or print name]

Its: _____

"Employee"

_____

_____

[type or print name]

Form EMPL-8: Amendment of Employee Agreement

1.   Introduction

This Amendment ("Amendment") is made and entered into as of _____, _____,

between _____ ("Employee") and _____, a
_____ ("Company").

2.   Purpose

Employee and Company are parties to a _____, dated as of
_____, _____ ("Original Agreement").

Employee and Company desire to amend the Original Agreement on the terms and conditions set forth herein. For good and valuable consideration, the receipt and sufficiency of which is hereby acknowledged, the parties agree as follows:

3.   Amendment

[ ]   Alternative # 1: Replacing a Clause

Section ___ of the Original Agreement is hereby deleted in its entirety. Section ___ shall now read in full as follows:

_____

_____

_____

[ ]   Alternative # 2: Deleting a Clause

Section ___ is hereby deleted in its entirety.

[ ]   Alternative # 3: Adding a New Clause

The following clause is hereby added to the Original Agreement as Section __. Section ___ reads in full as follows:

_____

_____

4. Applicable Law

This Amendment shall be governed by and construed in accordance with the laws of the State of _____.

5. Entire Agreement; No Other Change

This is the entire agreement between the parties. It supersedes and replaces any and all prior oral or written agreements between Company and Employee that relate to the matters covered by this Amendment. Except for the provisions modified by this Amendment, all the provisions of the Original Agreement shall remain in full force and effect. If there is any conflict between the provisions of this Amendment and the Original Agreement, the provisions of this Amendment will control.

6. Counterparts

The parties may execute this Amendment in counterparts, each of which shall be considered an original, and all of which shall constitute the same document.

IN WITNESS WHEREOF, the parties have executed this Amendment as of the day and year first written above in Section 1.

"Company"

_____, a _____

By: _____

_____

[type or print name]

Its: _____

"Employee"

_____

_____

[type or print name]

Form IC-7: Independent Contractor Agreement (General Agreement)

1. Introduction

This agreement ("Agreement") is made and entered into as of _____, _____,

between_____ ("Contractor") and _____, a
_____ ("Company").

2. Purpose

Company is in the business of _____.

[] Alternative # 1: New Contractor

Company would like to retain Contractor as a _____. In exchange for
Company's retaining Contractor's services, and for other good and valuable consideration,
the receipt and sufficiency of which is hereby acknowledged, Company and Contractor
agree as follows:

[] Alternative # 2: Existing Contractor With Prior Oral Agreement

Contractor was previously retained by Company as a _____ pursuant to an
oral independent contractor agreement dated which began on _____, _____.

Company shall continue to retain Contractor's services as a _____, but on the
terms and conditions set forth in this Agreement.

As _____, Contractor has access to Company's Confidential Information, as
defined in this Agreement. In exchange for Company's retaining Contractor's services as a
_____, and for other good and valuable consideration, the receipt and
sufficiency of which is hereby acknowledged, Company and Contractor agree as follows:

3. Duties

Contractor's duties will include:

_____

_____

_____

Contractor acknowledges that because Contractor is an independent contractor, Company will control only the results of the services Contractor provides to Company and not the means by which Contractor provides services.

4.   Compensation

In exchange for the services to be rendered by Contractor under this Agreement,

[ ]   Alternative # 1: Flat Fee

Company shall pay Contractor the sum of _____ Dollars ($_____), payable as follows: _____.

[ ]   Alternative # 2: Weekly or Monthly Fee

Company shall pay Contractor the sum of _____ Dollars ($_____) per [week/month], beginning on the ___ day after the date of this Agreement and continuing on the same day of each [week/month].

[ ]   Alternative # 3: Hourly Fee With Invoice

Company shall pay Contractor the sum of _____ Dollars ($_____) per hour. Contractor shall submit invoices to Company each [month/week] detailing the hours worked and services performed and the total fee due. Company shall pay Contractor the invoiced amount within _____ (___) days of receiving an invoice.

5.   Term of Services

[ ]   Alternative # 1: Fixed Term

This Agreement will begin on the date set forth in Section 1 and will continue for _____ (___) [weeks/months/years], ending on _____, _____.

[ ]   Alternative # 2: Project-Based Term

This Agreement will begin on the date set forth in Section 1 and will continue until _____ but shall not end later than _____.

6.   No Withholding or State Insurance

Because Company is retaining Contractor as an independent contractor and not as an employee, Company will not withhold from Contractor's compensation any state or federal income taxes, and Company will not withhold or pay any Social Security, Medicare, federal unemployment insurance (FUTA), workers' compensation insurance, state unemployment or disability insurance payments on Contractor's behalf. Contractor agrees and covenants to report all income received from Company and make all required income tax and other tax payments in connection with Contractor's compensation. Company will provide Contractor with a Form 1099 summarizing Contractor's compensation for each tax year.

7. No Partnership

This Agreement does not create any partnership or joint venture between Company and Contractor or any relationship other than client and independent contractor. Except as described in Section 3, or unless Contractor obtains Company's written consent, Contractor shall not have the authority to and shall not bind the Company to any contract or agreement.

8. No Other Benefits

Except as specifically set forth in this Agreement, Company is not responsible for providing and will not provide Contractor with any benefits, including but not limited to health insurance, pension benefits or any other benefits Company provides to its employees.

9. Termination of Services

If either Contractor or Company violates, breaches or fails to perform any provision of this Agreement, either party shall have the right, with written notice, to immediately terminate services under this Agreement.

10. Additional Agreements

Company and Contractor additionally agree that:_____

_____

_____.

11. Nondisclosure of Confidential Information

a.   Company may need to disclose to Contractor or give Contractor access to Confidential Information so that Contractor may properly fulfill his or her duties to Company. "Confidential Information" means Company's trade secrets, including, but not limited to, customer lists (including names, addresses, attributes, requirements, special needs and other data); names, locations of and agreements with vendors, suppliers and strategic business alliance partners; contemplated new products or services; _____; or any other information that is not generally known and from which the Company derives an economic benefit. The Confidential Information may be written, such as computer source code, programs, hardware and software, tapes, disks, documents, drawings, data or product specifications, or unwritten, such as unwritten knowledge, ideas, processes, practices or know-how. Confidential Information does not include information that is in the public domain, information that is generally known in Company's industry or information that Contractor acquired completely independently of his or her services for Company.

b.   For as long as the Confidential Information is not generally known and Company derives an economic benefit from the Confidential Information, Contractor shall not use or disclose to any other person or entity any Confidential Information or any copy or summary of any Confidential Information unless Contractor is required to do so to perform Contractor's duties to Company or as required by law.

c.   While Contractor is performing services for Company and afterward, Contractor shall not remove or copy any Confidential Information or participate in any way in the removal or copying of any Confidential Information without Company's written consent. Contractor shall immediately return to Company all Confidential Information when Contractor ceases performing services for Company, or any time Company requires such Confidential Information to be returned.

d.   Contractor will not obtain or attempt to obtain any Confidential Information for any purpose whatsoever except as required by Company to enable Contractor to perform his or her duties.

e.   Contractor will not disclose to Company or misuse any third party's trade secrets, including any trade secret information of Contractor's former employer or client, _____. Contractor represents and warrants that the execution of this Agreement by Contractor will not violate or conflict with the terms of any other agreement to which Contractor is a party.

12. Noncompetition

Contractor agrees that in order to protect the Confidential Information described above, while Contractor is performing services for Company, and for a period of _____ [years/months] thereafter (collectively, the "Term"), Contractor shall not:

a.   plan for, acquire any financial interest in or perform services for (as an employee, consultant, officer, director, independent contractor, principal, agent or otherwise) any business that would require Contractor to use or disclose any Confidential Information, or

b.   perform services (as an employee, consultant, officer, director, independent contractor, principal, agent or otherwise) that are similar to Contractor's current duties or responsibilities for any person or entity that, during the Term, engages in any business activity in which

Company is then engaged or proposes to be engaged and that conducts its business in the Territory.

c.   "Territory" means

[]   Alternative # 1: General Territory

any geographic area in which Company conducts its business during the Term.

[]   Alternative # 2: Specific Territory

_____ .

13. Nonsolicitation

While Contractor is performing services for Company, and for a period of _____ [years/ months] thereafter, Contractor shall not:

a.   employ, attempt to employ or solicit for employment by any other person or entity, any Company employees;

b.   encourage any consultant, independent contractor or any other person or entity to end their relationship or stop doing business with Company, or help any person or entity to do so or attempt to do so; or

c.   solicit or attempt to solicit or obtain business or trade from any of Company's current customers or clients with whom Contractor had contact or about whom Contractor acquired knowledge while performing services for Company, or help any person or entity do so or attempt to do so.

14. Right to an Injunction

Contractor acknowledges that his or her services to Company are special and unique and that, while performing these services, Contractor will have access to and Company may disclose to Contractor the Confidential Information described above. Contractor also acknowledges that performing services for Company will place him or her in a position of confidence and trust with Company and its employees, clients and customers.

If Contractor breaches or threatens to breach any of the provisions of Sections 11, 12 or 13 of this Agreement, Company will sustain irreparable harm. Company shall be entitled to an injunction to stop any breach or threatened breach of this Agreement, including the provisions of Sections 11, 12 or 13. Contractor acknowledges and agrees that monetary damages would not adequately compensate Company for any breach or threatened breach of these sections and that if Company seeks injunctive relief to put an immediate halt to the offending conduct, Contractor shall not claim that monetary damages would be an adequate remedy.

15. Reasonable Restrictions; Survivability

Contractor acknowledges that the restrictions set forth in Sections 11, 12, 13 and 14 of this Agreement are reasonable and necessary for the protection of Company, its business and its Confidential Information. The provisions of Sections 11, 12, 13 and 14 of this Agreement shall survive the termination, for any reason, of Contractor's employment with Company.

16. Severability

If a court determines that any provision of this Agreement is invalid or unenforceable, any invalidity or unenforceability will affect only that provision and shall not make any other provision of this Agreement invalid or unenforceable. Instead, such provision shall be modified, amended or limited to the extent necessary to render it valid and enforceable.

17. Applicable Law

This Agreement shall be governed by and construed in accordance with the laws of the State of _____.

18. Jurisdiction

Contractor and Company consent to the exclusive jurisdiction and venue of the federal and state courts located in _____, _____, in any action arising out of or relating to this Agreement. Contractor and Company waive any other venue to which either party might be entitled by domicile or otherwise.

19. Entire Agreement; No Other Change

This is the entire agreement between the parties. It supersedes and replaces any and all prior oral or written agreements between Company and Contractor that relate to the matters covered by this Agreement.

20. Assignment; Binding Effect

This Agreement shall bind the Company's successors and assigns, and Company may assign this Agreement to any party at any time, in its sole discretion, without Contractor's consent. This Agreement shall bind Contractor's heirs, successors and assignees. Contractor shall not assign any of Contractor's rights or obligations under this Agreement without Company's prior written consent.

21. Waiver

If Company waives any term or provision of this Agreement, that waiver shall be effective only in the specific instance and for the specific purpose for which Company gave the waiver. If Company fails to exercise or delays exercising any of its rights or remedies under this Agreement, Company retains the right to enforce that term or provision at a later time.

22. Amendment

This Agreement may be modified, changed or amended only in writing, and such writing must signed by both parties.

23. Counterparts

The parties may execute this Agreement in counterparts, each of which shall be considered an original, and all of which shall constitute the same document.

IN WITNESS WHEREOF, the parties have executed this Agreement as of the day and year first written above in Section 1.

"Company"

_____, a _____

By: _____

_____

[type or print name]

Its: _____

"Contractor"

_____

_____

[type or print name]

Form IC-8: Termination Agreement for Independent Contractor

1.   Introduction

This Termination Agreement ("Agreement"), dated as of _____, _____,

is entered into by and between _____ ("Contractor") and
_____, a _____ ("Company").

2.   Purpose

Company is in the business of _____.

[ ]   Alternative # 1: Contractor With Prior Written Agreement

Pursuant to an independent contractor agreement dated as of _____, _____

("Contractor Agreement"), Contractor has been performing services for Company as a
_____. Company and Contractor desire to terminate Contractor's performance of services under the Contractor Agreement and on the terms and conditions set forth in this Agreement.

In exchange for the mutual covenants and agreements contained in this Agreement, and for other good and valuable consideration, the receipt and sufficiency of which is hereby acknowledged, Company and Contractor agree as follows:

[ ]   Alternative # 2: Contractor With Prior Oral Agreement

Contractor has been performing services for Company as a _____. Company and Contractor desire to terminate Contractor's services with Company on the terms and conditions set forth in this Agreement.

In exchange for the mutual covenants and agreements contained in this Agreement, and for other good and valuable consideration, the receipt and sufficiency of which is hereby acknowledged, Company and Contractor agree as follows:

3.   Nondisclosure of Confidential Information

a.   While Contractor has been performing services for Company, Company has disclosed to Contractor or given Contractor access to Confidential Information so that Contractor could properly fulfill his or her duties to Company.

[ ]   Alternative # 1: Web engineers/designers and Software Engineers/Beta Testers

"Confidential Information" means Company's trade secrets, including, but not limited to, technology; equipment research, design and development; product formulas, pricing information, research, design and development; engineering or manufacturing processes or methods; database, website or network specifications or data; licensing arrangements; any titles, themes, stories, treatments, ideas, art work, computer hardware and software; _____; or any other information that is not generally known and from which the Company derives an economic benefit.

The Confidential Information may have been written, such as computer source code, programs, hardware and software, tapes, disks, documents, drawings, data or product specifications, or unwritten, such as unwritten knowledge, ideas, processes, practices or know-how. Confidential Information does not include information that is in the public domain, information that is generally known in Company's industry or information that Contractor acquired completely independently of his or her services for Company.

[ ]   Alternative # 2 Marketing/Market Research Consultants

"Confidential Information" means Company's trade secrets, including, but not limited to, customer lists (including names, addresses, attributes, requirements, special needs and other data); business plans or strategies; advertising, marketing or publicity campaigns; credit information; sales projections; market research and analyses (including focus group or survey results); personnel and hiring information (including salary, sales commission and bonus data); names, locations of and agreements with vendors, suppliers and strategic business alliance partners; accounting or financial data; licensing arrangements; product pricing information; contemplated new products or services; _____; or any other information that is not generally known and from which the Company derives an economic benefit.

The Confidential Information may have been written, such as computer source code, programs, hardware and software, tapes, disks, documents, drawings, data or product specifications, or unwritten, such as unwritten knowledge, ideas, processes, practices or know-how. Confidential Information does not include information that is in the public domain, information that is generally known in Company's industry or information that Contractor acquired completely independently of his or her services for Company.

[ ]   Alternative # 3: Salespeople and Brokers/Agents

"Confidential Information" means Company's trade secrets, including, but not limited to, customer lists (including names, addresses, attributes, requirements, special needs and other data); personnel and hiring information (including salary, sales commission and bonus data); sales projections; names, locations of and agreements with vendors, suppliers and strategic business alliance partners; product pricing information; contemplated new products or services; _____; or any other information that is not generally known and from which the Company derives an economic benefit.

The Confidential Information may have been written, such as computer source code, programs, hardware and software, tapes, disks, documents, drawings, data or product specifications, or unwritten, such as unwritten knowledge, ideas, processes, practices or know-how. Confidential Information does not include information that is in the public domain, information that is generally known in Company's industry or information that Contractor acquired completely independently of his or her services for Company.

[ ]   Alternative #4: Research and Development Consultants

"Confidential Information" means Company's trade secrets, including, but not limited to, technology; equipment research, design and development; product formulas, pricing information, research, design and development; engineering or manufacturing processes or methods; licensing arrangements; any titles, themes, stories, treatments, ideas, art work, computer hardware and software; _____; or any other information that is not generally known and from which the Company derives an economic benefit.

The Confidential Information may have been written, such as computer source code, programs, hardware and software, tapes, disks, documents, drawings, data or product specifications, or unwritten, such as unwritten knowledge, ideas, processes, practices or know-how. Confidential Information does not include information that is in the public domain, information that is generally known in Company's industry or information that Contractor acquired completely independently of his or her services for Company.

b.   For as long as the Confidential Information is not generally known and Company derives an economic benefit from the Confidential Information, Contractor shall not use or disclose to any other person or entity any Confidential Information, or any copy or summary of any Confidential Information unless Contractor is required to do so by law.

c.   Contractor shall not remove or copy any Confidential Information or participate in any way in the removal or copying of any Confidential Information without Company's written consent. On or prior to the Termination Date, Contractor shall immediately return to Company all Confidential Information.

4.   Noncompetition

Contractor agrees that in order to protect the Confidential Information described above, during the Term (as defined in Section 7 of this Agreement), Contractor shall not:

a.   plan for, acquire any financial interest in or perform services for (as a contractor, consultant, officer, director, independent contractor, principal, agent or otherwise) any business that would require Contractor to use or disclose any Confidential Information, or

b.   perform services (as a contractor, consultant, officer, director, independent contractor, principal, agent or otherwise) that are similar to Contractor's current duties or responsibilities for any person or entity that, during the Term, engages in any business activity in which Company is then engaged or proposes to be engaged and that conducts its business in the Territory.

c.   "Territory" means

[ ]   Alternative # 1: General Territory

any geographic area in which Company conducts its business during the Term.

[ ]   Alternative # 2: Specific Territory

_____.

5.   Nonsolicitation

During the Term, Contractor shall not:

a.   employ, attempt to employ or solicit for employment by any other person or entity, any Company contractors;

b.   encourage any consultant, independent contractor or any other person or entity to end their relationship or stop doing business with Company, or help any person or entity do so or attempt to do so; or

c.   solicit or attempt to solicit or obtain business or trade from any of Company's current customers or clients with whom Contractor had contact or about whom Contractor acquired knowledge while performing services for Company, or help any person or entity do so or attempt to do so.

6. Right to an Injunction

Contractor acknowledges that his or her services to Company were special and unique and that, while performing these services, Contractor had access to and Company may have disclosed to Contractor the Confidential Information described above. Contractor also acknowledges that his or her position in Company placed him or her in a position of confidence and trust with Company's employees, clients and customers.

If Contractor breaches or threatens to breach any of the provisions of Sections 3, 4 or 5 of this Agreement, Company will sustain irreparable harm. Company shall be entitled to an injunction to stop any breach or threatened breach of this Agreement, including the provisions of Sections 3, 4 or 5. Contractor acknowledges and agrees that monetary damages would not adequately compensate Company for any breach or threatened breach of these sections and that if Company seeks injunctive relief to put an immediate halt to the offending conduct, Contractor shall not claim that monetary damages would be an adequate remedy.

7. Reasonable Restrictions; Survivability

Contractor acknowledges that the restrictions set forth in Sections 3, 4, 5 and 6 of this Agreement are reasonable and necessary for the protection of Company, its business and its Confidential Information. The provisions of Section 3, 4, 5 and 6 of this Agreement shall survive the termination, for any reason, of the payments to Contractor pursuant to Section 10 of this Agreement.

8. Termination of Services

Contractor shall cease performing services for Company as of _____, _____ ("Termination Date"). On Termination Date, Contractor shall cease to be either a contractor or an agent of Company and Contractor shall not make any representation to any third party that he or she is a contractor or agent of Company or has the authority to bind Company to any agreement.

9. Payments

In consideration of Contractor's promises in this Agreement, Company shall pay Contractor certain payments, payable monthly on the _____ day of each month, of _____ Dollars ($_____), beginning on _____ , _____ and ending on _____ , _____ (the "Term").

10. Termination of Obligations

If Contractor breaches any of Contractor's obligations under this Agreement, Company's obligations under this Agreement will immediately terminate and Contractor will immediately refund to Company the full amount of any payments made to Contractor pursuant to Section 9.

11. Confidentiality

Contractor shall not directly or indirectly disclose either the existence of this Agreement or any of the terms of this Agreement other than to Contractor's attorney, except to the extent that disclosing such terms is required by law.

12. Notice

All notices, requests, demands and other communications hereunder must be in writing and shall be considered properly given if delivered by hand or mailed within the continental United States by first-class, registered mail, return receipt requested, postage and registry fees paid, to the applicable party and addressed as follows:

To Company:

_____

_____

_____

_____

with a copy to Company's attorney:

_____

_____

_____

_____

To Contractor:

_____

_____

_____

_____

with a copy to Contractor's attorney:

_____

_____

_____

_____

13. Severability

If a court determines that any provision of this Agreement is invalid or unenforceable, any invalidity or unenforceability will affect only that provision and shall not make any other provision of this Agreement invalid or unenforceable. Instead, such provision shall be modified, amended or limited to the extent necessary to render it valid and enforceable.

14. Applicable Law

This Agreement shall be governed by and construed in accordance with the laws of the State of _____.

15. Jurisdiction

Contractor and Company consent to the exclusive jurisdiction and venue of the federal and state courts located in _____, _____, in any action arising out of or relating to this Agreement. Contractor and Company waive any other venue to which either party might be entitled by domicile or otherwise.

16. Entire Agreement; No Other Change

This is the entire agreement between the parties. It supersedes and replaces any and all prior oral or written agreements between Company and Contractor that relate to the matters covered by this Agreement.

17. Assignment; Binding Effect

This Agreement shall bind the Company's successors and assigns, and Company may assign this Agreement to any party at any time, in its sole discretion, without Contractor's consent. This Agreement shall bind Contractor's heirs, successors and assignees. Contractor shall not assign any of Contractor's rights or obligations under this Agreement without Company's prior written consent.

18. Waiver

If Company waives any term or provision of this Agreement, that waiver shall be effective only in the specific instance and for the specific purpose for which Company gave the waiver. If Company fails to exercise or delays exercising any of its rights or remedies under this Agreement, Company retains the right to enforce that term or provision at a later time.

19. Amendment

This Agreement may be modified, changed or amended only in writing, and such writing must be signed by both parties.

20. Counterparts

The parties may execute this Agreement in counterparts, each of which shall be considered an original, and all of which shall constitute the same document.

IN WITNESS WHEREOF, the parties have executed this Agreement as of the day and year first written above in Section 1.

"Company"

_____, a _____

By: _____

_____

[type or print name]

Its: _____

"Contractor"

_____

_____

[type or print name]

Index

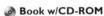

Your comments make a big difference in the development and revision of Nolo books and software. Please take a few minutes and register your Nolo product—and your comments—with us. Not only will your input make a difference, you'll receive special offers available only to registered owners of Nolo products on our newest books and software. Register now by:

PHONE
1-800-728-3555

FAX
1-800-645-0895

EMAIL
cs@nolo.com

or **MAIL** us
this registration card

REMEMBER:
Little publishers have big ears. We really listen to you.

fold here

REGISTRATION CARD

NAME _____ DATE _____

ADDRESS _____

CITY _____ STATE _____ ZIP _____

PHONE _____ E-MAIL _____

WHERE DID YOU HEAR ABOUT THIS PRODUCT? _____

WHERE DID YOU PURCHASE THIS PRODUCT? _____

DID YOU CONSULT A LAWYER? (PLEASE CIRCLE ONE)   YES   NO   NOT APPLICABLE

DID YOU FIND THIS BOOK HELPFUL?   (VERY)   5   4   3   2   1   (NOT AT ALL)

COMMENTS _____

WAS IT EASY TO USE?   (VERY EASY)   5   4   3   2   1   (VERY DIFFICULT)

DO YOU OWN A COMPUTER? IF SO, WHICH FORMAT? (PLEASE CIRCLE ONE)   WINDOWS   DOS   MAC

We occasionally make our mailing list available to carefully selected companies whose products may be of interest to you.
❑ If you do not wish to receive mailings from these companies, please check this box.
❑ You can quote me in future Nolo promotional materials. Daytime phone number

NOCMP 1.0

N O L O
I N   T H E
N E W S

"Nolo helps lay people perform legal tasks without the aid—or fees—of lawyers."

—USA TODAY

Nolo books are ..."written in plain language, free of legal mumbo jumbo, and spiced with witty personal observations."

—ASSOCIATED PRESS

"...Nolo publications...guide people simply through the how, when, where and why of law."

—WASHINGTON POST

"Increasingly, people who are not lawyers are performing tasks usually regarded as legal work... And consumers, using books like Nolo's, do routine legal work themselves."

—NEW YORK TIMES

"...All of [Nolo's] books are easy-to-understand, are updated regularly, provide pull-out forms...and are often quite moving in their sense of compassion for the struggles of the lay reader."

—SAN FRANCISCO CHRONICLE

fold here

- -

nolo
950 Parker Street
Berkeley, CA 94710-9867

Attn: **NOCMP 1.0**